THE OLD TESTAMENT
INTERPRETATION
OF HISTORY

THE OLD TESTAMENT INTERPRETATION OF HISTORY

By

CHRISTOPHER R. NORTH, M.A.

Professor of Hebrew
University College of North Wales
Bangor

THE EPWORTH PRESS
(EDGAR C. BARTON)
25-35 City Road, London, E.C.1

Published for the
FERNLEY HARTLEY TRUST

Made in Great Britain

TO

WILLIAM FREDERICK LOFTHOUSE
HENRY BETT
AND
WILBERT FRANCIS HOWARD

IN GRATITUDE FOR
FIFTEEN YEARS OF COLLEAGUESHIP
(HANDSWORTH 1925–40)

PREFACE

THIS Fernley-Hartley Lecture has been written in such spare time as I have had during a busy wartime pastorate—after years of teaching in a theological college—and a return to teaching, this time in a university college. I have wished sometimes that I could have treated the subject in a more objective and leisurely way: it might then have been less discursive than perhaps it is in places. On the other hand, what is here offered may have a note of challenge about it that would have been lacking if it had been written in academic seclusion. At least I have tried to look at the subject from the angle of the general-practitioner minister and interested layman, not simply from that of the Old Testament specialist.

Only after I had passed the first proofs did Dr. H. Cunliffe-Jones's recently published book, *The Authority of the Biblical Revelation*, come into my hands. In his Preface to this he expresses his conviction that

we are in the beginnings of a vast turning movement in Christian theology in which the critical historical labours of the last two centuries and a half are taken up into the older traditional understanding of the meaning of the Christian Revelation. On the one hand, we cannot return to the older understanding of Revelation, for it had many misunderstandings of the purpose of God from which these critical studies have delivered us. On the other hand, the achievement of the eighteenth, nineteenth, and early twentieth centuries is much more important as a corrective than as the positive exposition of Divine truth. We are called to strenuous theological labour, to the positive exposition of the Divine Revelation to which the Bible witnesses, in such a way as to do full justice to its historic actuality.

This, I think, is in some sort what I have tried to do.

Translations from Hebrew poetry are for the most part my own. Occasionally they assume emendations which I might not be prepared to justify if I were writing a critical commentary. I have tried to give the general sense of the original, but where an emendation has any bearing upon the exposition of the passage I have indicated the authority for it.

It will be obvious that I have learned much from the late Principal H. Wheeler Robinson. For the rest, my thanks are due to the Rev. Professor H. H. Rowley, D.D., who has read the typescript—he appears to read most books on the Old Testament before their authors venture into print!—and made several valuable suggestions. I am also indebted to my colleague, Mr. D. R. Ap-Thomas, M.A., B.D., who has compiled the Indexes of Scripture Passages and Authors Quoted. My wife has helped me with the reading of the proofs.

Finally, I wish to thank the Fernley-Hartley Trustees for the honour they have done me in inviting me to deliver this lecture.

C. R. N.

BANGOR
  Ascensiontide 1946

CONTENTS

PREFACE vii

INTRODUCTION xi

Event and Interpretation: 'Actuality' and 'Fact'—No 'bare'
facts for the Historian

1. THE HISTORY IN OUTLINE 1

2. THE SAGAS 20

The Primeval History—The Yahwist—The Elohist

3. THE PROPHETS: I. THEIR INTERPRETATION
OF PAST HISTORY 40

The Patriarchal Tradition—The Exodus and the Conquest of
Canaan—The Covenant—The Settlement in Palestine—The
Monarchy

4. THE PROPHETS: II. THEIR INTERPRETATION
OF CONTEMPORARY HISTORY . . 58

The Prophets as Actors in History—Prophetic Symbolism—
Yahweh, Lord of Universal Morality—The Doctrine of Moral
Retribution—Yahweh, Lord of History—Yahweh, Lord of
Nature—Yahweh, God of Israel

5. PROPHETICO-PRIESTLY:
THE DEUTERONOMISTS 85

The Laws—The History

6. PRIESTLY INTERPRETATION 107

The Priestly Code—Chronicles-Ezra-Nehemiah—The Final
Synthesis

7. ESCHATOLOGICAL AND APOCALYPTIC . 119

Pre-prophetic Eschatology (?)—Prophetic Eschatology: The Day of Yahweh, The Messiah—Apocalyptic: Transcendentalism, Determinism, Pessimism, Dualism

8. GOD IN HISTORY 141

Has God revealed Himself in history?—The Problem of Divine Personality—Theism and Pantheism—The Concept of Progressive Revelation—Modern Marcionitism—Berdyaev on the Essential Nature of the Historical—The Presentness of the Past

9. ISRAEL THE SERVANT OF YAHWEH . . 162

Did God choose Israel?—The Physical Factors—The Nature-miracles—Miracle of the Prophetic Consciousness—Prophetic 'Sympathy' with the Divine 'Pathos' a Bridge to the Incarnation—Israel the Prophet-nation—The Positive Achievement of Israel

10. ZION CITY OF GOD 183

Priest *versus* Prophet?—Post-exilic Judaism based upon Teaching of the Prophets—Localized Presence of Yahweh in Zion a Second Bridge to the Incarnation—Incompleteness of the Old Testament Revelation: Cultus and Spiritual Life, Paradox of National Monotheism, Transcendence and Immanence, Inadequacy of the Prophetic Theodicy—Lack of Dynamic Conception of the Holy Spirit

INDEXES 202

Authors Quoted—Biblical References—Subjects

INTRODUCTION

IT IS NOW generally agreed that we cannot make a summary outline of the Old Testament, and say, 'Here is the history of the Hebrews'. The Old Testament in its present form contains, not a straightforward account of Hebrew history, but that history as viewed from the standpoint of the Jewish Church in the period after the Exile. The total perspective is slightly, though not materially, modified if we take the books in the order in which they appear in the Hebrew Bible, namely, Law, Prophets, Writings, instead of that followed in the English Old Testament, namely, roughly, Law, Histories, Poetry, Prophecies. The Hebrew order is, of course, the more original, but even in the form it assumed in the Hebrew Bible the story is the result of a succession of editorial processes extending over several centuries. Thus, to take the Exodus, which occupied in Hebrew faith much the same place that the Resurrection has for the Christian: between the actual events of the Exodus and the final interpretation of those events in the Pentateuch as we have it there may be a period of almost a millennium. Obviously, if we are ever to know what really happened we must penetrate behind a series of 'defences in depth' within which the original citadel of the Hebrew faith in God and national destiny was guarded. This is equally true of the history as a whole. The main ramparts of this interpretative faith may be briefly enumerated: they are the Sagas (comprising the early documents of the Pentateuch and the stories of the heroes in Joshua, Judges, Samuel, and Kings), the Prophetical Writings from the eighth to the sixth century, Deuteronomy and the Deuteronomic historians, the Priestly Document of the Pentateuch, Chronicles, and the Book of Daniel.

Our task is twofold: (1) to outline the several stages in the Hebrew interpretation of history, and to consider whether that interpretation, either in the final synthesis, or in one or more or all of its several stages of development, was altogether or approximately true, and (2) to consider whether the actual course of Hebrew history, so far as it can be ascertained, warrants us in believing, as Jewish and Christian faith has always affirmed, that there was a special providence and purpose in God's dealings with Israel.

It is necessary, at the outset, to remind ourselves that these two tasks are not easily or, indeed, entirely separable. No historian today is content simply to chronicle events. If he were to try, he would be essaying the impossible. Even the contemporary diarist finds it impossible merely to record what he sees. He is bound in some measure to interpret it, and his interpretation will differ somewhat from that of another observer present. And when we come to deal with a sequence of events, 'remembered', it may be, centuries afterwards, the margin of difference between event and interpretation, and also between the several interpretations themselves, inevitably widens. Dr. H. Wheeler Robinson has reminded us

History is the interpretation of events seen in their proper sequence and relation. But the human consciousness, even in the first observer of an event, cannot take cognizance of it without in some degree interpreting it; there are no 'bare' facts for the historian. The observer's inevitable interpretation of the event may become, in turn, a new 'fact' of history.[a]

Elsewhere Wheeler Robinson uses the term 'actuality' to describe

the quality or status of the event as that which has 'taken place' once for all [and he goes on to point out that] if there is no objective fixity in the interpretation of the event, but its meaning so varies with the varying attitude of those whom it concerns, then the 'fact' constituted by event *plus* meaning is itself not unalterably fixed. The meaning of an event may be one thing to its contemporaries, and quite another to their successors. To a man reviewing his own past, that past will have different meanings, and so different values, at differing periods of his life. A transformation of attitude may profoundly alter, not the bare event (which is, however, always an abstraction), but the total 'fact' of an interpreted event.[b] . . . So it is with the longer and larger retrospects of history. . . . The actuality of history therefore remains, but does not rule out the possibility of a 'transvaluation' of the events of history.[c]

[a] *The Old Testament: Its Making and Meaning*, p. 76.
[b] *Redemption and Revelation*, p. xxx.
[c] ibid., pp. xl.f.

Event and interpretation, 'actuality' and 'fact', have a way of becoming blended with one another. The first task of the historian is to discover, so far as he can, the events that lie behind the theories. To quote Wheeler Robinson again:

This, so far as we can reach it, is the datum for a philosophy of revelation. Only when we have decided on a probable series of events, and a parallel series of human reactions to those events, can we usefully begin to ask how far and in what way they both *in their blended unity* serve to reveal God.[a]

Certain conclusions would seem to follow from these considerations:

(1) If the 'bare event' is an 'abstraction' we must not be surprised if we sometimes find it impossible to ascertain exactly what happened. Nor need we be unduly distressed by our failure. If revelation consists, not in the bare events, but in the events as interpreted by the religious consciousness, we can be content even though many of the details are obscure. Of course, if everything depended upon the credibility of a single event, we should have to be assured that the event really happened very much in the manner described. But that is not the situation that confronts us in the alleged revelation to the Hebrews. The foundation stone of the whole is the Exodus, and it is admitted that many of the details about the Exodus are obscure. But the Exodus is only the first of a series of 'mighty acts' in God's dealings with the Hebrews. What concerns us, therefore, is not the literal accuracy of this or that happening, but whether the interpretation as a whole is valid for the events in their broad totality.

(2) There must be a recognizable congruity between the events as a whole, and the revelational 'facts' that emerge from them. We must be sure that the interpreters are not just romancing, writing history out of the depths of their moral consciousness. Every religion, of course, has a history. But it is possible for a religion to consist of pure ideas for which no claim is made that they have been supernaturally revealed through events in history. Hinduism is the outstanding example. Outside Judaism and its derivatives, Christianity and Islam, indeed, religions make little pretence to be based upon revelations in history. With the

---

[a] *Record and Revelation*, p. 304.

religion of the Hebrews the case is different. It claims to be based
upon certain dealings of God with the nation, and by that claim
it must stand to be judged. If we find that the interpretative
'facts' are widely at variance with the 'actualities' we may
have to conclude that the interpretation of history proposed is
unwarranted.

(3) Nevertheless, we may allow for a certain measure of latitude,
and even of incongruity, between the original events and their
subsequent interpretation or interpretations, without being
obliged to conclude that the interpretations are false. In any
case, it is clear that the new 'fact' that emerges from the interpretation of an 'event' is often of immense power and significance,
even though it may sometimes be a 'travesty of the facts', as we
say. An extreme example is the Nazi legend that Germany was
not defeated in the First World War. The German nation was
persuaded to believe it, and that 'fact', as much as anything,
contributed to the outbreak of the Second World War. The truth
underlying the falsehood was that the German Army was defeated
militarily in 1918; but it was not annihilated. By all the standards
of previous wars, Germany was defeated, and surrendered; but
by the subsequent standards of totalitarian warfare it could be
plausibly claimed that she was not defeated. History is not
shaped by physical events simply, but by events compounded with
ideas, and the ideas, while suggested by the physical events, may
be the dominant force in the partnership. Indeed, long after the
generation that has witnessed the events has passed away, the
ideas to which the events gave birth may persist and grow. But
the ideas in the further stages of their development are not
necessarily untrue, even though their likeness to the original
events may ultimately be difficult to recognize. For example, in
the field of Hebrew history, the description in the Priestly Document of what happened at Sinai may be almost pure fiction, but
that is not to say without further ado that it is pure untruth. The
prophetic interpretation of Israel's history may be very different
from the priestly, but we are not in a position to say *a priori* that
if the one is true the other must be false. There may be truth in
all the several stages of the development of the Hebrew interpretation of history. The 'higher critic' may be right in his
analysis of the documents and in his presentation of the course
of Hebrew history and religion as based upon his analysis. At the

same time the 'fundamentalist', who takes the Old Testament in the completed form in which it has been handed down to him, may also be right in his broad conclusions. That remains to be seen. The first concern of the one is to ascertain the probable series of events; the other is desperately concerned to defend the truth of what is, on the whole, a late interpretation of the events. Both *may* be right. Nevertheless, each of them may be taking only a partial view, since, especially in the field of Old Testament religion, event and idea, if divorced from one another, are both abstractions. It has been well said that

the religious experience without the vision of history would be empty, the historical event without the religious experience blind.[a]

[a] Robert Winkler, in *Das Geistproblem*, p. 32, quoted by H. Wheeler Robinson in *Redemption and Revelation*, p. 16, note 1.

CHAPTER I

THE HISTORY IN OUTLINE

THE PURPOSE of this chapter is to outline the main course of Hebrew history. As we have seen, it may not always be possible to disengage the events of the history from the interpretations put upon them. We can but attempt to view the history as it might have appeared to an outside observer, as, indeed, it is viewed by the modern historical critic. There is no need for us to confine 'actuality' to physical happenings only, or to make believe that Hebrew history can be written without reference to Hebrew religion. Several writers, to mention only Ottley, Oesterley and T. H. Robinson, H. Wheeler Robinson, and Wardle in this country, have written separate and more or less parallel studies of the history and religion of the Hebrews; but, although this is a convenience for the student, the two subjects cannot be kept entirely distinct, and neither can be written without taking some account of the other. No ancient people was without religion, least of all the Hebrews. Even Wheeler Robinson, who has so clearly distinguished between original 'events' and interpretative 'facts', has said[a] that the work of Old Testament critical scholarship is to get behind later Jewish theories 'to the original history of both events *and ideas*' (italics mine). There are some religious 'ideas' which belong to the category of 'actuality'. Such ideas cannot be ignored without reducing the history to a bare skeleton, a thing without flesh and blood and sinews, let alone without the breath of life. No account of Hebrew history, however concise, can be reduced to a bare catalogue of physical events; it must *live*. We can but outline the course of Hebrew history as it might have appeared to a succession of intelligent outside observers.

Such a summary as is proposed in this chapter does not, therefore, preclude the mention of such religious 'ideas' as belong to the general stock of ethnic conceptions, inherited by Hebrew tradition from the pre-Mosaic past. It need not—since there are

[a] *Record and Revelation*, p. 304.

no 'bare facts' of history—altogether exclude ideas which are interpretative of events, so long as event and interpretation are
immediate and contemporary. It must be borne in mind, too,
that Deuteronomic and Priestly interpretations of Israel's past
are 'events' for the times when Deuteronomy and the Priestly
Code were written. If this means that it is not possible to present
the events of the history in a vacuum from which interpretative
'facts' are rigidly excluded, it cannot be helped. The best we can
do is to give as objective an account of what happened as we can,
reducing the interpretative content to a minimum.

Hebrew history proper begins with the Exodus. Even according to the Old Testament as we have it, only a *family* of seventy
males, not including Joseph, who was already there, migrated
with Jacob to Egypt (Genesis 46²⁷; Exodus 1⁵), later to emerge
as a nation. This is certainly a simplification of the actual facts.
The ancestry of the Hebrews, like that of all other nations, was a
good deal more complicated. There are good reasons for believing
that the patriarchs, the sons of Jacob, were in some sort tribes,
rather than individuals, prior to the descent into Egypt. This is
not to deny that there may have been individual originals for
some of the patriarchs in Genesis, notably for Abraham, though
what we are told of them largely reflects the movements of tribal
communities. Even so, it is not until the Exodus that we can
speak of the separate tribes as being welded into anything like
the semblance of a nation. It is also more than probable that some
at least of the traditional tribes were never in Egypt at all.
Whether we accept the Old Testament just as it stands, therefore,
or whether we think of the individual patriarchs as personifications of tribes, Hebrew history proper begins with the
Exodus.

There is not the slightest reason to doubt that the Exodus was
an event in history, even though it was a much smaller affair than
would ever have got into modern newspaper headlines. No
nation, let alone a nation so proud as the Hebrews, would ever,
if it had not been true, have gloried in saying that it owed its birth
as a nation to an escape from slavery, any more than the early
Christian apostles would have preached a crucified Messiah, if
Jesus had not been crucified. Neither the Exodus nor the Cruci-
fixion needs confirmation from external sources. Both at once
attest themselves as true.

When we come to details, however, it is at first disconcerting to find how little we know about an event of such fundamental significance as the Exodus for the nation that experienced it. We do not know with any finality when the Exodus took place. Exodus 1¹¹ seems to point to the reign of Merneptah (*circa* 1233–23), the son and successor of Ramses the Second. Twenty years or so ago it looked as if opinion was crystallizing in favour of a date in the fifteenth century,[a] but even more recently the thirteenth-century date has had its full share of advocacy.[b] It is generally admitted that dogmatism is impossible. Nor do we know how or where the passage of the Red Sea was made. The usual opinion has been that it was somewhat to the north of the Gulf of Suez, and that what made it possible was a strong wind that delayed the flow of the tidal waters over the low-lying marshland (cf. Exodus 14²¹, 15¹⁰). Latterly it has been argued that the Red Sea of the Bible (Hebrew: *yam suph*) was at the northern extremity of the Gulf of Akaba (cf. 1 Kings 9²⁶), and that the plagues, the crossing of the sea, the pillar of cloud, and the subsequent thunderings at the sacred mountain were all connected with a widespread series of seismic and volcanic disturbances.[c] But no matter when, or where, or how the crossing of the Red Sea took place, it made an instantaneous impression upon the Israelites, an impression which became ever more deep with the passage of the years. The couplet:

> Sing ye to Yahweh, for he is exalted in triumph;
> The horse and his rider hath he thrown into the sea,

which is found separately in Exodus 14²¹, and is also the opening couplet of the longer, and, in its present form, later ode Exodus 15¹⁻¹⁸, may well be contemporary with the event itself.

Having escaped from the pursuing Egyptians, the Israelites made their way to the mountain which was supposed to be the dwelling place of Yahweh, the God in whose name Moses had

[a] See J. W. Jack, *The Date of the Exodus*, 1925; Oesterley and T. H. Robinson, *A History of Israel*, Vol. I, 1932, p. 80.

[b] W. L. Wardle, *The History and Religion of Israel*, 1936, p. 33; H. Wheeler Robinson, *The History of Israel*, 1938, pp. 31ff.; H. H. Rowley, 'Israel's Sojourn in Egypt', in *Bulletin of the John Rylands Library*, 1938.

[c] cf. H. Gressmann, *Mose und seine Zeit*, 1913, pp. 108ff.; W. J. Phythian-Adams, *The Call of Israel*, 1934.

Jerusalem Temple, right down to the time of the Exile (2 Kings
15$^{12f.}$, 23^7; Ezekiel 8$^{9-18}$).

The period of the 'Judges' may be briefly described as that in
which Israelite influence became paramount. The newcomers,
fresh from the wilderness, and with still vivid memories of what
had happened at the Exodus, had a certain moral ascendancy.
The time came when they were able to accept the challenge of
the inhabitants of the plain. This they did under the leadership
of Deborah and Barak. The contemporary Song of Deborah
(Judges 5) gives a vivid description of the battle in the Kishon
Valley, in which contingents from several neighbouring tribes,
summoned in the name of their war-god Yahweh, routed Sisera
and his chariots. Like many another ancient poem, the Song of
Deborah was never intended to be an historical document, but
it is one nevertheless. Of the traditional twelve tribes it mentions
nine, together with Machir and Gilead (=Gad?), which at that
time evidently had equal status and responsibilities. Reuben,
Gilead, Dan, and Asher are censured for not obeying the sum-
mons. No doubt they were sufficiently far from the scene of the
combat to feel that it was no concern of theirs. But clearly they
were reckoned as members of a confederation bound together by
a common tradition and loyalties. Yahweh had a claim upon
them, and the fact that tribes on the east of Jordan were included
is evidence that the alliance was forged before the entry into
Canaan proper. It is significant that Judah is not mentioned,
not, in all probability, because it was too far distant, but because
it was not yet a member of the confederation.

The Israelites were now strong enough to take the lead in
repelling the attacks of other nomads who, like themselves some
generations before, attempted to invade the country. The heroes
who came to the fore in these times of crisis have come to be
known as the 'Judges'; but their functions were military rather
than judicial, though their exploits would naturally give them
authority in the conduct of civil affairs. It does not appear that
their influence was more than local, and some of them may well
have been contemporary with one another. It is likely that
Gideon attempted to found some kind of a monarchy. His half-
Canaanite son, Abimelech, certainly did, but he came to an
inglorious end. The nomad tradition of the Israelites, and the
long-standing rivalries of city-states in a deeply intersected land

like Canaan, made it impossible to establish a centralized authority, short of imperative necessity.

The necessity did become apparent when the Philistines, an Aegean people who had established themselves on the Mediterranean sea-board during the twelfth century, began to extend their power over the land which, after them, has come to be called Palestine. The Danites, who were their near neighbours, were constrained to migrate to the extreme north of the country. Advancing through the Plain of Esdraelon as far as Beth-Shean, the Philistines virtually cut the country in two, and reduced the Israelites to impotence and even servitude. But the immediate occasion for the rise of the monarchy was Saul's response to an appeal for help from the east-Jordan city of Jabesh Gilead, which was barbarously threatened by the Ammonites. Exactly how Saul became king, and what Samuel's early relations with him may have been, is obscure. The well-known story of how the young son of Kish went forth to seek for his father's lost asses, to be secretly anointed by Samuel, is not without its difficulties, since immediately upon his election Saul has a son who is already a warrior of prowess. It does, however, appear that the foundation of the monarchy was assisted by the patriotic fervour of prophets, who begin to be prominent about this time, and with whom Samuel was intimately associated. Saul was sufficiently able to curb Philistine pretensions as to prove that they were not invincible. But the area of his authority was restricted, and he seems to have had neither the ability nor the opportunity to establish much in the way of an administration. He was impulsive, and the balance of his mind was none too stable. It is clear that he fell out with Samuel, though we do not know the exact cause of the quarrel, and, to make matters worse, he became consumed with jealousy of David, a young Judahite warrior who had joined his standard. He finally fell in battle against the Philistines, and was succeeded by his son Ishbaal, a man in no way qualified to retrieve the situation.

David, who had had to flee from Saul and to seek refuge among the Philistines, was immediately installed as king over his native tribe of Judah. Some years of desultory warfare followed between his partisans and those of Ishbaal, until the murder of the latter—a crime to which David seems not to have been privy —afforded the opportunity to both north and south to unite under David. This was virtually a fresh declaration of war against the Philistines, and they were quick to move. Their power was broken, though they retained their independence alongside Judah for almost another three centuries. David's next move was to evict the Jebusites from the ancient and hitherto unconquered citadel of Zion-Jerusalem (Urusalim in the Amarna letters). This was not only a brilliant feat of arms but of political strategy as well. The city was a natural fortress, in territory neutral to Israel and Judah, in every respect an ideal capital for the now united monarchy. To it David brought up, with much trepidation, the Ark, which ever since the wilderness wanderings had been revered as the embodiment of Yahweh's warrior-presence among His people. For some time the Ark had been held as a trophy by the Philistines. It was now, with great cere-mony and—according to the notions of the times—reverential awe, deposited in a specially prepared tent close by the royal palace.

Whether to secure his own frontiers, or with the deliberate purpose of founding an empire, David subdued most of the adjacent territories. Edom and the country round Damascus were occupied by military governors; the rulers of Ammon and Moab sent him tribute; and treaties of friendship were concluded with Hamath, to the north on the Orontes, and the wealthy city of Tyre, on the Phoenician coast. A small standing army was established, chiefly of Philistine mercenaries, who could be counted on to have no interest in possible domestic dissensions. The reign also saw the organization of a rudimentary civil service. There was of course no popular franchise, but the power of the throne may truly be said to have rested upon popular consent, with some respect for the rights of the subject. The whole was a brilliant achievement, carried through in the space of a single generation. Beneath the surface, however, there lurked possibilities of disintegration. For all his great qualities of leadership, courage, and chivalrous generosity, David was a man of sometimes ungovernable physical passions, and his own conspicuous moral lapse made it well-nigh impossible for him to control his sons, to one of whom, Absalom, he came very near losing his throne. That the old tribal animosities were not yet dead is shown by the attempted revolt of a Benjamite named Sheba. When at length David had become senile, Solomon, a younger son, obtained the succession, largely as the result of a palace intrigue.

Solomon, who had been brought up in the enervating atmosphere of the harem, was no warrior, and in any case he was probably wise to consolidate his power by organizing the defences of the territories he possessed, rather than to try to conquer new ones. He accordingly built fortifications at strategic points, and added cavalry and chariots to the already existing armament. Even so the outlying provinces of Damascus and Edom succeeded in regaining their independence. The only gain to set over against these losses was the city of Gezer, on the borders of Philistia, which was conquered by the Egyptian Pharaoh and given as a dowry to one of his daughters who married Solomon. Solomon's building programme included not only defence works, but an extensive palace and administrative buildings in Jerusalem. Of all these sumptuous erections the Temple was destined to become by far the most important. Its size was much more modest than imagination has generally pictured it. At first intended as a royal chapel, adjacent to the palace, the very building of it was a definite, and even startling, departure from Israelite religious tradition. Hitherto Yahweh, as became a wilderness deity, had 'walked in a tent and in a tabernacle' (2 Samuel 7⁶). That the Ark was now housed in a permanent royal sanctuary was the symbol that He had at length consented to 'settle down'. Only gradually, however, did the Temple become a national sanctuary: it would hardly be accessible to the common people, even if they could undertake the pilgrimage to Jerusalem.

The grandiose building programme of Solomon, as well as his lavish private expenditure—his harem assumed Oriental proportions—was a severe drain upon the slender economic resources of the state, notwithstanding that those resources were energetically supplemented by customs dues on merchandise passing through the country, and maritime voyages based upon the Red Sea. To defray his expenses Solomon resorted to extensive labour conscriptions, and divided the country into administrative districts which ignored tribal boundaries, and thus flouted jealously guarded tribal sentiments. When, at Solomon's death, the people petitioned his son Rehoboam to remit something of their burdens, and Rehoboam lightheartedly refused, the northern tribes broke away from their loyalty to the house of David, and set up a kingdom of their own under Jeroboam, an Ephraimite commoner.

By far the larger part of the resources of Palestine lay within the area of the Northern Kingdom, and so long as the divided monarchy lasted Israel was of much more political and military consequence than Judah could even aspire to be. But its population was much less homogeneous, and it was constantly in danger of falling a prey to some military adventurer. No city could at once claim undisputed pre-eminence as its capital, as Jerusalem did in the south, and it would have needed a very great man to establish a dynasty with the prestige already enjoyed by the house of David. Judah, geographically isolated, and no great military prize, was able to pursue the modest tenor of its way without much outside interference. At first, relations between the sister states were hostile, and generally continued to be while no formidable foe threatened Israel from the north, Judah being more or less in a condition of vassalage to her more powerful neighbour. Jeroboam set himself to neutralize the potential religious hegemony of Jerusalem, and for this purpose set up bull-calf images of Yahweh in two important sanctuaries, Dan and Bethel. No doubt he did this without any conscious apostasy, though it must be said that he was a man without any vision beyond that of establishing a kingdom and dynasty reasonably secure. He was an energetic and capable ruler, but within two years after his death his dynasty came to an end, and his family was exterminated, by Baasha, a military usurper of the tribe of Issachar.

Baasha's dynasty was short-lived, and it was only after a period of civil war that Omri, the commander-in-chief of the army, succeeded in restoring order. Omri was an able ruler; he has been called 'the David of the Northern Kingdom', and his choice of the fortress-city of Samaria for his capital is an obvious parallel to David's choice of Jerusalem. He found himself menaced by the growing power of Damascus, and accordingly took steps to ally himself with Phœnicia. This was effected by the marriage of his son, Ahab, to Jezebel, a princess of Tyre. There is no doubt, too, that it was the need to establish a balance of power against Damascus that dictated a new policy of alliance with, instead of hostility to, Judah. Ahab's marriage had even more important consequences for religion than it had for power politics. Jezebel was a domineering woman, and a zealous propagandist. She tried to establish in Israel the cult of Melkart, the Baal of her cosmopolitan Tyre, even to murdering the prophets of Yahweh. She also took matters out of the hands of the more complaisant Ahab—who has been called 'the Solomon of the Northern Kingdom'—when he set covetous eyes upon the patrimony of one of his humble subjects. All this high-handed procedure called forth a vigorous protest from Elijah, a solitary prophet who came, very significantly, from east of the Jordan, where the ancient nomadic tradition was still cherished. Elijah insisted, and undertook to demonstrate, that the writ of Baal-Melkart did not run in Israel. Exactly what took place at the memorable encounter on Mount Carmel may never be known. We need not doubt that Elijah did succeed in checking the Baal menace, but since he was constrained forthwith to flee for his life, and the Baal cult had later to be extirpated by Jehu, it would appear that his triumph was not so immediately complete as the story in I Kings 18 suggests.

At the end of Ahab's reign an even more formidable danger than any that threatened from Damascus began to loom out of the north. An inscription of the Assyrian King Shalmaneser the Third records that in 853 B.C., at Karkar on the Orontes, he fought a coalition of western states which included both Damascus and Israel. Ahab's contribution of two thousand chariots was larger than that of any of his confederates. Despite his claims to total victory Shalmaneser does not seem to have followed up his advantage, and no sooner was the danger past than Israel and Damascus were once more at loggerheads over the disputed city of Ramoth Gilead. In the ensuing battle, at which Ahab was mortally wounded, Jehoshaphat of Judah appears as a vassal-ally of Ahab.

The kings who succeeded both Ahab and Jehoshaphat were men of little mark. The two reigning houses had become related by the marriage of Athaliah, the daughter of Ahab and Jezebel, to Jehoram the son of Jehoshaphat. In the year 842 B.C. or thereabouts we find Jehoram of Israel and Ahaziah of Judah once more at war with Damascus before Ramoth Gilead. Jehoram was wounded, and retired to Jezreel, whither Ahaziah went to visit him. Meanwhile Elisha sent a young prophet to Ramoth Gilead with orders to anoint as king a cavalry officer named Jehu.

that king Uzziah died', and his inaugural vision in the Temple
gives the keynote to his message. His emphasis was upon the
'holiness' of Yahweh, His majestic exaltation combined with His
incomparable moral purity. Yahweh was 'the Holy One of
Israel', a defence so sure that the making of security-treaties with
other states was apostasy from Him, the more so since such
alliances always involved a measure of recognition of the gods of
the treaty-power. It is an invariable rule in Hebrew history that
the kings who, like Ahaz and Manasseh, made foreign alliances
compromised the purity of the worship of Yahweh, while those
who, like Hezekiah and Josiah, attempted religious reformation
always tried to keep their country free from outside entangle-
ments. Isaiah's doctrine was so signally vindicated when, in
701 B.C., the army of Sennacherib had to make a panic-stricken
retreat, that the inviolability of Jerusalem became an established
dogma.

During the first half of the seventh century there was no dis-
puting the supremacy of Assyria, which, under Esarhaddon and
Ashurbanipal, even subdued Egypt. Manasseh, the contemporary
king of Judah, who reigned for more than fifty years, was in no
position to bar the Assyrian passage past his territory, and it may
be argued that his ready compliance did at least save his country
from being directly molested. But no sooner was Ashurbanipal
dead than the unwieldy empire began to totter under the combined assaults of Scythians, Medes, and a rejuvenated Babylonia.
In these circumstances Josiah, the grandson of Manasseh, was
able to reassert his independence, even, as it would seem, to
extending his control over parts of what had once been the
Northern Kingdom. His reforming zeal was encouraged by the
discovery in the Temple (621 B.C.) of a law-book which is generally
identified with some form of the book of Deuteronomy. When
in the year 612 Nineveh fell, and a few years later Pharaoh Necho
went to the assistance of the rump of the failing empire, Josiah
ventured to oppose his passage, and paid for his temerity with his
life, either on the field of battle, or, as some have suggested, by
the sentence of a court-martial. The Babylonian inheritance of
the power of Assyria was settled at Carchemish in 605 B.C., when
Necho was routed by Nebuchadrezzar.

The last days of the kingdom of Judah are chiefly memorable
for the long ministry of Jeremiah, whose position in relation to

the southern kingdom is remarkably parallel to that of Hosea in the north. Jeremiah began to prophesy some years before Josiah's reformation, and continued to be his country's mentor until after the fall of Jerusalem in 586 B.C. Whether or not he was at first sympathetic toward the programme of the Deuteronomists is disputed,[a] but it is generally agreed that his maturer judgement was that no organized reform of the externals of religion could avail to save the state. When, in 597, Jehoiachin and many citizens of consequence were deported to Babylon, Jeremiah wrote to the exiles bidding them make preparations for a lengthy stay, and to settle down as loyal subjects of the sovereign power. He seems to have been convinced that it was in the divine purpose that Temple and state should come to an end in the interest of a more inward and spiritual religion, that Nebuchadrezzar and his Chaldeans were therefore invincible until Yahweh's commission to them had been fulfilled; and during the final siege of Jerusalem he not only urged submission, but, when the vacillating king Zedekiah declined to follow his advice, even recommended individuals to give themselves up to the enemy. When at last, after 586, Nebuchadrezzar's conciliatory policy of attempting to govern Judah through a native commoner, Gedaliah, was frustrated by the stupid murder of his nominee, the conquered province was fully incorporated into the Babylonian empire.

Little is known of the fortunes of the Jews, as we may now call them, who continued to reside in Palestine during the period of the Exile proper (586–38 B.C.), except that their condition was indigent and unhappy. Nor is anything known of those who decamped to Egypt, forcibly taking Jeremiah with them. The centre of Jewish life and religion was now, and for many years continued to be, in Babylonia, whither the majority of the skilled and intelligent members of the nation had been transported. It was plain for all to see and ponder that the most unwelcome predictions of the prophets had been signally fulfilled, and since the prophets had always insisted that the impending disasters were Yahweh's chastisement for the wickedness and apostasy of His people, there was a noticeable deepening of the sense of sin. Ezekiel, a prophet who had been as vigorous as any in his denunciations, was actually resident in the exiled community, and he,

---

[a] Skinner, *Prophecy and Religion*, Chapter 6, and others think he was; Welch, *Jeremiah: His Time and His Work*, Chapter 5, thinks not.

political vicissitudes and disasters, were content. The monolatry of the early period had now given place to a genuine monotheism. The pre-exilic prophets had already proclaimed Yahweh as Lord of history and of universal morality, and from this the Deutero-Isaianic faith in Him as Lord of universal nature and human destiny, the one only God, was the inevitable corollary, now unquestioned. In the early days of monolatrous worship, when the existence of other gods besides Yahweh was taken for granted, the Hebrews had of course believed themselves to stand in a relation of peculiar intimacy with the national deity. It was therefore only natural that a sense of privilege and property in the one God should persist even now that His dominion was conceived to embrace the universe. This legacy from the past was further strengthened and reinforced by the obvious contrast between their own imageless worship and high standards of morality, and the idolatry and lax morals that were general in the contemporary world. On the whole, therefore, the Jew tended to be narrowly nationalistic in his religion; Gentiles had no part in the covenant mercies, though there were individuals, like the authors of Jonah and Ruth, whose sympathies were wider, and as time went on Jews of the Dispersion, particularly, were ready to receive and even to make proselytes, on the condition that they submitted to be circumcized and in other respects engaged to order their lives by the sacred Law. Animal sacrifices, which the pre-exilic prophets had viewed with suspicion and even contempt, were now organized into an elaborate system, the efficacy of which, as the chief external bond of the convenant, was un-questioned except by an occasional pious psalmist. Instead of affording the excuse for orgies of gluttony and drunkenness, sacrifice came increasingly to be related to the sense of sin. Al-though it is expressly stated that for deliberate and 'presumptuous' sin (Psalm 19[13]) there was no remission by sacrifice (Numbers 15[30f.]; cf. Hebrews 10[26f.]), and that even the sin-offering proper only availed for sins committed in ignorance (Leviticus 4), the general idea of making 'expiation'[a] was extended even to burnt-offerings.

It is only occasionally during the closing years of the Persian period, and the century that followed the conquests of Alexander the Great, that the veil of obscurity is sufficiently lifted for us to

---

[a] So Gray, *Sacrifice in the Old Testament*, p. 74, for E.V. 'atonement' (Lev. 1[4]).

be able to date and describe any particular event in the fortunes of the Jews. This lack of positive information is not a serious loss for the purposes of this essay, since the creative period of the religion was already past, and the main outlines of the Old Testament interpretation of history are clearly discernible in the sources that are extant. After the reconstitution of Judaism in Jerusalem, Babylonia ceased to be the centre of intellectual and spiritual activity; but new centres of thought and culture sprang up, particularly in Alexandria, where Jewish colonists were accorded special privileges. Other settlements were gradually founded in most of the great cities of the Mediterranean world. In them there developed a type of piety which had perforce to be kept alive, except for an occasional pilgrimage to the Holy City, without the daily ritual of sacrifices. Even in Palestine itself frequent worship at the Temple would only be possible for those who lived within a comparatively short radius of Jerusalem. For the great majority of Jews, therefore, religious life came to be centred in the Synagogue, and day-by-day piety to consist in the study of the law and obedience to its non-sacrificial precepts and obligations. This process of development, we may assume, went on silently during the third pre-Christian century, despite the disputes of Ptolemys and Seleucids for the possession of Palestine, and it was only when Antiochus Epiphanes (*reg.* 175–163 B.C.) tried to coerce his Jewish subjects into acceptance of a thorough-going Hellenism, and was aided and abetted in his attempt by some of the Jewish aristocracy, that they were goaded into revolt. The Maccabean struggle produced the book of Daniel, the first mature example of a new and distinctive interpretation of history, which deserves, perhaps, to be called a philosophy of the subject. According to Charles,

Daniel was the first to teach the unity of all history, and that every fresh phase of this history was a further stage in the development of God's purposes.[a]

[a] *A Critical Commentary on the Book of Daniel*, pp. cxiv.f.

CHAPTER II

THE SAGAS

THE ICELANDIC word *Saga* is a convenient designation for a considerable body of folk-poetry and story in the Pentateuch and historical books of the Old Testament. The materials it comprises are earlier than Deuteronomy, earlier, for the most part at least, than the eighth-century prophets. The sagas begin with the story of the Garden of Eden, and continue through the Pentateuch, Joshua, Judges, and Samuel, down to the stories of Elijah and Elisha in Kings.

The Saga element in the Pentateuch is contained in the so-called Yahwistic (J) and Elohistic (E) documents. It has long been recognized that these sources are continued into the book of Joshua; hence the term 'Hexateuch'. It is generally recognized, too, that the books of Judges and Samuel are composite, and that the saga materials in them consist of two main strands of interwoven narrative; but whether the stories in Judges and Samuel are actual continuations of J and E is uncertain. The latest 'Introduction',[a] by R. H. Pfeiffer, uses the symbols J and E to indicate the two old strands of narrative in Judges, but says this is 'merely a matter of convenience and need not imply that the same authors wrote J and E in Judges as well as J and E in Genesis'.[b] In his analysis of Samuel, Pfeiffer uses the terms 'Early' and 'Late' Source, and says of them that

their relationship is similar to that of J and E in the Pentateuch and Judges, but it is by no means certain . . . that they are really a continuation of J and E in the Pentateuch or part of the same works.[c]

Most critics find indications that J and E are themselves composite, or at least contain secondary and even tertiary strata, and it is quite common to meet with the symbols J^1, J^2 and J^3, E^1, E^2 and E^3, for earlier and later components of these documents

---

[a] *Introduction to the Old Testament* (New York, 1941).
[b] op. cit., p. 315.   [c] ibid., p. 341.

respectively. Otto Eissfeldt[a] has sought to simplify these 'algebraic symbols' by the, at first sight, paradoxical expedient of resolving the saga materials into three documentary strands, which he designates L, J, and E. All three are continued into Judges[b] and, though less positively, into Samuel.[c] Eissfeldt's L is so called from *Laienschrift*, or 'Lay-writing', because, so he finds, it is the most primitive and secular of the sources, at the farthest extreme from the sacerdotal Priestly Code (P). His J and E are the documents which have long been recognized, except, of course, that much of their materials, especially from J, is taken away from them and assigned to L. L is said to reflect the nomadic ideal, with its protest against the Canaanizing of Hebrew life, and to date from perhaps the time of Elijah.

According to Pfeiffer,

the chief objection to Eissfeldt's theory is that, outside of Genesis, his L and J either supplement each other or consist of mere snatches of narrative or isolated stories, hence, unless we assume that large portions are lost, no 'sources' or 'documents' can be reconstructed out of this literary debris.[d]

The hypothetical L

is characterized in the Pentateuch by archaic traits, exaltation of nomadic life, a certain coarseness, a primitive conception of the deity, and the lack of organic unity between the several stories. But after the end of Genesis, these characteristics fade away more and more, and it is often difficult to know on what criteria Eissfeldt separates J and L in the books from Exodus to Samuel.[e]

For his own part, Pfeiffer recognizes the presence, in Genesis, of elements which it is difficult to assign to J. These, including notably most of what earlier critics used to designate J¹, he

---

[a] *Hexateuch-Synopse* (Leipzig, 1922).

[b] *Die Quellen des Richterbuches* (Leipzig, 1925).

[c] *Die Komposition der Samuelisbücher* (Leipzig, 1931), in which the three narratives are designated I, II, and III; but cf. his *Einleitung in das Alte Testament* (Tübingen, 1934), p. 306, in which he says that Samuel is made up of 'three parallel threads of narrative, which are probably continuations of the three narrative threads of the Heptateuch—L, J, and E.' See also his article, 'Modern Criticism', in *Record and Revelation*, H. Wheeler Robinson, p. 84.

[d] op. cit., p. 159.

[e] ibid., p. 141.

treats as a separate document, which he denotes by the symbol S
(from South or Seir), probably Edomitic in origin. His J begins
with the call of Abraham (Genesis 12).

Whatever be our judgement on Pfeiffer's S hypothesis, his
criticism of Eissfeldt's attempt to carry through a three-document
analysis to the end of Samuel is certainly cogent. This lecture is
not concerned with the minutiæ of documentary analysis, and its
purposes will be sufficiently served by a separation of the Saga
materials into two main strands, the more so since Eissfeldt's L
and J are of approximately the same date, and therefore do not
differ very materially in their interpretation of history. The
'Early' and 'Late' strands may, with Pfeiffer, be labelled J and E
respectively, without prejudice to the question whether the actual
J and E are continued beyond the Hexateuch into Judges and
Samuel. At the same time, Eissfeldt's L and Pfeiffer's S are
attempts to deal with the problem presented by certain intractable early materials which it is difficult to incorporate into the
main body of J. Even if Eissfeldt's three-document hypothesis
should ultimately be accepted, it remains that the most marked
differences between his L and J are to be seen in the semi-mytho-
logical stories which tell of the primeval history (*Urgeschichte*) of
mankind in Genesis 1–11. These do present features which are
distinctive, and which hardly fit in with the normal outlook of J.
A short account of them seems therefore to be called for before we
proceed to consider the two main cycles of Saga.

1. *The Primeval History* (variously denoted J^1, L, or S).

The following are the principal sections of Genesis common to
Eissfeldt's L and Pfeiffer's S: 2$^{4-25}$ (in the main), The Story of
Creation; 3, The Expulsion from Eden; 4^1, $^{17-24}$, The Family of
Cain; 6$^{1-4}$, The Birth of the Nephilim; 9$^{21-7}$, Noah's Drunkenness;
11$^{1-9}$, The Tower of Babel; 19$^{1-26}$, The Destruction of Sodom;
19$^{30-8}$, The Incestuous Origin of Moab and Ammon; 34, The
Treachery of Simeon and Levi; 35^{21-2a}, Reuben's Incest; 36
(parts), The Annals of Edom; 38, Judah and Tamar. Of these
passages the most revealing for our present inquiry are those in
chapters 1–11, which tell the early history of mankind; the others
are mostly isolated and erratic blocks of matter which hardly fit
into any consecutive narrative, and whose chief common characteristic is a certain coarseness.

Eissfeldt's L, it may be noted, includes no story of the Flood, and while Pfeiffer includes the earlier (non-P) account of the Flood in S, he labels the section S², a designation representing 'additions made to S at various times during the two centuries 600–400 B.C.'.[a] It has frequently been observed that the section on the Cainite civilization (4^{17-24}) does not appear to anticipate the Flood:

The institutions enumerated are clearly those existing in the writer's own day; hence the passage does not contemplate a rupture of the continuity of development by a cataclysm like the Flood.[b]

The same is true of the section on the birth of the Nephilim (6^{1-4}), a fragment originally unrelated to the Flood story which now follows it; the race of Nephilim were not cut off by the Flood, as they surely deserved to be if anyone did, but survived as late as the days of Moses and Joshua (Numbers 13^{33}). It is only in its present context that the story is made to point the moral that mankind was so far gone in wickedness that there was only one remedy, the destruction of all except the family of Noah.

But although the L-S stories, when disengaged from the Flood-cycle, lose something of their monitory tone—the section on the Cainite civilization is not moralizing, even if we include in it Lamech's 'Sword Song' (Genesis $4^{23f.}$)—it is almost impossible not to discern in them the reflection that human happiness and even moral decency had progressively declined since man first ventured to taste of the forbidden tree of knowledge, in the belief that so he would become 'as God'. Something of the idea of the 'envy' of the gods is apparent both in the Eden story ($3^{22f.}$) and in that of the Tower of Babel ($11^{6f.}$). Man has impiously presumed to grasp after prerogatives which belong alone to deity; he must be put in his place, and deprived of all opportunity to repeat the attempt. Eden is for ever closed against him, guarded by Cherubim with swords of whirling flame. Henceforth he must contend with thorns and thistles, wresting a precarious sustenance from the soil by the sweat of his brow, perpetually at enmity with loathsome creatures like the serpent, his women subject to the pangs of childbirth, until he returns at last to the ground from whence he was taken. The Tower of Babel story, taken by itself, may only reflect the amused contempt of the nomad for the

[a] op. cit., pp. 160f.   [b] Skinner, *Genesis*, pp. 115f.

abandoned remains of some Babylonian *zikkurat*, but over the
stories as a whole there broods the sorrowful conviction that
civilization is labour and sorrow, a vanity of vanities attended by
violence and lust. Their theme is 'Paradise Lost'. This is not to
deny that the stories are patient of a more spiritual interpretation,
when viewed in the general context of religion, or even, in their
present form, as they stand. Their psychological verisimilitude
is astonishing, and it may be that their underlying pessimism is
an inheritance from the general stock of ethnic ideas about a
vanished golden age. The Old Testament cannot be accused of
treating sin lightly; yet, apart from the Eden story, it does not
concern itself much, if at all, with the problem of the origins of
evil, but only with sin in its empirical manifestations. It was not
until the inter-testamental period that the doctrine of the Fall
came to receive much attention in Jewish theological speculation,
as, for example, in Wisdom 2^{24}: 'By the envy of the devil death
entered into the world.' The Old Testament as a whole takes a
healthy and optimistic view of life and the good things of life;
there is nothing virtuously or disappointedly ascetic about its
outlook. Except in Ecclesiastes, it betrays no sourness in its
contemplation of existence as such. If, therefore, some of the
early stories in Genesis answered the 'envy' of the gods with stolid
defiance, such an attitude was only temporary, and left no
permanent mark upon the religion.

2. *The Yahwist* (J in the Hexateuch; the earlier strand of narrative
in Judges-Samuel).

There is not the least doubt that many of the stories of the
Yahwist in Genesis originally circulated at Canaanite sanctuaries
like Bethel, Beersheba, and Penuel, long before the Israelite
conquest of the country. This conclusion may even be drawn
from the stories as we have them, which relate how a patriarch
worshipped at, and even founded, such and such a sanctuary.
The theory of the Yahwist is of a kind of shadow occupation of
the country by the patriarchs, in obedience to the divine promise
of ultimate possession, prior to the descent into Egypt and the
final conquest. Without denying that some Israelite clans or
tribes may have been in Canaan before migrating to Egypt, the
inference lies near to hand that some of the stories, and even the
names of some of the heroes, were native Canaanite before ever

they came to be Hebrew. The name of one of the great patriarchs, Jacob, is found (in the form $y'qb'r$=Jacob-El) as a *place* name in central Palestine on a list of Thutmose the Third about 1500 B.C.[a] Asher, the name of a patriarch tribe, appears in Egyptian as the name of a district in north-west Palestine early in the eighteenth dynasty. Pfeiffer seems justified in saying that

the Palestinian origin of the sanctuary legends is indubitable, notwithstanding their far-reaching adaptation to Israel's nationalistic and religious ideals.[b]

The Yahwist, with consummate literary and religious genius, took from the assortment of Canaanite sanctuary and other legends materials which he combined with native Israelite traditions to frame an epic of Hebrew origins. He baptized the originally Canaanite stories into the Hebrew religion as it was embodied in his own soaring faith in his people's calling and destiny. What he produced far exceeds in majesty any Scandinavian saga; the only things comparable with it are the *Iliad* and the *Mahabharata*. The whole has been wrought according to a definite plan, and presents a conception of history that is unique for so early a period. No shadow of impending political decline obscures the robust optimism of the writer. The date can hardly be much later than 850 B.C.

Pfeiffer's submission that the Yahwist began his story with the call of Abraham has some bearing upon the scope of his conception of history. If he began with the Creation, and then continued with the account of the Flood, which only the family of Noah survived, and then proceeded to trace the genealogy of Shem through 'all the children of Eber' (i.e. the Hebrews—the initial consonants are the same—Genesis 10²¹) to Abraham and his descendants, he already thought in terms of the doctrine of election, of a divine choice gradually narrowed down from the race as a whole until it centred upon Abraham. This is certainly what P does. But if with Pfeiffer we detach the primeval history from J, it may be that the Yahwist was only thinking in terms of a particular divine providence attending some of Abraham's

[a] Skinner, *Genesis*, p. 360; A. Jirku, *Altorientalischer Kommentar zum Alten Testament* (Leipzig, 1923), p. 69.

[b] op. cit., p. 153; cf. Eissfeldt, *Einleitung*, pp. 42–5.

seed, not in terms of an election of that seed from the widest circle
of mankind. An unambiguous doctrine of election requires for
its foundation a monotheistic conception of God, and the general
opinion is that monotheism did not emerge until at least the
eighth century.[a] But it is clear that the Yahwist thought of
Yahweh's power as extending beyond the confines of Palestine
and the environs of Sinai; He was with Jacob at Paddan-aram,
with Joseph in Egypt, and the gods of Egypt were powerless
against Him even within their own territory. If we must date J
a century earlier than Amos, we must concede that at least one
thinker before Amos thought of Yahweh as in some sense Lord of
history. It may be said that any fourth-rate people is ready to
wager that its god is more powerful than any of his rivals. Be
that as it may,

Yahweh said unto Abram, Get thee out of thy country, and from thy
kindred, and from thy father's house, unto the land that I will show
thee: and I will make of thee a great nation, and I will bless thee, and
make thy name great; and be thou a blessing: and I will bless them that
bless thee, and him that curseth thee will I curse: and in thee shall
all the families of the earth be blessed (Genesis 12$^{1-3}$).

Something like the note of universalism is already struck in these
words.

Abraham's sojourn in the land of promise was cut short by a
famine, and he was fain to descend into Egypt. There he came
near to losing the wife who should bear him seed; she was taken
into the harem of the Pharaoh. But 'Yahweh plagued Pharaoh
and his house with great plagues because of Sarai Abram's wife'
(Genesis 12^{17}). The patriarch was sharply rebuked by Pharaoh
for his prevarication in persuading his wife to pass herself off as his
sister. He was given an escort to the frontier, and presumably
allowed to keep the wealth which had been lavished upon him
(Genesis 12^{16}, 13^{2}). On their re-entry into Canaan, Abraham
gave to Lot the first choice of location, and his title to the
promised land would have been compromised had his nephew not
greedily chosen the Plain of Jordan (Genesis 13$^{7-11}$). A reiterated
assurance of numerous seed (Genesis 13$^{15f.}$) must have seemed
remote from fulfilment, since Sarah was barren, and it looked as

[a] This notwithstanding the vigorous submission of W. F. Albright, *From the Stone
Age to Christianity* (Baltimore, 1940), pp. 207 *et passim*.

if Abraham would have to settle his estate upon one of his home-born slaves. But Yahweh insisted that a child of his own should be his heir (Genesis 15$^{3f.}$), even though it would only be after centuries of servitude that his descendants would come into their landed inheritance (Genesis 15$^{13-16}$). Sarah continued to be barren, and accordingly proposed to her husband that he should take her slave Hagar as his concubine: 'It may be that I shall obtain children by her' (Genesis 16^2), the child of the slave being legally reckoned as her own. No sooner had Hagar conceived than her mistress dealt harshly with her; but her child Ishmael was born, to become for a time the heir-presumptive of Abraham.

At length, when Abraham was old, and Sarah herself was past the normal age for child-bearing (Genesis 18$^{11f.}$), her own child, Isaac, was born. Ishmael now disappears from the story, to become the ancestor of the Bedawin. But where, when he grows up, shall a wife be found for Isaac? It is unthinkable that he should marry one of the daughters of the Canaanites (Genesis 24^3), equally unthinkable that he should return to the land from which his father came out (Genesis 24$^{5-8}$). There is nothing for it but that a wife shall be brought for him from among his father's kindred who are still beyond the Euphrates. Yet suppose the woman be unwilling to adventure? All is well again when Rebekah consents to the proposal. But for a time she also is barren, until Yahweh yields to Isaac's entreaty, and she bears twin boys. Their rivalry began while they were still in the womb, and even as they came to the birth Jacob had hold of his brother's heel, so eager was he to possess in himself the right of the firstborn. This was secured to him, when they grew to manhood, by Esau's sale of the birthright, and was later fully confirmed by Jacob's ruse to secure their aged father's blessing. This last stratagem had one untoward result; Jacob was obliged to do what Abraham had expressly forbidden for Isaac, go to Haran, for 'a few days', as Rebekah hopefully said, 'until thy brother's fury turn away' (Genesis 27^{44}). The 'few days' became instead twenty years, during which Jacob was cheated by an uncle every whit as crafty as himself, and it seemed as if the promised seed must be re-absorbed into the family which Abraham at Yahweh's command had forsaken. Even when, at some peril, Jacob got clear of Laban, he had to face the long-deferred encounter with Esau; and how would Esau receive him? He summoned up all his mingled piety

and shrewdness, and the meeting passed off more happily than he
had anticipated. Not wishing to run any further risks, however,
he politely declined Esau's suggestion that they should now be
neighbours, and continued on his leisurely way, while Esau went
on to Seir. Esau, in his turn, like Ishmael, now disappears from
the main narrative.

This brings us to the Joseph saga. Its main interest, from the
standpoint of the Yahwist interpretation of history, lies in its
account of how, when famine threatened to reduce his kin to
starvation, Joseph, after almost incredible reverses of fortune,
was raised to such an eminence that he was in a position to secure
for them something more than a bare sustenance in the land of
the Pharaohs. Once more the seed of Abraham were under the
necessity of leaving the land of promise; but Yahweh anticipated
their plight, and opened a way before them. The words of
Joseph to his brethren, 'So now it was not you that sent me
hither, but God' (Genesis 45[8]), and 'Ye meant evil against me;
but God meant it for good' (Genesis 50[20]), are by common
consent assigned to E, but they admirably sum up the Yahwist's
faith in a providence that overrules the stubbornness of nature
and the perversities and wickednesses of men.

After the death of Joseph, 'and all his brethren, and all that
generation' (Exodus 1[6]), a new king arose over Egypt, 'which
knew not Joseph' (Exodus 1[8]). The Israelites were put to slave
labour, and when notwithstanding they continued to multiply
alarmingly, orders were given that all male children born to them
should be thrown into the Nile. The chivalrous but rash action
of Moses in slaying an Egyptian taskmaster only made matters
worse; he was obliged to flee into the land of Midian, where, 'in
the course of those many days' (Exodus 2[23]) until the death of the
Pharaoh, probably the long-lived Ramses the Second (Exodus
1[11]), he married and became naturalized. He met Yahweh's
commission to him to go back and deliver his brethren with every
excuse he could think of, but Yahweh would brook no refusal.
While he was on the way to Egypt he fell dangerously ill,[a] and
his first encounter with the Pharaoh only resulted in harsher
treatment of the hapless Israelites. With regard to the ensuing
plagues,

[a] So McNeile's and Driver's interpretation of Exodus 4[24]; Eissfeldt assigns the
passage to L.

It has long since been remarked by commentators that the plagues stand in close connexion with the actual conditions in Egypt; and were in fact just miraculously intensified forms of the diseases and other natural occurrences to which Egypt is more or less liable.[a]

While there is no need for us to pretend that there is no 'miraculous' element in J's description of the plagues, this feature is less obtruded than it is in E and P. The formula with which a plague is introduced in J is that Moses is bidden to obtain an audience of the Pharaoh, and demand the people's release; if the demand is refused, Yahweh will do so and so; this, since Pharaoh is obdurate, He proceeds to do, without further action on Moses' part; the plague is likewise removed by Yahweh, on Pharaoh's request that Moses will entreat for him. There is no mention of the wonder-working rod of Moses.[b]

The same is true of the Yahwist's account of the crossing of the Red Sea; it stands in a closer relation to natural phenomena than do the accounts of E and P.

And Yahweh caused the sea to go along by a strong east wind all the night, and made the sea dry land (Exodus 14^{21b}; cf. 15^{10}). . . . And it came to pass in the morning watch, that Yahweh looked forth upon the host of the Egyptians through the pillar of fire and of cloud, and discomfited the host of the Egyptians. And he bound[c] their chariot wheels, and made them drive heavily; so that the Egyptians said, Let us flee from the face of Israel; for Yahweh fighteth for them against the Egyptians (Exodus 14$^{24f.}$). . . . And the sea returned to its wonted flow when the morning appeared; and the Egyptians fled against it; and Yahweh shook off the Egyptians in the midst of the sea (Exodus 14^{27}).

The story is anthropomorphic enough, but it is just as conspicuously theocentric. Both these features are characteristically Hebrew. As John Macmurray has put it:

Jewish reflection thinks history as the act of God. Where our historians say, 'Caesar crossed the Rubicon', or 'Nelson won the battle of Trafalgar', the Jewish historian says, 'God brought his people up out of the land of Egypt'. This is no mere concession to religious prejudice, but

[a] Driver, Exodus, p. 57.   [b] Driver, loc. cit.
[c] So Samaritan, LXX; cf. R.V. margin.

the continuous form which all Hebrew reflection takes. It means that
Hebrew thought is at once religious and empirical. It is religious in
that it thinks history as the act of God. It is empirical in that it reflects
upon history in order to discover the nature of God and the laws of
divine agency.[a]

The Yahwist's account of the transactions at Sinai is contained
in Exodus 19–40. From this long section it is comparatively easy
to separate out passages belonging to P; the Decalogue and the
Book of the Covenant (Exodus 20–3) are by general consent
assigned to E; otherwise it is often impossible to separate J from
E with any confidence. This is not to be wondered at in a section
which, from the standpoint of later Judaism, was the most important in the whole revelation, and so was edited and re-edited
until much of it is in inextricable confusion. Two points common
to J and E may be noted, since they have an important bearing
upon our subsequent investigation. (1) Both the early sources
speak of a 'covenant' made between Yahweh and Israel at the
sacred mountain, Exodus 19[5] (J?),[b] 24[7f.] (E), 34[10] (J), 34[27f.] (J).
There is also the very early passage, 24[1-2, 9-11,c] which describes
how Moses, Aaron, Nadab, and Abihu, and seventy of the elders
of Israel went up the mountain:

And they saw the God of Israel; and there was under his feet as it were
a paved work of sapphire stone, and as it were the very heaven for
clearness. And upon the nobles of the children of Israel he laid not his
hand: and they beheld God, and did eat and drink.

Although the word 'covenant' is not used—but note verses 7f. in
the interjected context from E—evidently something very like a
covenant is intended by the sacred meal in the divine presence.
This may well be the most primitive story of the covenant between
Yahweh and Israel.[d] A covenant with Abraham has already
once been recorded in J (Genesis 15[18]). On the other hand

P says nothing of such a covenant (at Sinai); the only covenant mentioned by him in this connexion is the covenant with the *patriarchs*, to

[a] *The Clue to History*, p. 38.
[b] J, Driver; E, Eissfeldt; R[D,] Baentsch, *Exodus und Leviticus*, p. 172; McNeile.
[c] L, Eissfeldt; J, Driver and McNeile; E[1], Baentsch.
[d] cf. Eissfeldt, *Hexateuch–Synopse*, pp. 49f.

which Jehovah gives effect by delivering their descendants from Egypt, and settling them in Canaan (see Exodus vi. 4–8).[a]

(2) Both the early sources are perfectly frank about the murmurings and rebellions of the Israelites in the wilderness. The most important passages in this sense are: Exodus 14[11f.] 'Were there no graves in Egypt?'; 15[23f.], the Waters of Marah; 17[3-7], Massah and Meribah; 32[1-24], the Golden Calf; 32[25-34], the Consecration of the Levites; Numbers 11, Dissatisfaction with the Manna and the Gift of the Quails; parts of Numbers 14, the Report of the Spies, the present Generation condemned to die in the Wilderness; parts of Numbers 16, the Rebellion of Dathan and Abiram. These passages present a different picture from what we should expect from Hosea 2[15] [(Heb. 17)] and Jeremiah 2[2f.], which speak of the wilderness wanderings in terms of honeymoon happiness. On the other hand, the picture is not so unrelievedly dark as that painted by Ezekiel, who has it that Israel 'committed whoredoms' even in Egypt (Ezekiel 23[3, 8, 19, 27]). There are reasons for believing that the story of the Golden Calf, which represents the conduct of the people as gross idolatry and apostasy, comes from the later stratum of E;[b] while the final tragedy of all, in which Moses, who otherwise displays almost incredible patience, is condemned to die without entering the promised land, is from a composite narrative, mainly P (Numbers 20[1-13]). The murmurings in the wilderness are only what we should expect in the circumstances. It seems inevitable, too, that at least a generation would have to elapse before the tribes were in a position to attempt the conquest of Canaan. The murmurings and the delay were accordingly related as cause and effect, to show why Yahweh's purpose to give to His people the promised land was so long in being accomplished. It is one more example of the Yahwist's thesis that the promise made to Abraham was at long last fulfilled, though only after many hindrances had been overcome. The effect is to heighten the impression of Yahweh's power and longsuffering.

It may be assumed from the way in which the Yahwist loves to dwell upon the promise that Abraham's and Jacob's seed

[a] Driver, *Exodus*, p. 170. Leviticus 26[45] may perhaps be an exception. But the passage belongs to the Law of Holiness (H), and, even so, may refer to the patriarchs (cf. v. 42).

[b] McNeile assigns it to E[2], and Baentsch (much of it) to a supplementary stratum of E.

should possess the land of promise (Genesis 12^7, 13$^{15ff.}$, 15^{18}, 24^7, 26^3, 28^{13}, Exodus 33^1), that his story included an account of the conquest. That, indeed, would have been an appropriate and adequate conclusion to his work. We accordingly expect to find it in the Book of Joshua. When we analyse the Book of Joshua, it is at once evident that its main narrative of the conquest is older than the Deuteronomic and Priestly writers, whose work is discernible throughout. But it is more difficult to analyse this presumably JE material into its components J and E than it normally is in the Pentateuch. There are indications of composite narrative, but many scholars hesitate to attempt a precise or final analysis, and content themselves with the designation JE for the earlier story as a whole. Embedded in the Book of Joshua, however, are some *disjecta-membra* (13^{13}, 15$^{14-19, 63}$, 16^{10}, 17$^{11-18}$, 19^{47}) which present a very different picture of the conquest from that of the normal 'JE'. Most of them are repeated in the summary account of the conquest now extant in Judges 1. They may, or may not, actually be from the Yahwist; but if it is a characteristic of his to dwell upon the difficulties that attended the fulfilment of Yahweh's promise, they are entirely in his vein. Most scholars are ready to assign them to J, and it is mainly upon them that the modern historian of Israel relies for his conclusion that the conquest of Canaan was at first only partial, and attended throughout with difficulty. Not only do these fragments show clearly that the Canaanites were by no means exterminated, but they make it certain that the occupation of Judah, at least, was in part effected by clans like the Kenites (Judges 1^{16}) and Kenizzites (Joshua 15^{17}, Judges 1^{13}; cf. Genesis 36$^{11, 15, 42}$), which were not even of pure Israelite blood. All this accorded ill with the later idealized conception of a rapid conquest of the whole country under one leader, Joshua, and it would seem that the Yahwist's story was almost entirely suppressed. Only a few fragments of it have survived, while other parts, no longer individually recognizable, may have been assimilated to E in the now extant JE.

The oldest sagas in the Book of Judges have all the brilliance of the Yahwist, whether or not they are actually his. They appear to know nothing of a separate period of the 'Judges' in between the (supposedly) complete conquest of Canaan and the establishment of the monarchy. They are quite frank in their admission of the lawlessness of the country. The repeated observation, 'In those days there was no king in Israel: every man did that which was right in his own eyes' (Judges 17^6, 18^1, 19^1, 21^{25}), indicates a recognition of the need for a monarchy. The Philistine menace pointed in the same direction; the tribe of Dan was so straitened in its original settlement on the Philistine border that it was reduced to a few hundred warriors in the villages of Zorah and Eshtaol (Judges 13^{25}, $18^{2, 8, 11}$), and had to seek a home elsewhere. Even Judah was threatened (Judges $15^{9ff.}$). The writer appears to have Saul and David in mind when he makes the angel of Yahweh say of Samson, 'he shall begin to save Israel out of the hand of the Philistines' (Judges 13^5). So far from his having any prejudice against the monarchy, he impresses his readers with the urgency of the need for it.

The picture of humiliating Philistine oppression is continued in some of the early stories of 1 Samuel (chapters 4^{1b}-7^1), in which matters are represented as now far worse than they had been in the days of Samson. The Israelites were heavily defeated in a pitched battle at Aphek (1 Samuel 4^{1-3}), and when they sought to retrieve the situation by placing the sacred Ark in the forefront of another battle, it was carried off as a trophy by their enemies. But although the Ark wrought such havoc among the victors that they judged it wise to restore it to its owners, their domination over Israel was continued. This was the situation in which Saul rose to power.

In the older of the two generally recognized accounts of the rise of the monarchy, Saul, going out to seek his father's lost asses, is secretly anointed by Samuel, and bidden to 'do as occasion serve' (1 Samuel 9^1-10^{16}). Accordingly, 'about a month later' (so 10^{27b}, LXX; cf. R.V. margin) he went to the relief of Jabesh Gilead (1 Samuel 11), and was acclaimed king at Gilgal. His first encounter with the Philistines, in which his son Jonathan is the hero, cannot have been long delayed, and is related in 1 Samuel 13f. We have already had occasion to remark[a] that the story of the bashful youth is hardly consistent with that of the yeoman farmer with a valorous son of military age, and it is probable that the earlier account of the rise of the monarchy is itself composite. Of its two components, the story of the lost asses is unquestionably of later date than the exploits of the warrior-

[a] *supra*, p. 7.

D

king. Even so it still belongs to the category of saga. There are, no doubt, legendary and idealistic features in it, but it gives an accurate picture of a sacrifice at a local 'high place', and of the wandering bands of ecstatics. In it the monarchy is still regarded as a divine ordinance. Yahweh has 'seen the affliction' (so read in 1 Samuel 9[16] with LXX, Targum) of his people at the hands of the Philistines, and himself takes the initiative in their deliverance by instructing Samuel to anoint Saul. Samuel is the comparatively unknown 'seer' of a small country town.

In the 'Court History' of King David (2 Samuel 9–20, 1 Kings 1–2) we pass for a while from the mystic twilight of saga into the clear daylight of history proper. Most scholars regard it, apart from a few minor additions, as contemporary, or very nearly so, with the events it narrates. If so, it is older than the main body of J. It is a brilliant piece of historical writing, five centuries older than Herodotus, 'the father of history'. It is not merely annalistic, like the earliest sources we have for the reign of Solomon; nor is it didactic and pragmatic, like the work of the Deuteronomic historians; it is thoroughly objective and impartial, as free from moralizing as the sagas at their best. Like the sagas, too, it is psychologically profound and convincing. The writer does not go out of his way to point out that the sorrows which overtook David in the later years of his reign were largely due to his own weaknesses of character; but we get the impression that he knew that perfectly well, and knew that his readers would recognize it too. Any historian is in duty bound to reinterpret the work of his predecessors. We are at liberty, therefore, if we feel ourselves competent, to place a different construction upon some of the characters and motives from that which the 'Court Historian' himself would have done; for example, it is quite likely that Hebronite jealousy of Jerusalem had in it the seeds of rebellion, quite apart from the wounded vanity of Absalom, and it may be more obvious to us than it was to the Court Historian that Solomon's accession to the throne was the result of a rather sordid palace intrigue. But with the writer's main enthusiasms we can be in cordial agreement; with his admiration for David's character and achievement as a whole; with his robust faith in his nation's destiny; and his conviction that the monarchy, thus far, was a beneficent thing, a veritable gift of God.

3. *The Elohist* (E in the Hexateuch; the later strand of narrative in Judges-Samuel).

The work of the Elohist, considered as a whole, has neither the completeness nor the organic unity of J. Consequently, the suggestion has been made by responsible critics[a] that E is a series of editorial notes to J, rather than a separate 'document'. Even if this were so—and most scholars remain unconvinced of it—it would still remain that a writer set out to improve upon J, and in so doing presented a viewpoint of his own, a viewpoint which we must now proceed to consider, in so far as it has a bearing upon the interpretation of history.

It is generally believed that the original E was written a century later than J, about the middle of the eighth century. The writer has still much of the buoyant confidence of the Yahwist, which is quite understandable if he wrote in the prosperous reign of Jeroboam the Second. It is quite certain, however, that the original document has been extensively added to. These supplementary elements—usually denoted by the symbol E^2—must presumably be dated after the fall of the Northern Kingdom, and thus are of approximately the same date as Deuteronomy. Their tone, too, is similar to that of the Deuteronomists, and it is often difficult to designate them exactly. The reader who will take the trouble to work through a number of commentaries on, say, Exodus 32–4 will see how difficult it is to distinguish between the later hand of E (E^2 or E^S=Supplementer), the editor who combined J and E (R^{JE}), and a Deuteronomic supplementer (R^D); for example, Exodus 32 [9-14] (part of the story of the Golden Calf) is assigned by Baentsch to E^S, by Driver to R^{JE}, and by McNeile to R^D. It is obvious that the broad designation E covers a good deal of material which cannot by any stretch of imagination be called saga, material which can be as didactic as anything in Deuteronomy, and which may even be of as late a date. This applies, for the reason already indicated,[b] chiefly to the Elohist's account of the transactions at Sinai. The stories in Genesis and the first half of Exodus are comparatively free from later expansions. Even in the more complicated sections, sufficient remains of the original E for us to be able to draw

---

[a] P. Volz and W. Rudolph, *Der Elohist als Erzähler, ein Irrweg der Pentateuchkritik?* (Giessen, 1933).

[b] See *supra*, p. 30.

Canaan from their base at Gilgal, having together crossed the Jordan from the east. The only setback they encounter is before Ai, and that is accounted for by the trespass of one of their own number. The inhabitants of Gibeon, hearing that Jericho and Ai had been put to the ban (Joshua $6^{2\,of.}$, $8^{2\,6}$), beguiled the Israelites into making a treaty of peace with them (9^{3-15a}). When, three days later, their ruse was discovered (9^{16}), Joshua was unable to go back upon his pledged word; but he evidently felt that he had committed an error of judgement, and he condemned the Gibeonites to be 'hewers of wood and drawers of water' ($9^{22f.}$). We are led to suppose that the Gibeonites were the only people who obtained even this concession, and that conquered populations were regularly exterminated.[a] The occupation of the central highlands was speedily followed by victories against coalitions of kings in the south (10^{1-27}) and north (11^{1-9}). Only when the conquest was completed did the several tribes disperse to occupy the territories allotted to them (24^{28}). The occupation of the country in a series of lightning campaigns was facilitated by happenings which, whatever may be the natural phenomena of which they are reminiscent, are, in their present form, sheer miracles. The Jordan was crossed dry-shod (3^{11-17}); the walls of Jericho collapsed at the sound of Israelite trumpets and voices (6); even the sun stood still upon Gibeon ($10^{12ff.}$). This last marvel was first recited in a fragment of ancient poetry, which may not have intended it to be taken literally. It was, however, interpreted as prose by the later historian.

It is a moot point whether the story of the offer of the crown to Gideon in Judges $8^{22f.}$ has any literary connexion with the later (Deuteronomic?) account of the rise of the monarchy in 1 Samuel. If the paragraph in which the words are found (Judges 8^{22-8}) is a unity, and this there is little reason to doubt—note the close connexion between verses 23 and 24, as though Gideon, having declined the greater honour, asks for an alternative token of confidence—it is saga, presumably E. Jotham's parable of the trees going forth to anoint a king over them (Judges 9^{8-20}) shows no theocratic prejudice against monarchy as such, but is only directed against the pretensions of the upstart adventurer Abimelech. It even seems to imply that Jerubbaal-Gideon had established something like a hereditary dictatorship, at least in the

[a] This even though 10^{28-43}, 11^{10-23} are to be assigned to R^D.

neighbourhood of Shechem. This had probably been his intention. But according to Judges 8²²ᶠ·, when 'the men of Israel'—
not, be it noted, a local junta—approach Gideon with the request,
'Rule thou over us, both thou, and thy son, and thy son's son also:
for thou hast saved us out of the hand of Midian', he piously
declines the invitation with the words: 'I will not rule over you,
neither shall my son rule over you: Yahweh shall rule over you.'
This is somewhat in line with the situation presented in 1 Samuel
7f., 10¹⁷⁻²⁴, 12, but its attitude to the monarchy is much less
polemical, and Moore has it that 'a later writer (D) would have
no visible motive for introducing the offer and rejection of the
kingdom in this place'.ᵃ Probably the story should be assigned to
a secondary stratum of E, which in this instance, notwithstanding
its condemnation of the Ephod, has still preserved something of
the character of saga.

We have already noted that the 'Court History' of David is
history, not saga. This, of course, does not mean that the saga
form now falls out of use, nor even that it ceases to be a narrative
medium for events after the reign of David. After all, the saga
of the Yahwist is almost certainly later than David's reign, and
although we now emerge more clearly into the light of history,
there are still personalities and events the records of which are
saga rather than history. This is conspicuously true of the Elijah
and Elisha stories, which are of North-Israelitish provenance,ᵇ and
are best mentioned here under the heading E. They do not, however, add anything to our knowledge of the saga interpretation of
history, though it is worth while to note that Elijah's journey to
Horeb is testimony to the place which Horeb-Sinai had in primitive Israelite tradition; while his prayer, 'O Yahweh, the God of
Abraham, of Isaac, and of Israel', is independent confirmation of
the fact that the patriarchal tradition was already well established
in Israel.

ᵃ *Judges, I.C.C.*, p. 229.

ᵇ Note 1 Kings 19³, 'Beersheba, which belongeth to Judah'; there are also gram-
matical forms which point to origin in North Israel.

CHAPTER III

THE PROPHETS

I. THEIR INTERPRETATION OF PAST HISTORY

TO PASS from saga to eighth-century prophecy is to enter a different world. It is a world with a clearer historical background, a harsher and more realistic world. Instead of the third personal 'Now Yahweh said unto Abram', introducing a story which may be largely fiction, we have the first personal 'Thus the Lord Yahweh shewed me', introducing an experience which, however psychologically puzzling it may be, is nothing if not intensely real. The sagas describe how Yahweh revealed Himself to the heroes of the past; the prophets show Him at work in the immediate present, and under the eyes of His authorized interpreters:

Surely the Lord Yahweh does nothing,
Except he have revealed his secret unto his servants the prophets.
The lion hath roared, who will not fear?
The Lord Yahweh hath spoken, who can but prophesy? (Amos 3⁷ᶠ·)

The passage just quoted from Amos shows clearly how the prophets understood their office in its relation both to Yahweh and to those to whom they were commissioned. They were the spokesmen of Yahweh, intermediaries between Him and His people. Two passages from the story of the call of Moses serve to illustrate this. When Moses objected that he was slow of speech, and that Yahweh's call had not straightway cured him of this disability, Yahweh replied that his brother Aaron should do the speaking:

And thou shalt speak unto him, and put the words in his mouth . . . and he shall be thy spokesman unto the people: and it shall come to pass, that he shall be to thee a mouth, and thou shalt be to him as God (Exodus 4¹⁵ᶠ·). [And again] See, I have made thee a god to Pharaoh: and Aaron thy brother shall be thy prophet (Exodus 7¹).

Yahweh was ever wakeful over His word to perform it (Jeremiah 1¹²), making history, as we should say; the prophet's task was to interpret, and warn.

The prophetic 'word', as the prophets conceived it, was not their own; it was Yahweh's. The 'I' of a prophetic oracle is not the prophet, but Yahweh himself. Even the 'word' of a man, it was believed, if uttered in the solemn form of a blessing or a curse, had preternatural potency, and was irrevocable.[a] Nothing could recall the blessing pronounced by Isaac upon Jacob, even though it was at once evident that Jacob had obtained the blessing by deceit.

And Isaac trembled very exceedingly, and said (to Esau), Who then is he that hath taken venison, and brought it me, and I have eaten of all before thou camest, and have blessed him? yea, and he shall be blessed (Genesis 27³³).

Esau must make the best of what is left (verse 37). Even the 'blessing' he receives contains a *double entente* which turns it, in effect, almost into a curse.

Behold, away from[b] the fatness of the earth shall be thy dwelling,
And away from the dew of heaven from above (Genesis 27³⁹).

If such can be the power of the human word, how much more that of the 'word' of Yahweh, especially if He 'swears' it, and swears it 'by Himself'?

By myself have I sworn, the word is gone forth from my mouth in righteousness, and shall not return, that unto me every knee shall bow, every tongue shall swear (Isaiah 45²³). For as the rain cometh down and the snow from heaven, and returneth not thither . . . so shall my word be that goeth forth out of my mouth: it shall not return unto me void, but it shall accomplish that which I please, and it shall prosper in the thing whereto I sent it (Isaiah 55¹⁰ᶠ·). Is not my word like as fire? saith Yahweh; and like a hammer that breaketh the rock in pieces? (Jeremiah 23²⁹).

Against this general background of the prophets' conception of the divine activity in history, and of their own place as Yahweh's

[a] cf. J. Pedersen, *Israel: Its Life and Culture*, I–II (1926), pp. 182ff., 411ff.
[b] So R.V. margin; Hebrew: *min.*

spokesmen, we may now ask what was their interpretation of the past history of their people.

THE PROPHETIC INTERPRETATION OF PAST HISTORY

(a) The Patriarchal Tradition

References to the patriarchal tradition in the pre-exilic prophets are almost conspicuous by their absence. Amos mentions Isaac (Amos 7[9, 16]), Jacob (3[13], 6[8], 7[2, 5], 8[7]), and Joseph (5[6, 15], 6[6]). It may be assumed that he was familiar with traditions about them; but as the names appear they are nothing more than designations of the nation Israel, or of parts of it. The only event prior to the Exodus mentioned by Amos is the destruction of Sodom and Gomorrah (4[11]). Hosea also refers to this, with the difference that the doomed cities are named Admah and Zeboim (Hosea 11[8]; cf. Genesis 14[8], Deuteronomy 29[23]). The mention of Adam's transgression (6[7]) is difficult of interpretation,[a] and probably textually corrupt. What Hosea has to say of Jacob:

> In the womb he overreached ('*āqēbh*) his brother,
> And in his manly vigour he strove with God:
> Yea, he strove with the angel, and prevailed:
> He wept, and made supplication unto him (Hosea 12[3f.] (Heb. 4f.))

is probably, in the light of both the preceding and following (verse 7, *Heb.* 8) contexts, not intended as a commendation of the patriarch. This interpretation of the verses is supported by a passage in Jeremiah, whose close affinity with Hosea is often remarked:

> Take ye heed every man of his neighbour,
> And put no trust in any brother:
> For every brother will utterly overreach ('*āqôbh ya'aqôbh*),
> And every neighbour go about with slanders (Jeremiah 9[4] (Heb. 3)).

This, it may be noted, is Jeremiah's only allusion to the patriarchs, and it seems to be an intentional play upon the name Jacob. Isaiah's references to the past are few, and, apart from the bare mention of Sodom and Gomorrah (Isaiah 1[9f.], 3[9]), and the phrase 'Who redeemed Abraham' (29[22]), which is textually

<hr>

[a] cf. R.V. margin

suspect, none recalls the period before Moses. The same applies
to the genuine oracles of Micah.

It is not until the Exile that the patriarchal tradition assumes
any prominence in the utterances of the prophets, and then their
thought dwells particularly upon the first forefather Abraham.[a]
Ezekiel speaks of the 'land which I gave to my servant Jacob'
(Ezekiel 28[25]; cf. 37[25]). Of Abraham he has the people say:

> Abraham was but one,
> And he inherited the land:
> But we are many;
> To us is given the land for inheritance (33[24]).

The memory of this was prominent in Deutero-Isaiah's message
of comfort:

> Look unto Abraham your father,
> And unto Sarah that bore you:
> For he was but one when I called him,
> And I blessed him, and made him many (Isaiah 51[2]).

Abraham is given the honourable title 'Friend of God':

> But thou, Israel, my servant,
> Jacob whom I have chosen,
> The seed of Abraham my friend;
> Thou whom I have taken hold of from the ends of the earth,
> And called thee from the corners thereof,
> And said unto thee, Thou art my servant,
> I have chosen thee and not cast thee away (41[8f.]).

Trito-Isaiah has the people cry to Yahweh:

> For thou art our father,
> Though Abraham knoweth us not,
> And Israel doth not acknowledge us (63[10]).

A late passage in Micah also calls to mind Abraham:

> Thou wilt perform truth to Jacob,
> Mercy to Abraham,
> Which thou didst swear to our fathers
> From the days of old (Micah 7[20]).

[a] See K. Galling, *Die Erwählungstraditionen Israels* (Giessen, 1928), pp. 52f.

The contrast between Yahweh's abiding faithfulness and the faithlessness of Israel, despite unforgettable mercies, is the theme of a comparatively late oracle in the Book of Micah:

> Hear, O ye mountains, Yahweh's controversy,
> And give ear, ye foundations of the earth:
> For Yahweh hath a controversy with his people,
> And with Israel will he enter into argument.
> O my people, what have I done to thee?
> And wherein have I wearied thee? Testify against me!
> For I brought thee up from the land of Egypt,
> And from the slave-house did I redeem thee;
> And I sent before thee Moses,
> Aaron and Miriam with him.
> Remember now what Balak
> The king of Moab consulted,
> And what the answer given him
> By Balaam the son of Beor;
> (Remember) from Shittim unto Gilgal,
> That thou mayest know the righteous acts of Yahweh.
>   (Micah 6²⁻⁵).

Ezekiel, in the immediate prospect of the Exile, recalls the events of the Exodus as happening 'in the day when I chose Israel':

> Thus saith the Lord Yahweh:
> In the day when I chose Israel,
> And lifted up my hand (in token of oath) to the seed of the
>   house of Jacob,
> And made myself known to them in the land of Egypt,
> And I lifted up my hand to them, saying,
> I am Yahweh your God;
> On that day I lifted up my hand to them,
> To bring them forth from the land of Egypt,
> Unto a land which I had selected for them,
> Flowing with milk and honey,
> Which is the glory of all lands (Ezekiel 20⁵ᶠ·).

Deutero-Isaiah, the prophet of the Exile, loves to recall the Exodus. For him the approaching return from exile is to be a second and even more wonderful Exodus: once Yahweh had made the sea dry land for His people to pass over; now He is to do 'a new thing', turn the inhospitable desert into a well-watered plain, richly planted with forest trees:

> Thus saith Yahweh,
> Who made a way in the sea,
> And in the mighty waters a pathway;
> Who led forth chariot and horse,
> Army and power together;
> They lay down, they did not arise,
> They were extinguished, like flax they were quenched:
> Remember ye not the former things,
> Neither consider the things of old.
> Behold, I am about to do a new thing;
> Now shall it spring forth; do ye not know it?
> I will even make a way in the wilderness,
> Rivers in the waste.
> The wild creatures of the field shall honour me,
> The jackals and the ostriches,
> When I give waters in the wilderness,
> Rivers in the waste,
> To give drink to my people, my chosen.
>
> (Isaiah 43[16-20]; cf. 41[18ff.])

The chapters commonly assigned to 'Trito-Isaiah' contain a magnificent poem, which begins by recalling the past lovingkindnesses of Yahweh, and gradually passes into an impassioned plea for a renewal of His saving zeal. The text is in places uncertain, but the following is the gist of it:

> Of the lovingkindnesses of Yahweh will I make mention,
>   The praiseworthy acts of Yahweh,
> According to all that he did for us,
>   Yahweh, great in goodness;
> What he did for us according to his mercies,
>   And the abundance of his lovingkindnesses.
> For he said, Surely they are my people,
>   Children that will not deal falsely:
> And so he became their saviour
>   In all their affliction.
> It was no angel nor messenger,[a]
>   But his own presence that saved them:
> In his love and in his pity
>   He himself redeemed them;
>
>   [a] So read with LXX.

And he bore them and carried them
  All the days of old.
But they rebelled, and grieved
  His holy spirit:
Therefore he turned to be their enemy,
  And himself fought against them.
Then he remembered the days of old,
  Moses his servant.[a]
Where is he that brought up from the sea
  The shepherds of his flock?
Where is he that set his holy spirit
  In the midst of them?
That caused his glorious arm to go
  At the right hand of Moses?
That clave the waters before them,
  To make for himself an everlasting name?
That led them through the deeps,
  As a horse in the wilderness,
  That they stumbled not?
As cattle that go down into the valley,
  The spirit of Yahweh caused them to rest:
So didst thou lead thy people,
  To make for thyself a glorious name.
                              (Isaiah 63[7-14].)

To go back to Deutero-Isaiah: another striking, and also, it
seems certain, original feature about his references to the Exodus
is the way in which he illustrates it from the ancient myth of the
slaying of the chaos-monster. This is not in the least to suggest
that the Exodus tradition borders upon mythology, but rather
that the prophet took of the broken fragments of mythology to
furnish his description of Yahweh's mighty acts in history.

Awake, awake, clothe thyself with strength,
  O arm of Yahweh!
Awake, as in the days of old,
  The generations of ancient times!
Art thou not it that hewed Rahab in pieces,
  That pierced the dragon?
Art thou not it that dried up the sea,
  The waters of the great deep;
That made the depths of the sea a way
  For the redeemed to pass over? (Isaiah 51[9f.].)
    [a] So some MSS. and Syriac, text uncertain.

Here the 'deep' is Tehom, the primeval chaos of Hebrew cosmogony (Genesis 1², cf. Proverbs 8²⁷, Psalm 104⁶), the Babylonian Tiamat. Rahab is a mythical sea-monster (Job 9¹³, 26¹², Psalm 89¹¹); it is also a poetical synonym for Egypt (Isaiah 30⁷; Psalm 87⁴, 'Rahab and Babylon'). The 'dragon' (Hebrew *tannîn*) which is 'pierced' is likewise a mythological personification of chaos (Isaiah 27¹), and in Psalm 74¹³ seems to refer to Egypt.

This association of the deliverance from Egypt with the act of creation becomes henceforward a definite motif in Hebrew psalmody. The Hebrews believed that the world had its origin in a creative act, or series of creative acts, as distinct from emanation out of chaos; but the doctrine of creation was always, in their thinking, subordinate to that of redemption, the Creation being, as it were, a kind of prelude to Yahweh's redemptive activity. This association of Creation with the redemptive fact of the Exodus has its literary origin in the oracles of Deutero-Isaiah. Apart from one passage, Jeremiah 32¹⁷⁻²³, which in its present context is a later insertion in the spirit of Deuteronomy,ᵃ most of these poems are to be found in the book of Psalms. It would take us beyond the scope of this chapter to quote them *in extenso*, but this seems the most convenient place at which to subjoin a list of the principal historical psalms which may be said to have their origin in the prophetic rather than in the priestly and legalistic tradition. They are Psalm 44 (verses 1–3 (*Heb.* 2–4)), *74 (12–17)*, 77 (5–20 (*Heb.* 6–21)), 80 (8–11 (*Heb.* 9–12)), 81 (1–10 (*Heb.* 2–11)), *135 (6–12), 136*. The passages in italic are those which associate Creation with the Exodus in the manner characteristic of Isaiah 51⁹ᶠ. The finest of them is Psalm 74¹²⁻¹⁷:

> Yet God is my King of old,
> Working salvation in the midst of the earth.
> Thou didst divide the sea with thy strength:
> Thou didst break the heads of the dragons in the waters.
> Thou didst crush the heads of leviathan in pieces,
> Thou gavest him to be food for the denizens of the wilderness.
> Thou didst cleave fountain and flood:
> Thou didst dry up the perennial rivers.
> Thine is the day, thine also the night:
> Thou hast established luminary and sun.
> Thou hast fixed all the boundaries of the earth:
> Summer and winter, thou hast made them.

ᵃ See Peake, *Jeremiah, Century Bible*, Vol. II, p. 119.

E

This passage might be taken as commemorating either the Creation or the Exodus; in fact, it commemorates both.

Finally, the question may be asked: Did the prophets think of the Conquest as a slow and arduous process, as, in fact, we have every reason to believe it was? Or did they think of it as speedily accomplished? None of the above-quoted passages reads as if it ever occurred to the writer that the Conquest took years to accomplish, not even the earliest of them, Amos 2[9ff].[a] It seems fairly certain that they all depend upon historical tradition as late as, or later than, E. Further, since they all assume that the promised land was Yahweh's gift to His people, and that the conquest of it was His conquest, it must have been inconceivable to them that any obstacle could impede the triumph of so invincible a conqueror.

For they gat not the land in possession by their own sword,
Neither did their own arm save them:
But thy right hand, and thine arm, and the light of thy countenance,
Because thou hadst a favour unto them (Psalm 44[3] [(Heb. 4)].).

The Hebrew historians, even as early as the Elohist, may have been largely romancing; but the story as they told it was a logical consequence of their pride in Yahweh. A religion may have its roots in history; this does not, however, mean that history will not be written, and re-written, from the standpoint of doctrine, of doctrine that is a precipitate from the original events of history.

(c) The Covenant

The almost complete silence of the pre-exilic prophets about the patriarchs has already been noted.[b] If the prophets knew of any covenant with Abraham they do not mention it. Indeed, their allusions to any covenant at all are fewer than might have been expected. Amos's 'You only do I know of all the families of the ground' (Amos 3[2]), and his obvious contempt for blind reliance upon Yahweh's protection (5[14], 9[10]; cf. Micah 3[11]), presuppose that his contemporaries assumed that they stood in a special relation to Yahweh, though he nowhere speaks explicitly of a

[a] cf. J. Rieger, Die Bedeutung der Geschichte für die Verkündigung des Amos und Hosea (Giessen, 1929), pp. 9f.

[b] See supra, p. 42.

:ovenant. The cry, 'We know thee, O God of Israel',[a] in Hosea 8[2], s in close context with the charge that the people 'have trans-gressed my covenant' (verse 1, cf. 6[7]). When and where this :ovenant was entered into is not said, though we should imagine rom the prophet's general historical retrospect that it had some :onnexion with the Exodus. Isaiah has a scathing passage Isaiah 28[14ff.]) addressed to the 'scornful men, that rule this people which is in Jerusalem', in which he accuses them of poasting:

> We have made a covenant with death,
> And concluded a pact with Sheol.

This, they imagine, is their guarantee of safety:

> For we have made lies our refuge,
> And under falsehood have we hid ourselves.

The prophet is, of course, being ironical. What he means is that he covenant of security about which they congratulate themselves will serve them no better than if it had been made with death and Sheol. It is often said, and very truly, that the covenant-idea was the seed from which the ethical religion of the Old Testament developed; but, like other true doctrines, it was capable of perversion, and the pre-exilic prophets, to say the least, viewed it with some suspicion.

References to a covenant are more numerous in Jeremiah, though even there they are not always without difficulty. The prayer,

Yet thou, O Yahweh, art in the midst of us, and by thy name are we called; leave us not. . . . Remember, break not thy covenant with us Jeremiah 14[9b, 21b.]),

s uttered in a very different spirit from that of the frivolous contemporaries of Amos; but it does not indicate what covenant s meant. In the present text of Jeremiah 11[3ff.] 'this covenant' is defined as that 'which I commanded your fathers in the day that . brought them forth out of the land of Egypt . . .'; but if, with Skinner[b] and Erbt,[c] we regard these words as a later expansion,

[a] So read probably, see Kittel's text.   [b] *Prophecy and Religion*, pp. 98ff.
[c] *Jeremia und seine Zeit* (Göttingen, 1902), pp. 138ff.

the 'covenant' referred to is presumably Deuteronomy. The 'New Covenant' oracle, however, is quite explicit:

Behold, days are coming—'Tis the oracle of Yahweh—when I will make with the house of Israel[a] a new covenant: not like the covenant which I made with their fathers in the day when I took them by the hand to bring them forth from the land of Egypt; seeing that they have broken my covenant, and I have rejected them[b]—'Tis the oracle of Yahweh. But this is the covenant which I will make with the house of Israel after those days—'Tis the oracle of Yahweh—I will put my law in their inward parts, and in their heart will I write it; and I will be to them a God, and they shall be to me a people. . . . (Jeremiah 31[31–3]).

The metrical form of this, assuming that it is intended to be poetry, is not at all clear, and it is possible that the original oracle has been expanded. But the association of the Old Covenant with the Exodus is strongly supported by 7[22f.]:

For I did not speak with your fathers, neither did I command them in the day that I brought them forth from the land of Egypt, concerning burnt-offerings and sacrifices: but this thing I commanded them, saying, Obey my voice, and I will be to you a God, and ye shall be to me a people.

It may seem strange that whereas the Yahwist had already combined the patriarchal and the Exodus traditions, even to using the word 'covenant' in connexion with them both,[c] the prophets, on the other hand, only speak of a covenant at the Exodus. Even Ezekiel, who knows of the inheritance of Abraham (Ezekiel 33[24]),[d] apparently still associates the covenant with the wilderness wanderings (Ezekiel 16[5–8, 59f.]; cf. 20[5f.]), not with Abraham, and he describes it under the figure of the marriage relation, much as Hosea and Jeremiah had done. There is nothing in the prophets to indicate that the covenant was concluded at Sinai in particular, as distinct from the Exodus proper. This is not to say that the prophets were ignorant of the Sinai tradition,

[a] Deleting 'and with the house of Judah'; cf. verse 33.
[b] LXX and O.Lat.; cf. Hebrews 8[9].
[c] See *supra*, p. 30.   [d] cf. *supra*, p. 43.

though it may well be that Galling[a] is right in his surmise that for
their religious consciousness the act of deliverance, the Exodus
itself, was the immediate occasion of the covenant-relation between Yahweh and Israel, rather than any deliverance of specific
laws at Sinai. However that may be, Galling is surely right in
his conclusion[b] that the Exodus tradition, notwithstanding that
it early became partially obscured by the patriarchal, was the
more primitive. This conclusion, based upon an independent
examination of the prophets, entirely confirms the one we have
already been led to draw from the Canaanitish provenance of
many of the patriarchal stories.[c]

(d) The Settlement in Palestine

The prophets are unanimous in their judgement of the settlement
in Palestine as a time of religious and moral apostasy. Many of
the passages already cited illustrate this, and it is only necessary
here to supplement them. Amos follows up his reminder of
Yahweh's leading in the wilderness and His gift of the possession
of the land of the Amorite with the words:

> And I raised up some of your sons to be prophets,
> And of your young men to be Nazirites.
> Is it not even so, O ye children of Israel?
>   'Tis the oracle of Yahweh.
> But you gave the Nazirites wine to drink,
> And upon the prophets you laid
> The injunction not to prophesy (Amos 2[11f.]).

Not that the prophets were Wahhabis or Rechabites, not even
Jeremiah. They could conceive of Yahwism coming to terms
with civilization.[d] But it is significant that the most puritanical
of them, Elijah and Amos, came from the wild.[e] As Amos saw
it, the gluttonous sacrificial orgies at Bethel and Gilgal were
in complete contrast with the non-sacrificial worship of the
wilderness:

> Was it sacrifices and offerings you brought me
> In the wilderness forty years, O house of Israel? (Amos 5[25]).

[a] op. cit., pp. 26–37.   [b] ibid., p. 63.   [c] See supra, p. 24.
[d] cf. A. C. Welch, Jeremiah: His Time and His Work, p. 241.
[e] cf. T. H. Robinson, Prophecy and the Prophets, p. 66.

This seems to expect a negative answer. The point of Jeremiah's

> Thus saith Yahweh of hosts, the God of Israel:
> Add your burnt-offerings to your sacrifices
> And eat ye flesh (Jeremiah 7²¹)

is that the burnt-offering, no part of which was available for
human consumption, was a waste of good meat; Yahweh did not
want it. The prophet goes on to say that Yahweh gave no
commandment concerning burnt-offerings and sacrifices in the
day when He brought the fathers out of Egypt (verse 22). Whether
he and Amos were right in their assumption that worship in the
wilderness was completely non-sacrificial is open to question,
though it is practically certain that the covenant, whatever its
obligations for Israel, contained no prescription about sacrifices.
Its requirements were moral, as Amos (5²⁴) and Jeremiah (7²³)
both insisted. Also, it is certain that the sacrificial ritual of the
pre-exilic centuries was largely borrowed from the Canaanites.
Even so, Amos and Jeremiah may have been idealizing.

The idealization of the wilderness period is even more pronounced in Hosea and Jeremiah. In that happy time Israel had
been the pure bride of Yahweh, but when she entered the promised land she became guilty of 'adultery', even of common
harlotry (Hosea 2²⁻¹³ (Heb. 4-15), Jeremiah 2⁴⁻²⁸). This was the
prophets' way of saying that Israel had forsaken Yahweh to
worship the Baals (Hosea 2⁸, ¹⁶ᶠ· (Heb. 10, 18f.), 13¹, Jeremiah 2²³).
The service of other gods than Yahweh was a breaking of
the marriage bond. Ezekiel paints the picture in still darker and
even revolting colours (Ezekiel 16¹⁵⁻³⁴, 23¹⁻²¹), and has it that
Israel committed whoredoms even in Egypt (Ezekiel 23³, ⁸, ¹⁹, ²⁷;
cf. 20⁷ᶠ·). We may feel that the prophets were grossly exaggerating. But they were describing what they saw. Agricultural
religion of the Baal-type does tend toward emphasis upon sex,
and ritual-prostitution is its all-too-common accompaniment.
The prophets were not just stigmatizing idolatry, but an idolatry
that licensed and encouraged sexual orgies. The Astarte figurines
brought to light by the spade of the archæologist show how
thoroughly beastly it could be. Or, we may feel, even if the
prophets were not exaggerating the present, they were exaggerating the contrast between the present and the past. But, again,
the religion of the nomad, while it may be simple, and even crude,

is relatively pure in comparison with worship of the Baal-type.
Where the prophets may have been mistaken, and so led to over-
emphasis, is in their assumption that the conquest of Canaan was
complete, and that the Israelites started in their new habitation
without insistent temptation from a still surviving and vigorous
Baal-cult. They did not know—how were they to know, since
the earliest traditions of the Conquest had already been forgotten?
—that to cut off the entail of Baalism was, in the circumstances of
the settlement, impossible.

(e) The Monarchy

The first objections to the monarchy as such appear to have been
voiced by Hosea.[a] When he says (Hosea 3⁴) that

the children of Israel shall abide many days without king, and without
prince, and without sacrifice, and without *maṣṣēbhâh*, and without
ephod or teraphim,

he is probably grouping together things which in his judgement
are all alike abhorrent to Yahweh. 'In their wickedness' the
people 'anoint kings, and in their treacheries princes' (Hosea 7³).[b]
The prophet represents Yahweh as saying: 'They have set up
kings, but not by me; they have made princes, and I knew it not'
(8⁴). Notwithstanding their feverish political expedients, their
calling upon Egypt and Assyria, 'they shall soon cease from the
anointing of kings and princes' (8¹⁰).[c] 'Already they are saying,
We have no king . . . and the king, what can he do for us?' (10³).
More explicitly still,

Where is now thy king, that he may save thee? and all thy princes,
that they may judge thee,[d] of whom thou saidst, Give me a king and
princes? I give thee a king in my anger, and take him away in my
fury' (13¹⁰ᶠ.).

These passages may only refer to the short-lived and usurping
kings who succeeded Jeroboam the Second. But can they be

[a] See for the details my article 'The Old Testament Estimate of the Monarchy', in
The American Journal of Semitic Languages and Literatures, Vol. XLVIII (1931), pp. 1–19,
from which this summary is taken.

[b] Reading *yimshehû* for MT. *yeśammehû*.

[c] So read following LXX.   [d] So LXX.

interpreted as embodying a judgement upon the monarchy throughout its history?

There are good reasons for believing that when Hosea condemned the kings he was not particularizing. It is certain that his condemnation is not confined to the kings who followed Jeroboam the Second, since his judgement on the dynasty of Jehu is no less severe than that on the 'puppet-kings' who disgraced the throne in the last two decades of the kingdom (1⁴). We must therefore conclude that his condemnation goes back to the middle of the ninth century, and that to him the drastic political surgery of Elijah and Elisha was barbarous. Does it go back farther still? In 10¹⁰ the prophet speaks of 'the double iniquity' of Israel, which some commentators refer to the cultus and the monarchy, others to the golden calves at Dan and Bethel. In two passages, 9⁹ and 10⁹, we read of corruption from 'the days of Gibeah'. Gibeah was the home of Saul, and accordingly Wellhausen[a] thought that here was a condemnation of the monarchy since its very inception. The more usual opinion, however, is that the reference is to the unseemly deeds related in Judges 19–21.[b] The 'wickedness in Gilgal' (9¹⁵), again, is variously referred to the cultus,[c] and to the establishment of the monarchy (cf. 1 Samuel 11¹⁴ᶠ, 15).[d] Most commentators remark on the inchoative force of the words 'there I hated them'—'there I conceived a hatred for them'—as though the hatred sprang out of a definite historical situation; while the closely following context says that 'all their princes are rebels'.

The exact bearing of these passages may be in doubt, but the total impression that Hosea leaves upon us is that he condemned the monarchy as such. Sellin[e] remarks that the prophet was no systematizer. He was, however, at pains to show that again and again in the remoter past, rather than in the nearer present, the nation had gone astray and brought itself into a trackless and thorny waste from which there was neither egress nor retreat. Now it was Baal-peor, now Gibeah, now Jezreel, now Bethel, and now Gilgal that was the starting-point of the ruin. Ever since

[a] *Die Kleinen Propheten* (1898), p. 125.

[b] So G. A. Smith, Marti, Nowack, Sellin; Rieger, op. cit., p. 76.

[c] So G. A. Smith, Marti, Harper, Nowack.

[d] So Sellin; Rieger, op. cit., p. 77.

[e] *Das Zwölfprophetenbuch* (Second edition, 1929), p. 100,

their entry into Canaan the Israelites had forsaken Yahweh and made trial of every allegiance save that which alone could profit, until the tragedy of broken and divided loyalties must perforce hasten to its inevitable end. It is, in all probability, to Hosea that we must look for the beginnings of the judgement on the monarchy which represents it as sin and rebellion against Yahweh.

CHAPTER IV

THE PROPHETS

II. THEIR INTERPRETATION OF CONTEMPORARY HISTORY

(a) The Prophets as Actors in History

WITH SUCH a conception of their office as they held, it is not surprising that the prophets sometimes took a hand in the shaping of history. The beginnings of the prophetic movement coincide with the origins of the monarchy, and it seems certain that it was the prophets who focused the attention of their contemporaries upon the need of the hour. Nathan the prophet, so the story goes, was David's mentor (2 Samuel 12$^{1-15}$). It was a prophet, Ahijah the Shilonite, who put revolt into the mind of Jeroboam the son of Nebat (1 Kings 11$^{29ff.}$). Jehu's usurpation was instigated by Elisha (2 Kings 9). Amaziah of Bethel's report to Jeroboam the Second, 'Amos hath conspired against thee in the midst of the house of Israel' (Amos 7^{10}), though a perversion of what Amos had actually said may therefore, from the standpoint of the priest-courtier, have been honestly enough spoken. Isaiah tried, albeit vainly, to dissuade Ahaz from throwing himself upon the perilous protection of Assyria (Isaiah 7$^{1-17}$), and was later appealed to in the crisis of Sennacherib's invasion (Isaiah 37). Jeremiah besought Zedekiah to capitulate, and when the king refused, he advised the defenders of Jerusalem to desert to the Chaldeans (Jeremiah 38$^{1-4}$). Haggai (Haggai 2$^{20-3}$) and Zechariah (Zechariah 3f.) encouraged Messianic expectations of Zerubbabel, perhaps to Zerubbabel's undoing.

(b) Prophetic Symbolism

Sometimes a prophet would give added emphasis to a 'word' he delivered by accompanying it with a symbolic act.[a] Examples

[a] See the Article 'Prophetic Symbolism', by H. Wheeler Robinson, in *Old Testament Essays*, published for the Society for Old Testament Study by Charles Griffin, 1927.

recorded appear to indicate that acts of prophetic symbolism were performed on occasions which were particularly fateful for the course of history. Ahijah the Shilonite rent a new outer garment, which apparently he had put on for the occasion, into twelve pieces:

And he said to Jeroboam, Take thee ten pieces: for thus saith Yahweh, the God of Israel, Behold, I will rend the kingdom out of the hand of Solomon, and will give ten tribes to thee (1 Kings 11^{31}).

When Elisha was dying, King Joash of Israel came to visit him. The prophet bade the king take bow and arrows, then to put his hand upon the bow; as he did so, the prophet laid his hands upon the king's hands. As the arrow sped from the bow, Elijah said, 'Yahweh's arrow of victory, even the arrow of victory over Syria'. He then bade the king strike the arrows upon the ground. The king did so, but only three times. Whereupon

the man of God was wroth with him, and said, Thou shouldest have smitten five or six times; then hadst thou smitten Syria till thou hadst consumed it: whereas now thou shalt smite Syria but thrice (2 Kings 13$^{14-19}$).

We may think to explain this by saying that the king's neglect to strike more than three times betokened indecision of character. So no doubt, it did; but that is not a sufficient account of the matter, from the standpoint of prophetic symbolism.

The incident of Joash and the arrows is similar to one recorded of Moses during a battle with the Amalekites (Exodus 17$^{10-13}$). Moses, it is said, went up to the top of a hill in company with Aaron and Hur.

And it came to pass, when Moses held up his hand, that Israel prevailed: and when he let down his hand, Amalek prevailed. But Moses' hands were heavy; and they took a stone, and put it under him, and he sat thereon; and Aaron and Hur stayed up his hands, the one on the one side, and the other on the other side; and his hands were steady until the going down of the sun. And Joshua discomfited Amalek and his people with the edge of the sword.

Similar again is the incident of Joshua and the javelin (Joshua 8$^{18, 26}$):

And Yahweh said unto Joshua, Stretch out the javelin that is in thy hand toward Ai; for I will give it into thine hand. And Joshua stretched out the javelin that was in his hand toward the city. . . . For Joshua drew not back his hand, wherewith he stretched out the javelin, until he had utterly destroyed all the inhabitants of Ai.

The uplifted hands and javelin are evidently supposed to be more than the bare symbols of victory (is there, in ancient thought, any such thing as a 'bare' symbol?)—they are charged with dynamic power, the very agents of victory. It may be said that these stories are taken from saga, and that we have no reason to suppose that they are historical. Evidently, too, they have their roots in mimetic magic, the principle that 'like produces like'. They are therefore morally objectionable. Or again, if such ideas survived into the age of prophecy, the 'false', no less than the 'true', prophets served themselves of these means of releasing *mana*. Thus,

Zedekiah the son of Chenaanah made him horns of iron, and said, Thus saith Yahweh, with these shalt thou push the Syrians, until they be consumed (1 Kings 22¹¹).

But symbolic actions are recorded of even the greatest of the 'canonical' prophets. Isaiah, we are told, was bidden by Yahweh,

Go, and loose the sackcloth from off thy loins, and put thy shoe from off thy foot. And he did so, walking naked and barefoot (Isaiah 20²).

He continued to go about thus for three years 'for a sign and a portent' (Hebrew, *'ôth ûmôphēth*), in token that the inhabitants of Egypt and Ethiopia should be led away captive to Assyria in a like state of naked humiliation. The date, 711 B.C., had special significance: Egyptian military power had not long previously been considerably strengthened by the accession of a new, the Ethiopian, dynasty, and Isaiah would have Hezekiah and his counsellors understand that even so it was vain for them to trust to Egypt for protection against Assyria. It does not appear that Isaiah was successful in his endeavour to dissuade Hezekiah from joining an anti-Assyrian alliance; nor, as a matter of fact, did an Assyrian army even enter Egypt until forty years later, in the reign of Esarhaddon. But he was right in his insistence that no effective aid was forthcoming to Judah from Egypt. However, the question at the moment is not whether a prognostication accompanied by a symbolic action was always infallibly correct. We are simply describing how the prophets believed that the course of events could be shaped and determined by such symbolic actions.

One of the most remarkable instances of prophetic symbolism is recorded of Jeremiah. He was bidden by Yahweh,

> Go, and buy a potter's earthern bottle, and take of the elders of the people, and of the elders of the priests; and go forth unto the valley of the son of Hinnom, which is by the entry of the gate of potsherds (R.V. margin). . . . Then shalt thou break the bottle in the sight of the men that go with thee, and shalt say unto them, Thus saith Yahweh of hosts: Even so will I break this people and this city, as one breaketh a potter's vessel, that cannot be made whole again (Jeremiah 19[1f., 10f.])

Wheeler Robinson[a] calls attention to the fact that this was

> done in the presence of chosen witnesses *prior* to the public announcement of the doom in the temple courts; the order of events shows that the act was not intended to be an illustration of the message, but rather an instrument of its fulfilment, something which had to be done first in order that the word to be proclaimed might be fully efficacious.

On another occasion, shortly after the deportation of King Jehoiachin,[b] Jeremiah, at Yahweh's command, appeared in public wearing a wooden yoke, the symbol of the subjugation of the nations of Babylon. Meanwhile, a 'false' prophet, one Hananiah, publicly announced that Yahweh had broken the yoke of the King of Babylon, and that within two full years Jehoiachin would be back in Jerusalem (Jeremiah 28[1-4]). To give the more assurance to his words, Hananiah took the bar from off Jeremiah's neck, and broke it (Jeremiah 28[10]). Jeremiah, in his turn, was bidden,

> Go, and tell Hananiah, saying, Thus saith Yahweh: Thou hast broken the bars of wood; but thou shalt make in their stead bars of iron (verse 13).

There are instances of prophetic symbolism, notably some actions ascribed to Ezekiel, which either border upon the bizarre

---

[a] op. cit., p. 6.
[b] Reading 'Zedekiah' for 'Jehoiakim' in Jeremiah 27[1], see R.V. margin.

or seem physically incapable of performance. Such are his
eating of the roll of a book (Ezekiel 2⁹–3³), and his lying on his
left side for one hundred and ninety days,ᵃ to represent the one
hundred and ninety years of Israel's captivity, and a further forty
on his right side to represent the forty years of the captivity of
Judah (Ezekiel 4⁴⁻¹⁷). In such cases we can only suppose that
the symbolism was enacted in a visionary or ecstatic experience.

Probably [as Wheeler Robinson says], the prophet could have drawn
no hard and fast line between the psychical and the physical in his
experience, even if he distinguished them at all.ᵇ

But he seems right to insist that as a general rule these actions
were really performed—

Hananiah could not have broken a yoke that existed only in the mind
of Jeremiahᶜ

and that

they are not simply dramatic illustrations of a rather feeble kind; they
are partial realizations of that which is to come, and to its coming they
themselves will contribute in their own degree.

Granted that they are to some extent magical in form and origin,

their character has been transformed by their being taken up into the
will of Yahweh, to which the prophet has so fully surrendered his own
will.ᵈ

   Closely akin to symbolic actions are the symbolic names which
prophets gave to their children. Hosea's children were called
Jezreel ('God sows', 1⁴), Lo-ruhamah ('Uncompassionated', 1⁶),
and Lo-ammi ('No people of mine' 1⁹); Isaiah's, Shear-jashub
('A remnant shall return', Isaiah 7³) and Maher-shalal-hash-baz
('Speeds spoil, hastens plunder', 8¹ᶠᶠ·). The significance attached
by the Hebrews to proper names is everywhere evident in the Old
Testament.

The naming of a child, as by Isaiah or Hosea, was a real event, and
as such could be thought to influence other real events.ᵉ

ᵃ So LXX.   ᵇ op. cit., p. 13.   ᶜ loc. cit.
ᵈ ibid., p. 10.   ᵉ H. Wheeler Robinson, op. cit., p. 12.

If Isaiah's nakedness was an *'ôth ûmôphēth* upon Egypt and Ethiopia, no less so were he and his strangely named children for Judah:

Behold, I and the children whom Yahweh hath given me are for signs and portents (*'ôthôth wemôphethîm*) in Israel from Yahweh of hosts (Isaiah 8¹⁸).

(c) *Yahweh, Lord of Universal Morality*

The prophets seem to have started from the conception of Yahweh as Law; they moralized the conception of Yahweh. The presupposition underlying this is fundamentally different from that of ordinary monolatry. Monolatry is the worship of one god, each people having its own particular god, whom alone it may worship, while at the same time the existence of other gods, each of whom is in a similar relation of patronage to the people who worship him, is freely recognized. 'Chemosh for Moab, Milcom for Ammon, Yahweh for Israel', is the formula for this type of worship.[a] It follows that no god can contemplate the annihilation of his people, or what shall he do for worshippers? His people, therefore, can always, in the last resort, rely upon him for protection. Such a conception, it is plain, is hardly consistent with a high moral standard, either in the god or in his people, since the god is bound to his people by self-interest, no matter what their behaviour may be. 'Is not Yahweh in the midst of us? no evil shall come upon us' (Micah 3¹¹) is a positive insurance, even when no formal covenant lies behind it. The Moabites and Ammonites, whose relation to their gods had no covenant basis, could have spoken similarly. At the stage of simple monolatry the conception of God as moral law is impossible.

The god of a monolatrous people is nevertheless quite capable of treating his people with great severity, so long as that does not involve their virtual extinction at the hand of external foes. An extreme example of this in the religion of Israel is to be seen in the story of how 'again the anger of Yahweh was kindled against Israel, and he moved David against them, saying, Go, number Israel and Judah' (2 Samuel 24¹ᶠᶠ.). David accordingly ordered a census, but when he had completed it 'his heart smote him', and he confessed his 'sin' (verses 1of.). He was offered the choice of three evils, and the one he selected involved the death from

a cf. Judges 11²⁴.

pestilence of seventy thousand people. The explanation of the story, assuming that it has an historical basis, is, of course, that the census was followed by a pestilence, and when the reason for the pestilence was sought, it and the census, which was no doubt unpopular, were causally related to one another. But why should the anger of Yahweh have been kindled at all? The story offers no explanation, and it evidently puzzled the Chronicler sufficiently for him to substitute Satan for Yahweh: 'And Satan stood up against Israel, and moved David to number Israel' (1 Chronicles 21¹). This might satisfy the conscience of a later age; but the original story dates from a time when the conception of Yahweh was still very imperfectly moralized. He was of uncertain temper. Gods were like that, and one never knew how they might behave. Nor was it any use to charge them with immorality; you simply accepted them as they were, since they were possessed of superhuman power. Indeed, it would never even have occurred to a man to charge a god with immorality, as we understand it: 'sin' was a breach of *tabu* rather than of moral law. The story of Uzzah and the ark shows this very clearly (2 Samuel 6⁶ᶠ·).

The gravamen of Amos's charge against the Israelites of his day was that they were guilty of gross immoralities—greed, oppression, robbery, bribery, drunkenness, and lust. For these offences Yahweh would hold them to strict account:

> For three rebellions of Israel,
> Yea for four, I will not reverse it (Amos 2⁶).

That they were punctilious and even supererogatory in their performance of ritual only aggravated their guilt. Yahweh was not interested in ritual, but in righteousness:

> Let justice roll down like waters,
> And righteousness as a never-failing *wadi* (5²⁴).

So far from the Israelites being free to presume on Yahweh's favour because they were the only nation He 'knew', their relation of privilege entailed greater responsibility (3²). He expected from them not less, but more, than He did from others. Amos nowhere says in so many words that Yahweh is righteous, but it is clear that the unrighteousness of Israel is being judged by reference to a standard of absolute and immutable righteousness which has its ground in the very nature of Yahweh.

Such an absolute righteousness as Amos predicated of Yahweh must be universal. Amos never argues the point; his perception of it seems to have been intuitive, not the result of a logical deduction. Indeed, if the order in which his prophecies are recorded at all corresponds to the order in which he delivered them, he seems to have started with the universal, and then descended to particulars. This is exactly what we should expect from the whole tenor of his message: Damascus, Philistia, Tyre, Edom, Ammon, and Moab, are all arraigned before Israel, and with the same introductory formula (Amos 1³-2³). The charge against them all is some form of 'frightfulness', inhumanity in the conduct of war, or slave-raiding. The offences perpetrated by the Aramæans, Philistines, Phœnicians, Edomites, and Ammonites may all have been against Israelites, though this is not certain. Nor, for Amos, was it of primary consequence. For the oracle against Moab is concerned with a crime against Edom:

> Thus saith Yahweh,
> For three rebellions of Moab,
> Yea, for four, I will not reverse it;
> Because he burned the bones
> Of the king of Edom into lime:
> But I will send fire against Moab,
> And it shall devour the palaces of Kerioth (Amos 2¹⁻²ᵃ).

What has this to do with Yahweh, on the postulates of ordinary monolatry? Let the god of the Edomites see to it, and avenge the wrong done to his people! No, says Amos in effect; any act of cruelty, no matter by whom or against whom it is committed, is Yahweh's concern, and He will avenge it. Yahweh, that is to say, is Lord of universal morality.

This conception of Yahweh as Lord of universal morality is already so clear in Amos that it becomes normative for subsequent prophecy. If in its universal aspect it is less evident in Hosea, that is because the situation with which Hosea was concerned was primarily domestic. It is found even in Nahum, whose 'Taunt-Song' over Nineveh is so savage that his claim to inclusion in 'the goodly fellowship of the prophets' has been questioned.

F

Ha! City of blood!
All of it lies,
Full of plunder,
No end of prey!
Hark to the whip!
Hark to the thunder of wheels!
Horses galloping,
Chariots jolting,
Cavalry charging!
The flashing sword,
The glittering spear!
Heaps of slain,
Masses of dead,
No end of corpses,
Men stumble over them!
For the multitude of the harlotries
Of the well-favoured harlot,
The mistress of sorceries,
That snared nations by her harlotries,
And peoples by her sorceries.
Behold! I am against thee,
'Tis the oracle of Yahweh of hosts (Nahum 3^{1-5a}).

This staccato, Skeltonian verse is not simply brilliant poetry; it is the expression of a genuine passion for humanity. So monstrous have the cruelties of Assyria been that none will bemoan her (Nahum 3^7). Nahum's is the first prophecy to be concerned solely with the doom of a foreign nation. Admittedly, it stands on a lower level of inspiration than that of the canonical prophets generally. But it is on a higher level than that of crude and unreflecting patriotism. The prophet is not just a jingoistic *nābhî*; it is the spokesman of outraged humanity that he concludes:

All that hear the tidings of thee
    Clap their hands over thee;
For upon whom hath there not passed
    Thy wickedness continually? (Nahum 3^{19}).

(d) The Doctrine of Moral Retribution

The inevitability of moral consequences follows so logically from the universality of the moral law that it is impossible to separate the two. In the preceding section we have not been able to avoid llustrating the one by reference to the other. It is convenient, nevertheless, to give to the doctrine of moral retribution a separate heading, if only for the reason that when the modern philosopher of history speaks of 'the prophetic interpretation of history' it is the doctrine of moral retribution that he has principally in mind. For him the chief emphasis in the prophetic interpretation of history is its insistence that righteousness exalts a nation, and that wickedness involves it in disaster. Thus, in the fourth of his Hulsean Lectures,[a] which has the title *The Prophetic Interpretation of History*, Professor H. G. Wood states the problem in these words: 'For the prophet, history is the scene of moral judgements. Does the study of history confirm this reading of the past?' And he quotes from Froude:

One lesson and only one history may be said to repeat with distinctness: that the world is built somehow on moral foundations: that in the long run it is well with the good: in the long run it is ill with the wicked. But this is no science: it is no more than the old doctrine taught long ago by the Hebrew prophets.[b]

We are here, therefore, face to face with one of the fundamental problems of the philosophy of history.

The principle of moral retribution, in its broad outlines, needs no further illustration from the prophetical writings. It is writ large over them all. Without exception, the pre-exilic prophets were prophets of judgement, and history, on the face of it, appears to have justified them. The judgement fell, and it was accepted as such by leaders and people alike. It is open to us, if we choose, to argue that even if the Hebrew kingdoms had been righteous, instead of wicked as the prophets declared they were, they would still have gone down before the might of empires like Assyria and Babylonia; that the fact that they did go down is no evidence that they were particularly wicked; that they were at least no worse than their neighbours, and that the prophets had no reason to expect them to be any better than they were. These are pertinent questions, but this is not the point in the discussion at which to attempt to deal with them. We may, however, at this stage refer to some particular applications of the principle of moral retribution as the prophets saw it in operation.

[a] *Christianity and the Nature of History* (Cambridge, 1934).
[b] *Short Studies in Great Subjects*, First Series, p. 21.

The prophets were not content with a generalization. They said more than that 'in the long run' it is well with the good and ill with the wicked. They did not hesitate to name specific crimes which should receive condign punishment. Every one of Amos's charges against surrounding nations, with the exception of that against Edom ($1^{11f.}$), which is probably an interpolation from the time of the exile, is concerned with a particular act of barbarity. The prophet also, it would seem, 'makes the punishment fit the crime', though the words 'I will send fire' is common to all the sentences of doom, and may well, with the details that accompany them, be largely rhetorical. We have of course no means of knowing to what extent these sentences were literally carried out, but it seems certain that Amos expected that they would not be long delayed. The judgement of Jezreel (Hosea 1^4) is of particular interest. Hosea is bidden to call his first child Jezreel, 'God sows':

for yet a little while, and I will avenge the blood of Jezreel upon the house of Jehu, and will cause the kingdom of the house of Israel to cease.

Jehu's ferocious purge at Jezreel (2 Kings 10^{11}) had taken place a whole century before (842 B.C.); but the prophet declares that in 'yet a little while' from now it will be avenged. And he appears to have been right.

Another feature of Amos's application of the principle of retribution is that he seems to have regarded natural calamities, famine, drought, blasting and mildew, locusts, and pestilence, as related to the divine judgement (4^{6-11}). He does not specify the immediate reasons for these visitations, and it may be that he only regarded them as preliminary warnings of the judgement proper. This is supported by what follows, which says that because these abnormal occurrences of nature have not brought about repentance, 'Therefore thus will I do unto thee, O Israel: and because I will do this unto thee, prepare to meet thy God, O Israel' (4^{12}). Two passages in Amos, which speak of Yahweh's touching the land so that it melts, and of the solid earth rising and falling like the Nile (8^8, 9^5), appear to anticipate earthquake, and the editorial superscription to the book says that Amos prophesied 'two years before the earthquake' (1^1), an earthquake so severe that it was long remembered (Zechariah 14^5). It seems clear that the prophet thought of physical calamities as immediate acts of God, with a definitely admonitory and even minatory purpose. In this, of course, he was like any other Hebrew; the Hebrews, no more than any other people in the ancient world, knew anything of secondary causes, 'laws of Nature' as we call them.

The prophets not only believed that the forces of judgement operative in the world were directed by a personal will; they did not hesitate to assert that judgement would fall upon particular individuals. This again is more specific than if they had only said in general terms that history is the scene of moral judgements, that in the long run it is well with the good and ill with the wicked. Amos's retort to Amaziah of Bethel (Amos 7¹⁷) may perhaps not be a valid example of this. In our English version it reads:

Therefore thus saith Yahweh: thy wife shall be a harlot in the city, and thy sons and thy daughters shall fall by the sword, and thy land shall be divided by line; and thou thyself shalt die in a land that is unclean.

But the Hebrew verb has no auxiliaries, and we are free to translate 'will' instead of 'shall' throughout. The prophet may only have meant that Amaziah and his family would as a matter of fact share the fate that commonly overtook notable citizens when the Assyrians overran a country. However that may be, what Jeremiah had to say to his antagonist Hananiah (Jeremiah 28¹²⁻¹⁷) is quite specific. After their first encounter over the yoke 'the prophet Jeremiah went his way', as though he had no clear instruction what he should answer further. 'Then', after an indefinite interval, 'the word of Yahweh came unto Jeremiah.' Concerning Hananiah's fate he was bidden to say,

Therefore thus saith Yahweh, Behold, I will send thee away from off the face of the earth: this year thou shalt die, because thou hast spoken rebellion against Yahweh.

So [the story concludes], Hananiah the prophet died the same year in the seventh month (verse 17).

We cannot conceive that Jeremiah hired assassins to put Hananiah out of the way, nor is it likely that the audience of so friendless a man contained sympathizers who took matters into their own

hands. Nor have we any reason to suppose that the prediction is
a *vaticinium post eventu.* Perhaps, after what Jeremiah had said,
Hananiah died of sheer fright? Or perhaps his death so soon
afterwards was pure coincidence? Or have we here, and perhaps
also in Amos's description of impending earthquake, cases of
prophetic clairvoyance, similar to that in which Ezekiel, in
Babylonia, witnessed the death of Pelatiah in Jerusalem (Ezekiel
11¹³)?[a]

It is sometimes said that it is unfair to judge men in positions
of public responsibility by the clear but somewhat narrow moral
standards which may legitimately be applied to private individuals.
A genius may be amoral, but a great man notwithstanding. A
king with the safety and welfare of a State on his hands may be
much less free to act virtuously than the private citizen is. He
may even be virtuous in his private life, and at the same time
unashamedly opportunist in his conduct of State affairs. Can the
standards of private morality be expected of a ruler, and do the
judgements of the prophets throw any light upon the problem?
It does not appear that any Hebrew king, with the exception of
David, was a genius. Some, say Solomon, Jeroboam the First,
Omri, Ahab, Jehoshaphat, Jeroboam the Second, Uzziah,
Hezekiah, and Josiah, were extremely capable rulers. Most of
the usurpers were mere adventurers; Jehoiakim was a mounte-
bank, and perhaps also Jehu; one or two, notably Zedekiah, were
weak men whose misfortune it was that they were called to the
throne in circumstances that would have taxed the capabilities
of far abler men, and it is difficult for us to feel anything but
compassion for them. In contemporary Assyria the outstanding
figures are the kings, and not least usurpers like Tiglath-Pileser
and Sargon; in Israel, on the other hand, the outstanding figures
are the prophets, not the kings. The judgements of the prophets
upon the kings are, on the whole, such as the modern historian,
who has the advantage of a distant perspective, can approve, and
they are always dictated by moral considerations. Jeremiah,
despite the piteous state of nervous exhaustion to which he had
been reduced by his incarceration in the dungeon, was restrained,
almost sympathetic, in his attitude to the hapless Zedekiah
(Jeremiah 37¹¹⁻38). Ezekiel, a sterner man, was forthright in his
condemnation; but on the ground that Zedekiah had signed a

[a] See G. A. Cooke, *Ezekiel, I.C.C., in loc.*

covenant with Nebuchadrezzar which he was bound by oath to keep, and then had wantonly broken it (Ezekiel 17^{11-21}). Even the milder Jeremiah foretold disaster if Zedekiah did not capitulate, and disaster, with all that it entailed of bodily torture for the king himself (2 Kings 25^7), was not long delayed. Jeremiah, indeed, could be scathing, and his philippic against Jehoiakim (Jeremiah 22^{13-19}) is only equalled in severity by Elijah's threat to Ahab (1 Kings 21^{19}). The charge against both was essentially the same, that they had invaded the rights of the private citizen for their personal pleasure and aggrandisement. Whether Jeremiah's prediction that Jehoiakim would be 'buried with the burial of an ass, dragged about and flung forth outside the gates of Jerusalem', was fulfilled, is not certain; though Skinner[a] thinks it was, and points out that although 2 Kings 24^6 'gives the impression that Jehoiakim died a peaceful death, it is noteworthy that nothing is said of his burial', and that the only other omission of the kind is in the case of Hezekiah (2 Kings 20^{21}), an omission which is 'certainly accidental'. Even if Jehoiakim fared better than he deserved, the iniquity of the father was visited upon his youthful son Jehoiachin and his half-brother Zedekiah. It was not just a case of 'in the long run', nor was the visitation delayed until the third and fourth generation, even though it continued as long.

The doctrine of strict measure-for-measure for the individual is stated with uncompromising logic by Ezekiel (Ezekiel 18). He will have it that the proverb, 'The fathers have eaten sour grapes, and the children's teeth are set on edge', has been abrogated.

As I live, saith the Lord Yahweh, ye shall not have occasion any more to use this proverb in Israel. ... The soul that sinneth, it shall die: the son shall not bear the iniquity of the father, neither shall the father bear the iniquity of the son; the righteousness of the righteous shall be upon him, and the wickedness of the wicked shall be upon him.

Ezekiel's conception of society is purely atomic: no man stands either to lose, or to gain, by anything his forebears may have done. Not only so; he is neither benefited nor penalized by his own past. If he turns from righteousness to wickedness, no good that he has done in the past can avail to excuse him; and if he turns from

[a] *Prophecy and Religion*, pp. 248f.

wickedness to righteousness, no evil that he has done will in the least inconvenience him. This, of course, is patent exaggeration. The discovery by Jeremiah of the worth and responsibility of the individual before God was epoch-making, and Ezekiel, in his enthusiasm for it, stated it too baldly. As Dr. S. A. Cook has pointed out,[a] too, Ezekiel's ruthless logic may partly be accounted for by the fact that

as a priest he would be familiar with the ritual occasions when a man passed from the condition of ordinary everyday life to a state of ceremonial purity and back again.

Against this background of ritual practice it was easy to regard sin 'as a matter of status rather than of ethical misbehaviour, as was the prevailing teaching of the prophets'. Ezekiel's teaching in due course inevitably raised the problem of the suffering of the righteous; but this is a question that lies on the periphery of the interpretation of history, and we need not pursue it farther here.

(e) Yahweh, Lord of History

We have seen that even in the Sagas the power of Yahweh was not thought to be confined to Sinai and Palestine; it could at least occasionally be exercised in the adjacent territories.[b] There is, however, one thing common to all incursions of Yahweh into the domains of other gods: it is always as the helper or deliverer of His own people that He goes; He has no direct dealings with other peoples, unrelated to the fortunes of His own worshippers. Ordinarily, if a man went outside Yahweh's land, he had no option but to transfer his allegiance to the god in whose territory he settled (cf. 1 Samuel 26[19]). Had the Hebrews succeeded in establishing an empire, the jurisdiction of Yahweh would no doubt have been extended to embrace its provinces. The result would have been a polytheism of the type familiar in the ancient world, with Yahweh as head of the pantheon. It was not thus that monotheism came to the Hebrews, but as a corollary of the doctrine of Yahweh the Lord of universal morality. Accordingly, Yahweh became Lord of History, of history in which His own people might or might not be directly concerned. This conclusion

[a] *The Old Testament: A Reinterpretation*, p. 112.　　　[b] See *supra*, p. 26.

was drawn by Amos, the first representative of the newer prophecy. He has Yahweh say:

> Are you not as the Cushites to me,
> You Israelites? (Amos 9⁷),

meaning that Yahweh has no more regard for Israelites than He has for African negroes. This was an epoch-making utterance, and it takes us at once far beyond the confines of Palestine. The oracle goes on:

> Did not I bring up Israel
> From the land of Egypt,
> And the Philistines from Caphtor,
> And Aram from Kir?

The exact locations of Caphtor and Kir are uncertain, but in any case they were beyond the near confines of Israel. In other words it was Yahweh who presided over the migrations of the peoples. The same presupposition underlies the oracle on the relations between Moab and Edom in Amos 2¹ᶠ·, though it is not so explicitly put.

Isaiah sees the ruthless Assyrians as an instrument in Yahweh's hand, with which to chastise his own people:

> Ho Assyrian, the rod of mine anger,
> The staff in whose hand is my indignation!
> Against a profane nation do I send him,
> And against the people of my wrath do I give him a charge,
> To take the spoil and to take the prey,
> And to tread them down like the mire of the streets (Isaiah 10⁵ᶠ·).

Not that the Ayssrians are aware of any such commission, or would have done otherwise than scoff had it been explained to them. Their only thought is 'to destroy, and to cut off nations not a few' (Isaiah 10⁷). All nations come alike to them (verses 9ff.), and Yahweh, so the Rabshakeh boasted, would no more be able to deliver Jerusalem than the gods of Hamath and Arpad and Sepharvaim, of Gozan, Haran, and Reseph, had been to deliver their peoples (Isaiah 37¹⁸ᶠᶠ·, 38¹²). Indeed, had not the fate of Samaria proved the powerlessness of Yahweh? (37¹⁹). Very well, as soon as the Assyrians have served the purpose for which

Yahweh called them, He will 'punish the magniloquence of the King of Assyria, and the glory of his high looks' (Isaiah 10¹²). Their overweening pride, their reliance upon their own might and cleverness, shall be humbled.

> Is the axe to boast itself against him that heweth therewith?
> Or the saw to magnify itself against him that wieldeth it?
> That would be as if a rod should brandish him that lifts it up,
> As if a staff should lift up him that is not wood (Isaiah 10¹⁵).

There are three passages in Jeremiah—namely, 25⁹, 27⁶, 43¹⁰—in which Yahweh speaks of the Babylonian King Nebuchadrezzar as 'My servant'. Although the LXX in all cases either omits or mangles the title, in 25⁹, probably quite rightly,ᵃ there is no reason to doubt its genuineness in the other two passages. We may well believe that the translator objected to such an honourable title being given to a heathen king. But as Jeremiah understood it, it was given to Nebuchadrezzar as the instrument of Yahweh's vengeance, not as one of His worshippers. In any case it is clear that Jeremiah thought of Nebuchadrezzar and his Babylonians as the executors of Yahweh's will, and as such invincible until their mission was accomplished (Jeremiah 21³⁻¹⁰, 38²ᶠ·). To resist them was therefore futile, and when Zedekiah and his courtiers refused to capitulate, the prophet went so far as to urge individual soldiers to desert to the Chaldeans.

More striking even than Jeremiah's description of Nebuchadrezzar as Yahweh's 'servant' are the titles given to Cyrus in Deutero-Isaiah. In Isaiah 44²⁸ Yahweh calls Cyrus 'My shepherd', and in 45¹ He addresses him as His 'anointed' (lit., Messiah).

> Thus saith Yahweh to his anointed,
> To Cyrus, whose right hand I have holden,
> To subdue before him nations,
> And the loins of kings I will unloose;
> To open before him the doors,
> And the gates shall not be shut:
> I myself will go before thee,
> And the rugged places I will make a plain;

ᵃ See Peake, *Jeremiah, Century Bible, in loc.*

> The gates of brass I will break in pieces,
> And the bars of iron I will hew down:
> And I will give thee the treasures of darkness,
> And the hidden riches of secret places,
> That thou mayest know that I am Yahweh,
> That calleth thee by thy name, the God of Israel.
> For the sake of my servant Jacob,
> And Israel my chosen one,
> I have called thee by thy name,
> I surname thee, though thou knowest me not.
> I am Yahweh, and there is none else;
> Beside me there is no God:
> I gird thee, though thou knowest me not:
> That they may know from the rising of the sun,
> And from its place of setting, that there is none beside me:
> I am Yahweh, and there is none else,
> That form the light, and create darkness,
> That make peace, and create calamity;
> I am Yahweh, that doeth all these things (Isaiah 45$^{1-7}$).

This is only one of many passages indicating that the Prophet of the Exile had fully grasped the implications of the ethical monotheism of his eighth- and seventh-century predecessors. He is satirical about the pretensions of the idol gods, and bids them 'do good, or do evil', show any signs of animation and intelligence, 'that we may know that ye are gods' (41^{23}). He is insistent that Yahweh, and Yahweh alone, can predict coming events (41$^{22f., 26}$, 44^7, 45^{21}, 46^{10}). He, and He alone, knows the course that history will take, because He shapes and is in unchallenged control of it.

> Turn unto me, and be ye saved,
> All the ends of the earth:
> For I am God, and there is none else.
> By myself have I sworn,
> The word is gone forth from my mouth
> In righteousness, and shall not return,
> That to me every knee shall bow,
> Every tongue shall swear (Isaiah 45$^{22f.}$).

This is monotheism, unambiguous and absolute, and the logic of it is universalism. 'The God of the whole earth shall he be called' (Isaiah 54^5).

(f) Yahweh, Lord of Nature

For Deutero-Isaiah Yahweh is not only Lord of history, He is
Lord of universal Nature. The prophet is fond of rhetorical
questions, which expect, and sometimes receive, the answer 'None
but Yahweh'.

> Who hath measured the waters in the hollow of his hand,
> And meted out the heavens with a span,
> And contained the earth in a tierce-measure,
> And weighed the mountains in a balance,
>   And the hills in scales?
> Who hath estimated the spirit of Yahweh,
> Or being his counsellor hath taught him?
> With whom took he counsel, and who instructed him,
> And taught him in the right path,
> And gave him to know the way of understanding?
> Behold, the nations are as a drop of a bucket,
> And are reckoned as the small dust in the scales:
> Behold, he taketh up the coastlands as a very little thing
>   (Isaiah 40^{12-15}).

The stars are the martial retinue of Yahweh, obedient to His
every word of command:

> Lift up to the height your eyes,
> And see who created these;
> That leads forth their host by number:
> All of them he calls by name;
> By the greatness of his strength, and by his mighty power,
> Not one lags behind (Isaiah 40^{26}).

The word 'create' (Hebrew *bārā*') in this last passage is a favourite
of Deutero-Isaiah. He uses it sixteen times, more than any other
Old Testament writer. It is the word used in the Priestly account
of creation in Genesis 1, and is used only of the divine activity.
No man can 'create'.

> For thus saith Yahweh,
> That created the heavens;
> He alone is God:
> That formed the earth and made it;

> He it was that established it:
> He created it not a waste,
> He formed it to be inhabited: —
> I am Yahweh, and there is none else (Isaiah 45[18]).

It goes without saying that any god of consequence must be credited with supernatural power, even though, if he is a departmental god, his power may be restricted to his own particular element. A national god like Yahweh will, of course, have absolute power within his own domain. Such power had always been conceded to Yahweh; indeed, He seems from the first to have been especially associated with storm phenomena. Very naturally, too, in any local form of creation myth the national deity will be the hero. We have such a myth in the Yahwistic story of creation in Genesis 2[4b-25]. But even though in it Yahweh Elohim 'made earth and heaven', the horizons are not very wide, and the description of the four rivers (2[10-14]) is probably a later amplification. It is folklore rather than cosmogony. We get the impression of a miniature universe, of an estate in which Yahweh takes His walk in the cool of the evening. It has not the cosmic sweep of Deutero-Isaiah. In the present text of Amos, besides the meteorological and earthquake passages already mentioned,[a] there are two 'doxological' verses which speak of Yahweh as

> He that formed the mountains, and created the wind,
> And declareth to man what is his thought,
> That maketh dawn and darkness,
> And treadeth upon the high places of the earth;
> Yahweh, the God of hosts, is his name (Amos 4[13]);

and

> That made the Pleiades and Orion,
> And turneth deep darkness to morning,
> And darkeneth day into night;
> That calleth the waters of the sea,
> And poureth them out upon the face of the earth,
> Yahweh is his name (Amos 5[8]).

These verses are very loosely connected with their contexts; they contain the word *bārā'* ('create'), which is otherwise not certainly attested before Ezekiel (21[30], 28[13, 15]) and Deutero-Isaiah; and the participial relative clauses of which they are largely made up are so characteristic of Deutero-Isaiah, that, without wishing to

[a] *Supra*, p. 68.

credit them to that prophet, we may conjecture that they are of approximately the same date as he. It is in Deutero-Isaiah that we meet with the conception of Yahweh as unambiguously and without qualification Lord both of universal history and of universal nature.

(g) Yahweh, God of Israel

It might be expected from the doctrines of the retributive judgement of Yahweh and His universal sovereignty that any special relation He may once have had to Israel would be broken off. Yet this is not so. It is one of the paradoxes of Old Testament religion that Yahweh, who was first worshipped as a national god, and then came to be recognized as the God of the whole earth, still continued to be in a peculiar sense the God of Israel. So far as we know, for both Amos and Micah the judgement upon Israel would be utterly annihilating. But a later generation evidently felt that their oracles of doom needed to be supplemented with words of comfort and restoration (Amos 9[8b, 9b-15], Micah 4-7). The suggestion that similar passages in Hosea should be treated as drastically as the concluding verses in Amos has not found acceptance. Hosea was just as clear-eyed as Amos about the fate that awaited Israel, but the man who could not cease to love his unfaithful wife could not conceive that Yahweh would finally reject Israel.

I will betroth thee to me for ever;
Yea, I will betroth thee to me in righteousness, and in judgement,
    And in lovingkindness, and in mercies.
I will even betroth thee to me in faithfulness:
    And thou shalt know Yahweh.
And it shall be in that day,
I will answer—'tis the oracle of Yahweh—I will answer the heavens,
And they shall answer the earth;
And the earth shall answer the corn,
    And the new wine and the oil;
And they shall answer Jezreel.
And I will sow him to me in the earth;
And I will have compassion upon Lo-ruhamah;
And I will say to Lo-ammi, Thou art my people;
    And he shall say, Thou art my God
                    (Hosea 2[19-23] (Heb. 21-5)).

Both in thought and in language these verses, and also 14¹⁻⁸, ring true to the message of Hosea.

The distinctive title of Yahweh in Isaiah is 'The Holy One of Israel'. That is the ground of Israel's condemnation: much as the vision of Yahweh in the Temple, and the antiphonal 'Holy, holy, holy, is Yahweh of hosts', of the Seraphim, smote Isaiah with a sense of his own uncleanness—'I am a man of unclean lips, and I dwell in the midst of a people of unclean lips' (Isaiah 6⁵)—so the holiness of Yahweh is a standing rebuke to all that is unclean in Israel. Condemnation was the more complete because the people had 'spurned the Holy One of Israel' (Isaiah 1⁴, 5²⁴; cf. 5¹⁹, 30¹¹ᶠ.). But if the Holy One of Israel is the ground of Israel's condemnation, He is equally the ground of Israel's confidence. Isaiah was firmly convinced that the Assyrians had been given a charge in the execution of Yahweh's devastating judgement against Israel; but he could not conceive that Israel would be entirely destroyed, and he was perhaps the more fortified in this conviction because of the blasphemous arrogance of Assyria. When, in the crisis of Sennacherib's invasion, Hezekiah sent a deputation to the prophet, the answer he received was:

Thus saith Yahweh, the God of Israel, Whereas thou hast prayed unto me against Sennacherib king of Assyria, this is the word which Yahweh hath spoken concerning him:

> Despised thee and laughed thee to scorn
>   Hath the virgin daughter of Zion;
> Her head hath she shaken at thee,
>   The daughter of Jerusalem.
> Whom hast thou reproached and blasphemed?
> And against whom hast thou exalted thy voice
> And lifted up thine eyes on high?
>   Against the Holy One of Israel (Isaiah 37²¹ᶠᶠ.).

Zion, the earthly dwelling place of Yahweh, was in the last resort impregnable.

> Thus saith the Lord Yahweh,
> Behold I lay in Zion a stone,
>   A tried stone,
> A precious corner-stone of sure foundation:
> He that believeth shall not get perturbed (Isaiah 28¹⁶).

We may easily lose sight of the fact that these words are part of
a stern denunciation. Not all did believe, as Isaiah was well
aware (cf. 7⁹). He had no illusions. He commenced his ministry
with no high expectations of success (6⁹ff.). He knew that it was
out of the fires of judgement that Israel would be saved. The
purblindness of Israel became the ground, as the menace of
Assyria was the occasion, of another of his characteristic doctrines,
that of the remnant. Instead of going down to Egypt for help,
and staying upon horses; and trusting in chariots because they are
many; and in horsemen, because they are very numerous, Israel
should look unto the Holy One of Israel, and Yahweh should
they seek! (Isaiah 31¹; cf. 30¹⁵). This they refused to do. Therefore a day is coming when 'the glory of Jacob shall be made thin,
and the fatness of his flesh shall wax lean'. Nought shall be left
to him save gleanings, like a few odd berries in the topmost
boughs of an olive tree after it has been stripped. Yet 'In 'that day
shall a man look unto his Maker, and his eyes shall have respect
to the Holy One of Israel' (Isaiah 17⁴⁻⁷). Another metaphor is of
the Holy One of Israel as a flame which 'shall burn and devour
his thorns and his briers in one day' (Isaiah 10¹⁷).

And it shall come to pass in that day, that the remnant of Israel, and
the fugitives of the house of Jacob, shall no more stay upon him that
smote them; but shall stay upon Yahweh, the Holy One of Israel, in
truth. A remnant shall return, the remnant of Jacob, unto the mighty
God (Isaiah 10²⁰f.).

The doctrine of the remnant exercised a profound influence upon
Judaism, as indeed it has done upon all subsequent religious
thought. It took shape in Isaiah's mind long before the Assyrian
crisis came to a head with the invasion of Sennacherib. As early
as the Syro-Ephraimitic invasion (735 B.C.) he took with him his
little son Shear-jashub ('A remnant shall return') when he went
to meet king Ahaz, and had to rebuke him for his want of faith
(Isaiah 7³).

The conception of Yahweh as 'the Holy One of Israel' is the
closest link of association between Proto- and Deutero-Isaiah.
The phrase occurs about thirty-five times in the Old Testament,
of which no fewer than fourteen are in Proto-, twelve in Deutero-,
and two in Trito-Isaiah (Isaiah 60⁹, ¹⁴). In Deutero-Isaiah it is
no longer used in a sense condemnatory of Israel, but is always

part of the prophet's dominant message of comfort. The Holy
One of Israel is Israel's 'Redeemer' ($g\hat{o}'\bar{e}l$, 41¹⁴, 43¹⁴, 47⁴, 48¹⁷,
49⁷, 54⁵), 'Saviour' (43³), 'Creator' (43¹⁵), 'Maker' (45¹¹), and
'King' (43¹⁵). The Holy One of Israel has 'glorified' Israel (55⁵),
and Israel shall 'glory' in the Holy One of Israel (41¹⁶). These
references could be multiplied if we were to take, as, of course,
we are free to do, every passage descriptive of the relation between
Yahweh and Israel as applying also to the relation between 'the
Holy One of Israel' and Israel. It is precisely the prophet who
is most universalistic in his outlook who is most emphatic that the
relation between Yahweh and Israel is one of peculiar intimacy.
He it is who says that Yahweh 'chose' Israel (41⁸, ⁹, 43¹⁰, 44¹, ²,
49⁷; cf. 43²⁰, 45⁴, 'my chosen one'). This choice is as old as the
birth of the nation. The only other Old Testament writers who
display a comparable interest in the conception of Yahweh's
'choice' of Israel are the Deuteronomists, and it is a moot point
whether the phrase originated with them. Ezekiel has one passage
which speaks of 'the day when I (Yahweh) chose Israel' (Ezekiel
20⁵). In Deuteronomy Yahweh 'chose' one central sanctuary
(Deuteronomy 12⁵ and frequently); he also 'chose' the Levites
to be priests (Deuteronomy 18⁵, 21⁵); and the Israelites are only
to make king him 'whom Yahweh thy God shall choose' (Deuteronomy 17¹⁵). But in the central portion of Deuteronomy, the
law-book proper (chapters 12–26), there is only one passage which
speaks of Yahweh's choosing Israel—namely, 14²,

For thou art a holy people to Yahweh thy God, and thee did Yahweh
choose to be a people of possession to himself above[a] all the peoples
that are upon the face of the earth.

This is an almost verbal repetition of 7⁶, and, since it is fairly
certain that the original law-book has been expanded, it is likely
that the words have been filled in from there. The other passages
in the Deuteronomic writings which speak of Yahweh's choice of
Israel are Deuteronomy 4³⁷, 7⁷, 10¹⁵, and 1 Kings 3⁸, all of which
may well be as late as Deutero-Isaiah. The associated phrase 'a
people of (treasured) possession' is a verbal link with Exodus 19⁵,
the provenance of which is uncertain, though it is probably
Deuteronomic.[b] Perhaps we may say that the divine choice of

---

[a] Or, perhaps, 'out of' (Hebrew: *min*).   [b] See *supra*, p. 36.

Israel was from the first implicit in the covenant-idea, but that it was Ezekiel and Deutero-Isaiah who first gave it explicit theological expression. That the God of the whole earth should be peculiarly the God of Israel is, to us, a paradox; but in the circumstances of the historical development of Hebrew religion it was a perfectly natural and even inevitable paradox, and it had to wait for clear theological expression until a fully monotheistic conception of God had been reached.

A similar aspect of this paradox confronts us in Jeremiah. The New Covenant in Jeremiah is both individual, and universal, in its application, but it is announced as being 'with the house of Israel' (Jeremiah 31 31-4). The prophet who awaited the destruction of the Temple and the dissolution of the state as the will of Yahweh; who could conceive of religion without sacrifice, thus stripping it of the larger part of its external ordinances; who could exhort the exiles in Babylon to settle down as loyal subjects of the sovereign power, and assure them that if they prayed to Yahweh they should find Him, even in Babylon, and thus have all of religion that mattered (Jeremiah 29 12ff.); was not altogether consistent when he anticipated a return from exile, with all the reorganization which that would necessarily involve.[a] But Jeremiah was not consistent, and for that we may be thankful. If he had been, the best that he stood for might have been lost. It would be unwarranted scepticism to deny the genuineness of some of the prophecies of restoration in the Book of Jeremiah, notably those in chapter 31. Even during the final siege of Jerusalem the prophet bought the estate of his cousin Hanamel in Anathoth. The transaction was carried through with as much publicity as his situation in the court of the guard would allow, and completed with full legal formalities, in token that 'Thus saith Yahweh of hosts, the God of Israel, Houses and fields and vineyards shall yet again be bought in this land' (Jeremiah 32 6-15).

But if there is ambiguity about Jeremiah's anticipations of Israel's future, there is none at all about Ezekiel's. There is, to our ways of thinking, something at once quaint, and even repulsive, about Ezekiel's view of the matter. As he sees it, 'when the house of Israel dwelt in their own land, they defiled it by their way and by their wanton doings' (Ezekiel 36 17). Wherefore

[a] cf. Skinner, *Prophecy and Religion*, pp. 308f.; Welch, *Jeremiah: His Time and His Work*, pp. 239ff.

Yahweh scattered them among the nations, and they were dispersed through the countries (verse 19). Even in the lands whither they were deported they profaned Yahweh's holy name, and men said of them, 'These are the people of Yahweh, and from his land they are gone out' (verse 20). It was exactly what the heathen, with their purely territorial notions of divine sovereignty, might be expected to say. That Yahweh should have suffered His people to go into exile, no matter how badly they had behaved, was for them evidence of a diminution of His sovereignty: obviously He was unable to prevent it. No self-respecting god, let alone Yahweh, could be expected to let matters rest there. He had a concern for His good name; He must vindicate His credit among the heathen.

But I had pity for my holy name, which the house of Israel profaned among the heathen, whither they came. Therefore say to the house of Israel, Thus saith the Lord Yahweh, Not for your sake am I about to act, O house of Israel, but for my holy name, which you have profaned among the heathen, whither you are come. And I will sanctify my great name, which has been profaned among the heathen, which you profaned in their midst, and the heathen shall know that I am Yahweh —'tis the oracle of Yahweh—when I shall be sanctified in you before their eyes. And I will take you from among the heathen, and I will gather you out of all the countries, and I will bring you into your own land (Ezekiel 36$^{21-4}$).

This is not simply a belated reversal of sentence. It must be a different Israel that returns to the holy land of Palestine. This also Yahweh will accomplish.

A new heart will I give you, and a new spirit will I put within you: and I will take away the stony heart from your flesh, and I will give you a heart of flesh. And my own spirit will I put within you, and make you to walk in my statues, and my judgements you shall keep, and do them. And you shall dwell in the land which I gave to your fathers, and you shall be to me a people, and I myself will be your God (Ezekiel 36$^{26ff.}$).

The land shall be fruitful, its cities rebuilded, and its people prosperous as never before. In view of Ezekiel's doctrine of a changed heart, this is not just crass materialism; material prosperity is for the prophet the outward and visible sign of an inward and spiritual grace. Ezekiel is a realist, but he has learned much from the idealism of Jeremiah. The last nine chapters of his book (Ezekiel 40-8) are a kind of blue-print containing detailed prescriptions for a reconstituted Judaism. It is not certain that the whole section is from the hand of Ezekiel himself. The first draft of it may well be his, but the chapters as we now have them seem to have been a depository for tentative proposals which were later given authoritative form in the Priestly Code.

CHAPTER V

PROPHETICO-PRIESTLY: THE DEUTERONOMISTS

THE LITERARY activities of the Deuteronomic school extend over more than two centuries, from about the middle of the seventh to the end of the fifth century B.C. During the past quarter of a century the date of Deuteronomy itself has been much in dispute. Ever since the time of de Wette (1805) it had come to be accepted critical orthodoxy that the law-book found in the Temple in 621 B.C., which was the basis of Josiah's reformation, was some form of Deuteronomy. This opinion has now been challenged from two sides: on the one hand, Welch would date the main part of the book in the period not far removed from the time of Solomon;[a] at the other extreme, Kennett[b] and Hölscher[c] would make it post-exilic, dating from about 500 B.C.[d] Neither of these suggestions has met with wide acceptance, and even if it had, the sequence of the documents, JE, D, Ezekiel 40–8, P, would, as Peake insisted,[e] still be unaltered. Of the relative date of Deuteronomy we may therefore be quite certain, and of its absolute date, in the years following the reign of Manasseh, almost equally so.

The original Deuteronomy, it may be assumed, contained the central corpus of laws (chapters 12–26), substantially in the form in which we have them, together with some of the introductory sections, of which there are at least two,[f] now embedded in

[a] The Code of Deuteronomy (1924); Deuteronomy: The Framework to the Code (1932).

[b] Deuteronomy and the Decalogue (1920); Old Testament Essays (1928).

[c] 'Komposition und Ursprung des Deuteronomiums', in Zeitschrift für die alttestamentliche Wissenschaft, 40 (1923), pp. 161–255.

[d] On the whole subject see Eissfeldt, Einleitung in das Alte Testament (Tübingen, 1934), pp. 188–91; Siebens, L'origine du code deutéronomique (Paris, 1929).

[e] 'Recent Developments in Old Testament Criticism', Rylands Library Bulletin, Vol. XII, No. 1 (January, 1928), p. 18; also printed in The Servant of Yahweh and other Essays (1931).

[f] cf. Deuteronomy 1¹, 4⁴⁴.

chapters 1–11. It is likely, too, that Josiah's law-book had chapter 28 for its conclusion, since the curses threatened there are such as may well have moved the king to rend his garments (2 Kings 22^{11}), when he realized how ill the requirements of the law had been met. In subsequent editions further introductions and appendices were added, until the whole assumed its present form. The exact details of these editorial processes are obscure, and there is no need to discuss them here. What is important for our purpose is that the editors of a revised corpus of laws should think it necessary to place them in a definite historical setting— namely, in the mouth of Moses at the close of the wilderness wanderings. The introductory chapters contain long historical retrospects (1^6–3$^{3.9}$; 9^1–10^{11}) and plentiful reminiscences (4$^{3f.}$, 10-14, 32-5, 5$^{22-31}$, 6$^{20-3}$, etc.), and even the laws are interspersed with frequent reminders of the slavery in Egypt (e.g. 13^{10}, 15^{15}, 16$^{3, 12}$, 23^7) and the rigours of the wilderness (23$^{3f.}$, 24^9, 25$^{17ff.}$). It is as though what we call the concept of revelation in history was already so deeply rooted in the Hebrew consciousness that no attempt at a reformation of religion had the slightest prospect of success unless it was presented in a framework of history. We shall find occasion to believe that the Deuteronomic and Priestly 'historians' manipulated their materials, and even, as time went on, unashamedly invented incidents which are not historical at all. But before we declaim against their history as 'untrue', we should consider whether their method was not a tacit recognition of the importance of the principle that revelation is mediated through history.

Deuteronomy knows of Yahweh's oath to Abraham, Isaac, and Jacob, that their descendants should possess the land of Canaan (1^8, 6^{10}, 9$^{5, 27}$, 29^{13}, 30^{20}). It also refers to Jacob, though it does not actually name him, as a 'wandering Aramean' (Hebrew '*ôbhēdh*), with some suggestion that he was in a precarious plight (26^5). It tells briefly of his descent into Egypt, 'few in number', of the multiplication of his seed there, of their sufferings in 'the house of bondage', and of their mighty deliverance (26$^{5-8}$). Otherwise its historical retrospect begins with the transactions at Horeb, and continues with a narration of the adventures which befell the Israelites between their departure from there and their arrival on the plains of Moab.

A Deuteronomic version of Israel's history from the Conquest to the Exile is contained in Joshua, Judges, Samuel, and Kings, the 'Former Prophets' of the Hebrew Canon. These books have all passed through the hands of writers who shared the ideals and wrote in the characteristic style of the original Deuteronomy. They have left their mark most clearly on Judges and Kings. Kings, indeed, may be described as a Deuteronomic writing. Not that it is a free composition of the historian: the style is not homogeneous throughout, and it is clear that the author quoted extensively from prior-existing sources; he also refers, though only for information which he has not had occasion to include in his own composition, to 'The Book of the Acts of Solomon' (1 Kings 11⁴¹), and, frequently, to 'The Book of the Chronicles of the Kings of Israel (and Judah)'. But the selection and arrangement of materials was his own. He had the field to himself; his estimate of the period of the monarchy was not hampered or obscured by the judgement of previous writers like the Yahwist and Elohist, whose work in any case was not continued beyond the establishment of the kingdom. It is all but certain, too, that the period from Solomon to the extinction of the Kingdom of Judah was the first to engage the attention of the Deuteronomic historians. The prior purpose of the compiler of the laws in Deuteronomy had been to establish the primacy of the sanctuary at Jerusalem, 'the place which Yahweh your God shall choose out of all your tribes'. The Temple had been built by Solomon, and it was naturally from the period during which the Temple had stood that the writer could best illustrate the consequences of the neglect of his programme of centralized worship.

After Kings the book in which the work of the Deuteronomists is most clearly in evidence is Judges, for the reason that the saga materials relating to the period lent themselves readily to the exposition of another of their characteristic doctrines, that of the inevitability of moral retribution. In Joshua the work of the Deuteronomists is found chiefly in the first half of the book (chapters 1–12), where the theory of a swift and total conquest of Palestine is even more emphasized than it had been in E. The Deuteronomic revision of Samuel was less thorough; there was not much in the records of Saul and David to which the writer could take exception. To be sure, there was one flagrant incident in the career of David which might be expected to incur the censure of a moralizing historian; but the 'Court Historian' had

that your generations may know that I made the children of Israel
to dwell in booths when I brought them out of the land of Egypt
(Leviticus 23⁴³).

The original reason, no doubt, was that the Israelites, like the
Canaanites before them, spent the days of this rollicking festival
in the vineyards for sheer busyness and lightness of heart. In the
Old Testament no historical event is commemorated by the
Festival of Weeks, which as late as P (Numbers 28²⁶ᶠ·) is still a
purely harvest festival. By New Testament times Pentecost, to
give it its more familiar Greek name, had come to be commemora-
tive of the giving of the Law on Sinai, an interpretation somewhat
dubiously based on Exodus 19¹ᶠ·. In one sense this giving of historical interpretations to the festivals, with the exception perhaps
of the Exodus, was a taking of liberties with history. But it had
the effect of purging the harvest festivals of some of their grosser
accompaniments, and it was a perfectly logical development from
the conviction that revelation is mediated through history.
   A second feature of the laws in Deuteronomy is their humani-
tarian emphasis. This again is immediately due to the influence
of the prophets, though the compiler, very characteristically,
gives as the reason for Yahweh's demand for human-kindness,

And thou shalt remember that thou wast a slave in the land of Egypt,
and Yahweh thy God redeemed thee: therefore I command thee this
thing today (Deuteronomy 15¹⁵; cf. 5¹⁵, 16¹², 24¹⁸, ²²).

Love toward Yahweh, and lovingkindness toward man, are to
be man's response to the love of Yahweh, who redeemed and by
that act 'chose' (7⁶ᶠᶠ·) Israel.
   The third characteristic of Deuteronomy, and in this also it
reflects the direct influence of prophecy, is its emphasis upon
retribution. Yet it is worth noting that whenever a law calls for
the exercise of humanity, it is never said that failure to observe
it will bring down punishment. In such cases the appeal is to
love for Yahweh in gratitude for His lovingkindness, not to fear
of the consequences of disobedience. Exhortations to remember
the slavery of Egypt, whenever they occur (5¹⁵, 10¹⁹, 15¹⁵, 16¹²,
24¹⁸, ²²), always follow a law which, whatever the original
purpose underlying it may have been, is now given a humani-
tarian motive. In other words, what we should call moral laws

in their truest sense have love for their sanction, not fear of retribution. This is as it should and must be where the highest morality is inculcated. Sometimes to the appeal for humanity there is subjoined the prospect of reward (14^{29}, 15^{10}, ^{18}, 16 ^{15}, 22^{7}, 23^{20} (Heb. 21), 24^{19}).

Crimes such as are reprobated in any decently ordered society, offences against the rights of property or the inviolable sacredness of human personality, are punishable. The execution of justice is still governed by the *lex talionis* (19^{21}), but it is distinctly stated, for the first time in any Hebrew law-code, that

the fathers shall not be put to death for the children, neither shall the children be put to death for the fathers: every man shall be put to death for his own sin (24^{16}).

Murder ($19^{11ff.}$), adultery (22^{22-7}), man-stealing (24^{7}), and obstinate disobedience to parents (21^{18-21}), are to receive the death penalty. But it is when he deals with the worship of 'other gods', rather than with these gravest offences against the civil code, that the Deuteronomist is most expansive and rhetorical. Quite evidently he regards this, and the idolatry which was its inevitable accompaniment ($17^{2f.}$), as the most heinous offence of all. The worship of other gods is punishable by death, and a man is not to spare even his brother, or his son, or his daughter, or his wife, or his friend, if they entice him secretly to it (13^{6-11}; cf. 17^{2-7}). Any city that is found turning away to other gods is to be put to the ban (13^{12-18}). We may think it due to fanaticism or lack of true moral insight that the Deuteronomist should treat idolatry as even more deserving of capital punishment than murder. But we should remember that he was attempting to deal with a situation which for him was of extreme urgency. He put the laws into the mouth of Moses, but they were intended to meet a present crisis. Deuteronomy is not history for the time of Moses, but it is an historical document of the greatest importance for the seventh century. As the compiler of the laws saw it, on the observance of the law of the one sanctuary, with the prospect it gave of eliminating the worship of 'other gods', depended the welfare and even the very existence of the State. The prophets had asserted that Israel's sole and sufficient protector was Yahweh, and that if the nation would trust Him it would have no need to depend upon foreign alliances, with all the recognition of alien gods which such alliances always involved. We can afford to be complaisant toward idolatry, as if it were a cultic rather than a moral offence, but the judgement of the Hebrews may be summed up in the words of the Book of Wisdom: 'For the devising of idols was the beginning of fornication, and the invention of them the corruption of life' (Wisdom of Solomon 14[12]). To that judgement the Deuteronomist would certainly have assented, and if the curses he enumerates in chapter 28 are in length and severity almost in a ratio of seven to one to the blessings (cf. verses 7, 25), it was because he envisaged the possibility, even the probability, of approaching disaster, and exerted all his eloquence and fervour to steer the nation clear of it.

II. THE HISTORY

History as written by the Deuteronomists was 'history with a purpose'. Never have historians been more didactic, or so concerned to point the moral for their contemporaries. Their style is hortatory and sermonic, and can easily be recognized even in translation. Their work on the historical books, and in the latest strata of Deuteronomy proper, may be taken to be of later date than the fall of Jerusalem, so that the object lesson they were concerned to teach was clearly apparent to their readers.

The historical retrospects in Deuteronomy itself, like the laws, are uniformly dependent upon JE, and appear to know nothing of stories which are peculiar to P. For example, the story of the rebellion of Korah, Dathan, and Abiram in Numbers 16 is generally recognized as being a conflation from two sources, the Korah element being from P, the Dathan and Abiram from JE. Deuteronomy (11[6]) refers to Dathan and Abiram, but is silent about Korah. It was facts like these which first led critics to discern that P, not D, is the latest document in the Pentateuch. Deuteronomy keeps closely to the substance of JE, though it usually adds comments

designed to bring home to the Israelite reader the theocratic signific-ance of the history, and to arouse in him emotions of becoming grati-tude toward the divine Leader and Benefactor of his nation.[a]

[a] Driver, *Deuteronomy*, *I.C.C.*, p. xvii.

The Deuteronomic story of the Conquest goes even farther than the later stages of E in representing it as complete and almost effortless on Israel's part. The rout of Sihon king of the Amorites, in Transjordania (Numbers 21²¹⁻³²), has in Deuteronomy become annihilation (Deuteronomy 2²⁶⁻³⁷):

We utterly destroyed [i.e. treated as *herem*, put to the ban] every inhabited city, with the women and the little ones; we left no survivor (verse 34).

The destruction of 'Sihon king of the Amorites' is followed by that of 'Og the king of Bashan' (Deuteronomy 3¹ff·). The annihilation of Og and his people is recorded also in the present text of Numbers (21³³ff·), but the language of the section is different from the general style of JE in Numbers, and some of its expressions are Deuteronomic. Hence it is generally accepted that the passage was copied back into Numbers from Deuteronomy. The Deuteronomist, perhaps to account for the location of half the tribe of Manasseh in the region north of the Jabbok, seems to have invented the story.

Og's people, like Sihon's, were put to the ban, treated as *herem* (Deuteronomy 3⁶). The root idea underlying *herem*, which is cognate with the Arabic *harîm*, 'harem', is that of *tabu*, inviolable sacredness to the deity. What was 'devoted' to the deity was made over to him by being destroyed, so alienating it from common use and rendering it innocuous to those who would otherwise be injured by contact with it. The custom goes back to immemorial antiquity, and there is no reason to doubt that it was practised by the Hebrews in their first onslaughts upon Canaan (cf. Joshua 6¹⁷⁻²¹, 8²⁶, JE). The Deuteronomist multiplies instances of it: in eight short summary paragraphs (Joshua 10²⁸⁻⁴³) he uses the expression 'treated as *herem*' no less than five times, and the three that want it have it that the Israelites left no survivors. But he was not really so savage as he sounds. With him it has become almost a bloodless formula, and the purpose for which he uses it is a utilitarian one. When the Israelites fight against a city which is 'very far off', not one of the cities of the Canaanites, they are to offer it peace. If the offer is not accepted, they are to besiege it, and when it falls they are to smite all the males, but spare the women and children and the spoil (Deuteronomy 20¹⁰⁻¹⁴).

Thus shalt thou do unto all the cities which are very far off from thee,
which are not of the cities of these nations. But of the cities of these
peoples, which Yahweh thy God giveth thee for an inheritance, thou
shalt save alive nothing that breatheth: but thou shalt put them to the
ban; the Hittite, and the Amorite, the Canaanite, and the Perizzite,
the Hivite, and the Jebusite; as Yahweh thy God hath commanded
thee: that they teach you not to do after all their abominations, which
they have done unto their gods; so should ye sin against Yahweh your
God (*ibid.*, verses 15–18).

The purpose of the *ḥerem*, according to Deuteronomy, is to save
the Israelites from temptation to idolatry. This is quite obviously
idealizing.

One of the Yahwistic narratives in Joshua (Joshua 15¹³⁻¹⁹; cf.
Judges 1¹⁰⁻¹⁵) tells how the fortress-town of Kiriath-arba (Hebron)
was taken by Caleb, who had Edomite connexions, and how
Othniel the son of Kenaz took Kiriath-sepher (Debir), and was
rewarded for his prowess by being given his cousin, the daughter
of Caleb, in marriage. For this lively and charming story the
Deuteronomist has substituted two colourless paragraphs, written
according to formula, to the effect that both cities were conquered
by 'Joshua . . . and all Israel with him' (Joshua 10³⁶⁻⁹).

The unreality of the Deuteronomist's picture of the Conquest
may be further illustrated from the exemptions he allows from
military service (Deuteronomy 20⁵⁻⁹, 24⁵). These are peculiar to
Deuteronomy. They cover anyone who has built a house and
not yet dedicated it, or planted a vineyard and not yet used its
fruit, or is newly-wedded or betrothed, and even the fearful and
faint-hearted. Whether these exemptions were ever granted in
practice we have no means of knowing. Since they are put into
the mouth of Moses, it must be supposed that the writer would
allow such of them as were relevant to apply to the conquest of
Canaan now impending, as well as to his own time. Even if that
were not so, one passage (Deuteronomy 2¹⁴) emphasizes that
during the wilderness wanderings 'all the generation of the men
of war were consumed from the midst of the camp', as though the
generation of the Conquest were totally unskilled in the conduct
of war. Whether the writer realized this implication of his state-
ment is no matter: the Israelites have no need at all to fear, 'for
Yahweh your God, he it is that fighteth for you' (3²²; cf. 1³⁰, 20⁴;

Joshua 10⁴², 23³). One man, therefore, is capable of chasing a thousand (Joshua 23¹⁰).

It is against the suppositious occupation of a land which had been cleared of its autochthonous inhabitants, that we must set the Deuteronomic estimate of the period of the 'Judges'. The introductory section (Judges 2⁶–3⁶) to the Deuteronomic recension of Judges is not altogether consistent. It is probable that it is not homogeneous, and that the editor who gave it its present form was working upon an already existing JE summary, though 'the analysis is difficult and doubtful'.[a] According to 3³ 'the nations which Yahweh left' were

the five tyrants of the Philistines, and all the Canaanites, and the Sidonians, and the Hittites [so read] inhabiting Mount Lebanon, from Baal-Hermon as far as the Pass of Hamath.

This agrees well with the description of 'cities which are very far off' in Deuteronomy 20¹⁵, as though all but their inhabitants were exterminated. On the other hand 2²³ speaks of nations which Yahweh 'left . . . without driving them out quickly; neither delivered he them into the hand of Joshua', which accords well with the standpoint of J; while 3⁵ᶠ· has it that

the children of Israel dwelt in the midst of the Canaanites; the Hittites, and the Amorites, and the Perizzites, and the Hivites, and the Jebusites: and they took their daughters to be their wives, and gave their own daughters to their sons, and served their gods.

The reason why some of the pre-Israelite population were left is variously explained, as a punishment for Israel's apostasy (2²⁰ᶠ·, E?), as a means whereby the Israelites might not lose their skill in war (3², J?), and, finally, as a test of Israel's faithfulness,

to know whether they would hearken unto the commandments of Yahweh, which he commanded their fathers by the hand of Moses (3⁴, D?).

In a verse which is indubitably Deuteronomic (2¹²; cf. Deuteronomy 6¹⁴), Israel's sin consists in the worship of foreign gods, and the appropriate punishment is that they are 'sold into the hands of their enemies round about' (2¹⁴ᵇ). This is the distinctive Deuteronomic note, rather than that which represents

[a] Moore, *Judges*, *I.C.C.*, p. 63.

Israel's sin as the worship of Baal and Astarte, with consequent
deliverance into the hands of 'plunderers' nearer by ($2^{13, \ 14a}$, E?).
For the Deuteronomic historians the Baal controversy was largely
a thing of the past; the nearer peril, as they remembered it, was
imperial cults. Canaan, according to their theory, had been
practically cleared of inducements to heathenism from within,
and that the Israelites should go out of their way to invite temptation from without was utterly gratuitous and graceless on their
part. The prophets had been right; the settlement in Palestine
had been a time of religious and moral apostasy.

That the period of the settlement was marked by a certain
declension from the ideals of Moses and the simple praxis of the
wilderness wanderings admits of no question. But in the circumstances of the time that was almost inevitable. Yahwism was
the faith of a minority in a very mixed population, and most of
the minority were not spiritually enlightened at that. Their task
was to apply the principles of Mosaism in a situation far more
complex than any they had hitherto experienced, and they had
to do it in the face of a conservative mass of religious tradition
rooted in the soil, of the earth, earthy. There were the makings
of a faith far richer than any that was possible under conditions
of nomadism, but long centuries were needed for its full development. The period of the settlement marks the first growing-pains
of what is destined still to be the faith of universal mankind; but
the actors in it were novices, and they had little or no conception
of the part they were called upon to play. They were beset by
urgent and for the most part mundane necessities, and they often
stumbled badly. We are able to view the stupendous drama—for
such it is—in something like its entirety, and are moved much
more to sympathy than to censure. The Deuteronomic historians
were living in the exile, when it was still touch-and-go whether
Yahwism would survive. They were not concerned with nicely
balanced erudite judgements upon the distant past, but with the
clamant realities of their present. Things had gone sadly wrong,
and if the sagas of that far-off time lent themselves—as they
conveniently and most plausibly did—to point a moral, who is
to censure them? We can afford, or we think we can afford, to
be superior to the moralizing historian; but he has had his uses.

As the Deuteronomic historian saw it, then, the period of the
Judges was marked by a monotonously recurring cycle of Israelite

apostasies from Yahweh, their oppressions at the hands of enemies, their sorrow for their parlous plight and their cries for deliverance, Yahweh's response in the raising up of 'Judges', the deliverances effected by the Judges, the periods of peace and order that followed, until at the death of the Judge the process was set in motion all over again (Judges 2¹¹⁻¹⁹); the whole lighted up with vivid pictures of the valorous deeds of Gideon, Barak, Samson, Jephthah, and other less conspicuous heroes. Most of the stories could be made to illustrate the theory of the Deuteronomist that the oppressors were foreigners, Moab (3¹²), Midian (6ff.), Ammon (10⁶ᶠᶠ·), the Philistines (13ff.). He leads off with one which is summary and colourless, about an eight years' oppression by 'Cushan-rishathaim king of Aram-naharaim (Mesopotamia)', from whom the Israelites were delivered by Othniel the son of Kenaz, Caleb's nephew and son-in-law, who already figured in an early story of the conquest (Joshua 15¹⁷; Judges 1¹³). The traditional pronunciation of Cushan-rishathaim is probably to be interpreted as 'the Nubian of double-dyed villainy'. He may have come from Midian (Habakkuk 3⁷; cf. Numbers 12¹), and not from Nubia proper, but what connexion he can even then have had with Aram-naharaim, the region between the Euphrates and the Tigris, it is impossible to conjecture. Tradition may have preserved a story of the repulse of Bedawin (Midianite) raiders by the Kenizzites of southern Judah; but the Deuteronomic editor seems to have known no details, and the story in its present form appears to be a homiletical invention of his own, perhaps because he felt that the list of Judges would be incomplete if it included no name from Judah.

There is no clear break between the Deuteronomic Book of Judges (Judges 2⁶–16³¹; chapters 17–21 were not included in the Deuteronomic edition of the book) and the early chapters (1–12) of 1 Samuel. We expect from an author so didactic, not only an introduction, but a conclusion, something analogous to Joshua 24, which marks the close of the Elohistic story of the Conquest. There is nothing of the kind at the end of chapter 16, and when we pass to 1 Samuel the formula that Eli (4¹⁸) and Samuel (7¹⁵) 'judged' Israel is exactly the same as that used of Samson and others of his predecessors (10²ᶠ·, 12⁷, ⁹, ¹¹, ¹⁴). Samuel, indeed, is said to have judged Israel 'all the days of his life', from which we may infer that the editor did not recognize the legitimacy of

H

Saul's reign, but divided it between the judgeship of Samuel and the reign of David. It is all but certain that the speech of Samuel in 1 Samuel 12 marked the close of the Deuteronomic book of Judges. The period preceding the judgeship of Samuel is depicted in the darkest colours, in some ways justly so, since the fortunes of Israel had fallen to a very low ebb under the pressure of the Philistines. But the editor carried his doctrine of moral retribution too far, and he was less than fair to Eli, Hophni, Phinehas, and Saul, all of them brave men who, on his theory, deserved much better than they received. Instead of saying that here were noble men who ought therefore to have prospered, he started with the undoubted fact that they had died violent deaths, that their work had ended in failure, and concluded therefrom that they must have been reprobates.

The attitude of the original Deuteronomy to the monarchy (Deuteronomy 17^{14-20}) is one of qualified acceptance rather than of enthusiasm. The injunction 'thou mayest not put a foreigner over thee, which is not thy brother' (verse 15) is puzzling, since there is no reason to suppose that the Israelites, so long as they were free to choose, would ever have contemplated any such step. If the people desire a king they are to have one, under safeguards. He is to be one 'whom Yahweh thy God shall choose: one from among thy brethren'. He is not to 'multiply horses to himself, nor cause the people to return to Egypt'; that would be a reversal of the nation's destiny. 'Neither shall he multiply wives to himself.' Both these cautions appear to have Solomon in mind, as also does the reiterated emphasis that the relation of the king to his subjects is to be that of a 'brother'—'that his heart be not lifted up above his brethren'. The Hebrew ideal of monarchy was essentially democratic, and accordingly when Samuel was faced with the demand for a king, Yahweh bade him warn the people that they would forfeit many of their cherished freedoms (1 Samuel 8^{9-18}); this again, no doubt, with the high-handed despotism of Solomon in mind.

It is going beyond the evidence to argue that the author of 1 Samuel 7^2–8^{22}, 10^{17-24}, 12, was inveterately hostile to the monarchy as such. His attitude does not differ essentially from that of the permissive law in Deuteronomy. Theocracy was his ideal; but even so Yahweh would need a vicegerent, either a judge or a king, through whom He could act. Nobody imagined that He proposed to rule directly, and after four centuries of monarchy, with memories of kings like David, Solomon (as a later age pictured him), Hezekiah, and Josiah, of whom they write very appreciatively, the Deuteronomists can hardly have condemned the whole institution. That the prophet Hosea, living in the death-throes of the Northern Kingdom, should have done so is one thing; but the Deuteronomists were historians, of sorts, and however didactic they may have been, they had to take a reasonably long view. They nowhere say, nor do they even infer, that the monarchy was, from start to finish, a mistake, even though they may have regarded it as a second best. What they condemned was the manner of its inception, and their judgement on that incident may have been coloured by the fact that in their view Saul was a poor substitute for Samuel. They appear not to have recognized any Philistine menace. On the contrary, the Philistines had been routed by divine thunderings in response to the prayers of Samuel:

So the Philistines were subdued, and they came no more within the border of Israel: and the hand of Yahweh was against the Philistines all the days of Samuel (1 Samuel 7$^{5-14}$).

When, therefore, the people approached Samuel with the request for a king, their request was interpreted as base ingratitude, both to Yahweh and His representative.

The history of David has been practically untouched by the Deuteronomists, except possibly in 2 Samuel 7, though that may well be later than they, based upon Psalm 89, rather than the Psalm upon it. David was the beau idéal of Hebrew kingship, and his reign offered little scope for the moralizing so characteristic of the Deuteronomic school. The sources clearly pointed to a revival of Yahwism; it was not, as the period of the Judges had been represented, a time when the nation might have enjoyed peace had it not deliberately turned away to heathenism; and although there was as yet no Temple, David had done everything in his power to prepare the way for it by providing a resting-place for the Ark. Solomon's conduct and policy might be expected to arouse the denunciatory rhetoric of the Deuteronomists, and, indeed, the cautionary clauses in the Deuteronomic law of the kingdom and the later account of the foundation of the monarchy

had him in mind as much as any king that reigned. But it was
clearly impossible to represent the builder of the Temple otherwise than as a pious Deuteronomist (1 Kings 8¹⁴⁻⁶¹). Also, his
reign was too prosperous, outwardly at least, to provide a very
sensational illustration of the thesis that unrighteousness does
not prosper. Nevertheless, the editor was not altogether happy
about him, and the immediate sequel to his death, the disruption
of the monarchy, called for a moralizing explanation. This was
found, not in the spendthrift prodigality of Solomon, his economic
oppression and excessive taxation, but in the fact that 'when he
was old, his wives turned away his heart after other gods'
(1 Kings 11⁴).

Wherefore Yahweh said unto Solomon, Forasmuch as this is done of
thee, and thou hast not kept my covenant and my statutes, which I
have commanded thee, I will surely rend the kingdom from thee, and
will give it to thy servant. Notwithstanding in thy days I will not
do it, for David thy father's sake: but I will rend it out of the hand of
thy son (1 Kings 11¹¹ᶠ·).

This typically Deuteronomic paragraph is followed by accounts,
taken from old sources, of the loosening of Solomon's hold upon
the outlying provinces of Edom and Damascus (1 Kings 11¹⁴⁻²⁵).
There is no reason to suppose that these defections, or at least that
of Damascus, occurred so near the end of the reign as the present
order of contents in 1 Kings suggests. Nor, perhaps, should we
stress Solomon's fondness for women 'when he was old' as much
as the editor appears to do. But the order in which he arranged
his materials was his own, and it seems to have been his intention
that his readers should relate Solomon's large harem and the
consequent building of chapels for his wives, and the rebellions
of Edom and Damascus, as cause and effect. And he put both at
the close of the reign as a foreshadowing of the greater misfortune
that was to follow.

For the period of the divided monarchy the work of the Deuteronomic editor consisted mainly of verdicts, more often than not
adverse, upon the several rulers. We have seen[a] that the prophets
did not hesitate to mete out praise and blame to individual kings,
and that their judgements were always prompted by ethical

[a] cf. *supra*, pp. 69ff.

considerations. The verdicts of the Deuteronomist are, by comparison, less penetrating, even shallow. They had but one standard of reference, the attitude of the king to the cultus, which for them meant the law of the one sanctuary. The rulers of the Northern Kingdom, therefore, instead of being judged for their conduct in the circumstances in which they found themselves, were condemned for non-observance of a law which only became statutory, and even then not very securely, in the sister kingdom a century after their own realm had ceased to exist. It is true that the actual wording of the case against them was that they maintained the worship of the golden calves, but Jeroboam's motive for instituting these gaudy attractions is said to have been fear lest, 'if this people go up to offer sacrifices in the house of Yahweh at Jerusalem', they would be seduced from their allegiance to himself (1 Kings 12²⁶ᶠᶠ·). He might have said with some justice that the claims of Dan and Bethel were older and better attested than those of the upstart sanctuary in the south. But as the Deuteronomist saw it, he not only flouted the law of the one sanctuary, but added thereto a particularly repulsive form of idolatrous symbolism. Hosea had regarded it so, and the Deuteronomists were his disciples. But what had for the prophet been physical and moral revulsion became for his disciples a stereotyped formula, to be applied by rule of thumb.

He did that which was evil in the sight of Yahweh, and walked in all the way of Jeroboam the son of Nebat, and in his sin wherewith he made Israel to sin:

this or the like form of words is used of every one of the kings of Israel with the exception of Shallum ben Jabesh, a usurper whose power lasted only a month (2 Kings 15¹³), and Hoshea ben Elah, the last of them all, on whom the comparatively lenient estimate, for which no reason is given, is that 'he did that which was evil in the sight of Yahweh, yet not as the kings of Israel that were before him' (2 Kings 17²). Even to the account of Zimri, the murderer of Elah ben Baasha, whose reign lasted but seven days, and who, when Omri besieged him in Tirzah, burnt the palace over his head and perished in the flames, the editor adds,

for his sins which he sinned in doing that which was evil in the sight of Yahweh, in walking in the way of Jeroboam, and in his sin which he did, to make Israel to sin (1 Kings 16¹⁹).

Another manifestation of the editor's bias is to be seen in his
scanty treatment of the reigns of Omri (1 Kings 16$^{23-8}$) and
Jeroboam the Second (2 Kings 14$^{23-9}$), who are allowed only
half a dozen verses apiece, mostly his own comment. All that he
has preserved of the history of the one is that he made Samaria
his capital, and of the other that he recovered territory which had
long been lost to the Aramæans. Yet Jeroboam reigned for forty-
one years, and his country prospered as it had not done since the
days of Solomon. That Omri was a conspicuously able man is
evident from external sources. The Moabites, as the Mesha
inscription testifies, had good cause to remember him, since he
brought them under a subjugation which lasted for forty years.
On the Black Obelisk of Shalmaneser the Third, Jehu, who
destroyed Omri's dynasty, is nevertheless called 'the son of Omri',
and the regular description of Israel on Assyrian monuments even
in the eighth century is 'the land of the house of Omri', as though
Omri was regarded as its founder. But, according to the Deuteronomist, Omri 'dealt wickedly above all that were before him'
(1 Kings 16^{25}). Wherein his exceptional wickedness consisted is
not explained, though Micah 6^{16} speaks of 'the statutes of Omri',
as of something very reprehensible. Since, however, to the
expression there is added 'and all the works of the house of Ahab',
it is probably a generalization.

We have more materials from which to review the Deuteronomic estimate of Ahab. The judgement of the modern historian,
that Omri was the David, and Ahab the Solomon, of the Northern
Kingdom, is perhaps rather less than just to Ahab. In the affair
of Naboth's vineyard (1 Kings 21$^{1-16}$) the king's initial request
to his subject was studiously polite, even generous, and he
accepted Naboth's curt refusal, albeit with a bad grace. We are
reminded of the story of Frederick the Great and the miller of
Potsdam. That Ahab was peeved is no doubt true, but we need
not assume that he was hen-pecked. He clearly knew nothing of
Jezebel's forged letter until Naboth and his sons were dead, and
he set out to take possession of the vineyard. His unprotesting
acceptance of the *fait accompli* brought down upon him a frightful
denunciation from Elijah, which put him in such abject fear that
'he rent his clothes, and put sackcloth upon his flesh, and fasted,
and lay in sackcloth, and went softly' (1 Kings 21 $^{17-20a,\ 27ff.}$—
the intermediate verses, 20b–26, are Deuteronomic). These

tokens of repentance, which may have been sincere, secured a remand of the threatened vengeance. The LXX twice has it (at verses 16 and 27) that Ahab put on sackcloth as a show of mourning as soon as he heard that Naboth was dead, thus attributing to him 'an unnatural refinement of hypocrisy'.[a] The fact is that the farther we get away from the judgement of his contemporaries the wickeder is Ahab made to appear. But the Old Testament has preserved one story, written not from the religious but the political standpoint, in which Ahab appears as a gallant and chivalrous gentleman, every inch a king (1 Kings 20). His marriage to Jezebel was dictated by politico-military considerations. Together with that of his own daughter Athaliah to Jehoram, the son of Jehoshaphat of Judah, it was designed to strengthen the balance of power against the persistent encroachments of Damascus. The names of his children, Ahaziah, Jehoram, and Athaliah, are all compounds of the divine name 'Yah' (Yahweh), and Ahab would certainly have repudiated the accusation that he was consciously apostate from Yahweh. At Karkar in 853 B.C. he and Benhadad so far forgot their mutual rivalry as to offer a common front to the growing menace of Assyria. Ahab, naturally enough in his position and circumstances, looked at things from the angle of power-politics, Elijah from that of religion. For Ahab, Elijah was an unmitigated nuisance: 'Is it thou, thou troubler of Israel?' Elijah's retort was that the real troubler of Israel was the king himself (1 Kings 18[18]). Of course, Elijah and Micaiah ben Imlah were fundamentally right; they discerned intuitively what Ahab was incapable of seeing, that however politically advantageous his policy might be made to appear, from the standpoint of the nation's loyalty to Yahweh, it was disastrous. This was the abiding testimony of the higher conscience of Israel; but what was delivered by Elijah in the white heat of moral and religious indignation became for a later generation a second-hand prescription to be dealt out to all and sundry who did not conform to their standards of orthodoxy.

Of all the kings of Judah, it is naturally Josiah who comes in for the highest encomiums.

He did that which was right in the eyes of Yahweh, and walked in all the way of David his father, and turned not aside to the right hand or

[a] Skinner, on 1 Kings 21[16], in the *Century Bible.*

to the left. . . . And like unto him there was no king before him, that
turned to Yahweh with all his heart, and with all his soul, and with all
his might, according to all the law of Moses; neither after him arose
there any like him (2 Kings 22², 23²⁵);

truly a king after the Deuteronomic ideal. Similar praise is
bestowed upon Hezekiah, the first king of whom it is said that 'he
removed the high places'.

He trusted in Yahweh the God of Israel; so that after him there was
none like him among all the kings of Judah, nor among them that were
before him (2 Kings 18⁴ᶠ).

Asa (1 Kings 15⁹⁻¹⁵), Jehoshaphat (1 Kings 22⁴¹ᶠᶠ), Jehoash
(2 Kings 12¹ᶠᶠ), Amaziah (2 Kings 14¹⁻⁴), Azariah-Uzziah (2
Kings 15¹⁻⁴), and Jotham (2 Kings 15³²⁻⁵) are commended in
proportion to their zeal in suppressing idolatry, but always with
the qualification 'howbeit the high places were not taken away;
the people still sacrificed and burnt incense in the high places'.

It is often remarked that during the period of Assyrian ascendancy the kings who are praised for reform of the cultus are those
who strove to keep the country free from foreign alliances, while
those who accepted the suzerainty of the paramount power were
lax in their devotion to the Deuteronomic ideals. The reason
for this is clear: acceptance of political overlordship always
involved at least a token recognition of the gods of the State to
whom allegiance was paid, and this was probably demanded as
part of the terms of submission. The case of Ahaz and Assyria is
a case in point, and it has behind it the authority of no less a
prophet than Isaiah. Isaiah regarded Ahaz's throwing of himself
upon the protection of Tiglath-Pileser as both unnecessary in
itself, and faithless to Yahweh besides (Isaiah 7¹⁻⁹). Let Ahaz
'Take heed, and be quiet': the great king would not suffer Rezin
of Aram, and Pekah of Israel, 'these two tails of smoking fire-
brands', to attack a third party with intent to do injury to himself.
The sequel to Ahaz's obstinate persistence in his own policy might
have been anticipated, and no doubt was anticipated by Isaiah.
Ahaz went to Damascus to meet Tiglath-Pileser—no doubt he
was summoned there—and from there he sent to Jerusalem the
pattern of an Assyrian altar he had seen, with orders to Urijah
the priest to have one made like it against his return from Damascus, and to put it in the place of the ancient altar of Solomon.

This, together with other rearrangements of the Temple precincts and furniture, was done 'because of the king of Assyria' (2 Kings 16[10-18]).

Both the political and religious policy of Ahaz were reversed by Hezekiah, the account of whose religious reformation is followed by the words, 'and he rebelled against the king of Assyria, and served him not' (2 Kings 18[7]). While there is no reason to question the sincerity of Hezekiah, there is little doubt that his religious and political policies were closely related, and that his bid for political independence would be assisted by a purification of the cultus. The principle that foreign alliance involved religious syncretism is clearly illustrated, in both its positive and negative aspects, by the reigns of Manasseh (*circa* 696–641 B.C.) and Josiah (639–608 B.C.) respectively. The account of Manasseh's reign, which comes entirely from the Deuteronomists, is brief but definite (2 Kings 21[1-18]). Any reformation his father Hezekiah may have effected was completely reversed. Canaanitish idolatries and superstitions were restored, and astral worship of the type that had its origin and centre in Babylonia-Assyria was introduced: 'He built altars for all the host of heaven in the two courts of the house of Yahweh' (2 Kings 21[5]; cf. 17[16], 23[5]). This worship became prevalent in Judah in the years preceding the exile (cf. Zephaniah 1[5], Jeremiah 8[2], 19[13]), and Deuteronomy is emphatic in its condemnation of it (Deuteronomy 4[19], 17[3]). Manasseh's reign coincided with the period of the greatest expansion of Assyria, when Esarhaddon (680–668 B.C.) and Ashurbanipal (668–625) even invaded Egypt. The Chronicler relates that the Assyrians invaded Judah and carried Manasseh in fetters to Babylon (2 Chronicles 33[11ff.]). There is nothing in Kings to confirm this, but there is some reason to believe that Manasseh did actually go to Nineveh at the bidding of Esarhaddon.[a] If he was summoned he was in no position to refuse. By the time Josiah came to the throne circumstances had changed: the military power of Assyria was past its zenith. Egypt had reasserted its independence in 652 B.C. Scythians and Medes began to press in upon the exhausted empire. On the death of Ashurbanipal in 626 the Babylonians became free under Nabopolassar, and in 612 Nineveh fell. During these years in which the hold of Assyria upon its outlying provinces

[a] Oesterley and Robinson, *A History of Israel*, Vol. I, p. 400.

was visibly weakening, Josiah, it is said, was able to exert his authority as far north as Bethel (2 Kings 23[15]). It seems clear that his policy of religious reformation, if not prompted by political considerations, was at least facilitated by the altered political conditions. It is no business of ours to excuse Manasseh or to belittle the achievements of Josiah. But we can scarcely help asking what Manasseh *would*, and what Josiah *could*, have done, if each had been in the position of the other? We have not the means to answer the question, but to ask it should keep us on our guard against taking the rather mechanical judgements of the Deuteronomists exactly at their face value.

CHAPTER VI

PRIESTLY INTERPRETATION

THE PRIESTLY interpretation of history is embodied in two works, the Priestly Code in the Hexateuch, and the books of Chronicles-Ezra-Nehemiah. The first of these, generally denoted by the symbol P, deals with the origin and sacred institutions of Israel, beginning with the creation of the world, and ending with the settlement of the tribes in Canaan. Of 1 Chronicles, the first nine chapters consist of genealogies, and are followed by a history of David's reign (1 Chronicles 10–29). The Second Book of Chronicles is occupied with the reign of Solomon (2 Chronicles 1–9), and the kingdom of Judah to its termination (2 Chronicles 10–36). The history of the Jews to the times of Ezra-Nehemiah is contained in the books of those names, books which in their present form are from the hand of the Chronicler, who composed them as a sequel to his main work. This is evident from the fact that they follow it without any break; indeed, the liberation edict of Cyrus, with which Ezra opens (Ezra 1^{1-3a}), is, in the present text, a doublet of the concluding verses of Chronicles (2 Chronicles 36$^{22ff.}$).

It has long been recognized that P is not all from one hand, and Gerhard von Rad[a] has argued that, apart altogether from minor secondary additions, the whole consists of two parallel strands which have been interwoven. A similar conclusion in regard to Chronicles has been proposed by von Rad[b] and A. C. Welch.[c] The suggestion is that alike in P and Chronicles the later materials are more pronouncedly priestly and clerical in their outlook than the earlier; in particular both von Rad and Welch lay stress on the affinity of the earlier narrative of Chronicles with Deuteronomy. It is unnecessary for our purpose to enter minutely into

[a] *Die Priesterschrift im Hexateuch, Beiträge zur Wissenschaft vom Alten und Neuen Testament,* IV, 13 (Stuttgart, 1934).

[b] *Das Geschichtsbild des chronistischen Werkes, Beiträge zur Wissenschaft vom Alten und Neuen Testament,* IV, 3 (Stuttgart, 1930).

[c] *The Work of the Chronicler: Its Purpose and Date* (1939).

analytical discussions of this kind. Our concern is with the broad
priestly interpretation of history, and we may therefore take both
works in the final form in which we have them. What happened
to both P and Chronicles is one more illustration of the fact that
once clericalism gets under way it is usual for clerics to become
ever more clerical.

I. THE PRIESTLY CODE

The Priestly Code, though it undoubtedly contains materials from
a time later than Ezra (?397 B.C.), is in the main a work of the
fifth century. Its place of origin was presumably Babylonia, and
it arose in circles which busied themselves with the problem of
the reconstitution of Judaism, which at the time was going
forward slowly and amid many difficulties and hindrances, in
Palestine. Either Ezekiel, or his disciples, or both, had already
put forward proposals concerned mainly with the Temple, its
priesthood and ritual (Ezekiel 40-8). These proposals were
taken up, sometimes in modified form, and expanded on the basis
of materials already extant in J, E, and D, into the much larger
corpus which we know as P. The difference between the Ezekiel-
ian programme and that of P is that in the former the proposals
are put into the form of a vision of the future, while in P they are
projected back to the age of Moses, which at once gave them the
sanction of antiquity. The formula, 'And Yahweh spake unto
Moses, saying', with which so much of the Priestly legislation is
introduced, gave to the laws absolute divine authority. The
consequence was that a later age found difficulty with Ezekiel,
because he appeared sometimes to be making proposals that ran
counter to the Law. Really it was he more than any man who set
the course of Judaism in the direction of legalism.

The purpose of the Priestly writers was essentially practical.
They were concerned with the realities of their contemporary
situation. Under the Persian rule they were accorded a large
measure of religious freedom, and they had to devise means
whereby they could exercise this without coming into conflict
with the imperial authorities. Having elected to throw their
proposals into the form of commandments delivered in the time
of Moses, which was, to be sure, the creative age of their religion,
they found it desirable, and indeed, perhaps, even necessary, to

present their legislation in a framework of history. This took the form of a summary account of how the Creator of the world had gradually narrowed down the circle of His choice from mankind as a whole to Abraham and his descendants, whom He finally brought into the land of their inheritance completely provided with all the ordinances needful for them to live there henceforth as His people. The whole corpus of history and laws is so erudite, even to the point of pedantry, that it took the critics a century to discover that P was the latest, not the earliest, of the components of the Pentateuch. In reality it is a *midrash*, or interpretation of history, rather than history proper. This is not to deny that in another and very true sense, P is history. In it we can read the essentials of Jewish history in a period, that of the Persian dominion, which is otherwise very inadequately documented. If we want to know, for example, how sacrifices were conducted or how High Priests were consecrated in the time of our Lord, we can find all we need in the Priestly Code and its supplement the Mishna, which is largely a commentary upon it. It cannot be too strongly insisted that an interpretation of history, however fanciful it may be, can yet become a determining factor in the making of history. Of nothing is this more true than of P, which still exercises authority over millions of practising Jews.

For P, the God who subsequently revealed Himself by the name of Yahweh is the sole and omnipotent Creator of the universe. It does not appear that He created the world *ex nihilo*. He worked upon the formless chaos of Babylonian mythology, but His power over it was absolute. No physical means or contact with matter is employed; creation is by fiat, and the recurring formula for each successive act is 'Let there be . . . and it was so'. When the stage is reached for the creation of man, God communicates His intention to His heavenly council, but there is nothing to suggest that He defers to its opinion or is assisted by it in any way. The whole creation, with man as its crown, is complete in six days, and at the end 'God saw every thing that he had made, and, behold, it was very good' (Genesis 1 31). On the seventh day God rested, thus Himself ordaining and keeping the Sabbath (Genesis 2 2f.).

It would almost seem as if the story of creation was told, not for its own sake, but as an explanation of how the Sabbath came to be instituted. This is supported by the fact that for the period

prior to Moses it is only when the origin of some sacred ordinance
has to be explained that the writer permits himself to enter into
details. Otherwise his story is mainly confined to genealogies.
The sequel to the Flood is the rainbow-covenant with Noah and
his sons (Genesis 9$^{8-17}$). The next section of any length is that
which tells how the covenant of circumcision was made with
Abraham and his descendants (Genesis 17). The story of Abraham's purchase of the burial-cave of Machpelah from the Hittites
(Genesis 23) may seem an exception; but it is evident that the
writer attached great importance to it, no doubt because he
regarded the purchase as constituting a kind of earnest or title-
deed to the inheritance of Canaan by Abraham's descendants.
Not again until the divine name Yahweh is revealed to Moses
(Exodus 6), and the stage is set for the Sinai legislation, does the
Priestly writer become expansive.

P conceived of history from the creation of the world to the
time of Moses inclusive as consisting of four eras or world-ages,
each of which was inaugurated by one of the permanent ordinances enumerated in the preceding paragraph. The first era,
during which the deity was known as Elohim, was that from the
Creation to the Flood; its permanent institution was the Sabbath,
and during it both men and animals were vegetarian (Genesis
1$^{29f.}$). During the second era, that from Noah to Abraham, the
Divine Being continued to be known as Elohim; covenant was
made with all living creatures by means of the rainbow-sign
that no more should the earth be destroyed by flood, and henceforward men were permitted to eat flesh, on the strict condition
that it was properly drained of blood (Genesis 9$^{3f.}$). In the third
era, that from Abraham to Moses, God announced Himself as
El Shaddai (Genesis 17^1), and circumcision was enjoined as the
outward sign of a covenant now made with Abraham and his
descendants. The fourth era, that of Moses, was the occasion for
the revelation of the name Yahweh, and, in due course, of the
fully developed Mosaic ritual. Only in this fourth era are sacrifices
prescribed, and the writer is quite consistent with this in that he
is silent about any distinction between 'clean' and 'unclean' (i.e.
sacrificial and non-sacrificial) animals at the time of the Flood,
nor does he ever betray himself into saying that the patriarchs
built altars, much less that they offered sacrifices. The slaughter-
ing of animals for food which was sanctioned after the Flood was,

of course, non-sacrificial, similar to that permitted at a distance
from the central sanctuary in Deuteronomy (12[15f.], [20ff.]). P was
antiquary enough to make what for the Deuteronomist was an
innovation the custom of a much earlier age.

We have already noted that, according to P, when God looked
upon His finished work of creation, His judgement upon it was
that it was 'very good'. Nor has the conception of a Fall any
definite place in the writer's scheme. Instead, he appears to think
of four progressive stages in the knowledge of God, culminating
in the revelation to Moses. At the same time it would seem as if
the almost universal notion of a series of descents from an initial
Golden Age has unobtrusively got into his picture.[a] Only in the
first world-age were men and beasts not carnivorous. A later age
looked forward to such a happy condition as the ideal (Isaiah 11[7]),
perhaps as a return to primeval blessedness, and the permission
to eat flesh which marks P's second era looks like a concession
to the unideal. On the eve of the Flood, P has it that 'the earth
was corrupt before God, and the earth was filled with violence'
(Genesis 6[11]), though he offers no clear explanation of how it
came to be so. It has been suggested that he traced the beginnings
of degeneracy from the time of Jared (Genesis 5[15]), in the sixth
generation from Adam. The name, which may be an intentional
modification of its opposite number, Irad ('*îrād*), in the Yahwistic
genealogy (Genesis 4[18]), signifies 'descent'. It must be admitted,
however, that if P intended to convey this suggestion, he could
easily have been more explicit. Still, if longevity be reckoned as
a mark of the divine favour (cf. Proverbs 10[27]; Isaiah 65[20],
translating 'he who falls short of being one hundred years old
shall be reckoned accursed'), it is significant that the span of life
in the first era was anything up to ten centuries, in the second from
two to six, in the third from one to two, and in the fourth a mere
seventy or eighty years.

From the strictly historical standpoint Old Testament religion
is the story of how the god of a small confederation of nomads
came to be recognized as the God of the whole earth. How that
came about is to be read in the sagas and the prophets. For P the
development was in the contrary direction: his is the story of how
the Creator of the universe gradually narrowed down the circle
of His choice to one people. There was some precedent for this

[a] Pfeiffer, op. cit., p. 199.

in the saga of the Yahwist, who represents Yahweh's attitude to
the first-born descendants of Abraham as selective, excluding
Ishmael, the son of the concubine, and Esau, who forfeited his
birthright. The Yahwist also, unless with Pfeiffer[a] we make his
work begin at Genesis 12, included in his survey a post-Noachic
genealogy to the time of Abraham, of which at least some portions
have been preserved (Genesis $9^{18f.}$, $10^{21, 24-30}$, $11^{28f.}$). (It will
be remembered that the Cainite genealogy of Genesis 4^{17-22}
comes from a source which knew nothing of the Flood, since the
civilization it describes is assumed to have continued unbroken
to the writer's own day.)[b] Even so, the Yahwist's story is much
less deliberately theorizing than that of P. It has also a certain
historical basis: the Hebrews, of whom Abraham was the reputed
ancestor, were one branch of 'all the children of Eber' (Hebrew,
'*ēbher*: 'Hebrew' = '*ibhrî*), and Eber in his turn was a descendant
of Shem, the eponymous ancestor of all Semites (Genesis 10^{21});
Ishmael, who was excluded on the ground that his legitimacy was
contestable beside that of Isaac, was the eponym of the Arabs, a
people closely related to the Hebrews, but of wider habitat and
associations; as for Esau, the father of the Edomites, it appears
that the Edomites were closely akin to the Israelites, that they
settled in the country between the Dead Sea and the Gulf of
Akaba before the Israelites settled in Canaan, but that the
climatic conditions of their habitation never permitted them to
advance beyond the stage of semi-nomadism, so that while they
might have a claim to primogeniture, they could be said to have
forfeited their birthright. What P did was to superimpose upon
these broad facts of historico-geographical selectivity a theory of
absolute divine selectivity, purposed from the creation of the
world. The reason for Esau's exclusion was not that he forfeited
his birthright, but that he married outside the family circle of
Abraham (Genesis $26^{34f.}$, $27^{46}-28^9$). Isaac and Jacob, on the
other hand, had been scrupulously careful to preserve racial
purity by marrying within the family from which Abraham had
come. Jacob-Israel, therefore, when Ishmael and Esau have been
excluded, is the heir in an unbroken succession of first-born son
going back to the creation itself, truly the first-born among the
nations. History is set within the framework of genealogies
headed 'These are the generations of . . .': the first is that of heaven

[a] *Supra*, p. 22.   [b] See *supra*, p. 23.

and earth (Genesis 2⁴ᵃ), followed by those of Adam (5¹), Noah (6⁹), Shem Ham and Japheth (10¹), Shem (11¹⁰), Terah the father of Abraham (11²⁷), Ishmael (25¹²), Isaac (25¹⁹), Esau (36¹, ⁹), and Jacob (37²). Thereafter no account is taken of generations other than Israelitish. Indeed, the only other occurrence of the superscription 'These are the generations of . . .' in exactly that form is at Numbers 3¹, 'Now these are the generations of Aaron and Moses', though the verses that follow relate only to Aaron and his sons, as if to say that the Israel within Israel, the real centre of the theocratic community, is the priests.

Such, indeed, was the view of P. The sagas had spoken of 'the tent of meeting' (*'ōhel mô'ēdh*) which Moses used to take and pitch 'without the camp, afar off from the camp' (Exodus 33⁷; cf. Numbers 11²⁶ᶠ·, 12⁴, E), and which was guarded by a single attendant, the Ephraimite Joshua. In P this has become an elaborate structure, guarded by a host of ministering Levites (Numbers 3–4), whose presence as a protective cordon between it and the secular multitude serves to insulate the 'holiness' inherent in it (Numbers 1⁵³). Its place is in the centre of the camp (Numbers 2¹⁷), which is ranged round it in an idealized replica in miniature of the land of Palestine (Numbers 2). In the saga of the Elohist, too, the Ark, which presumably was housed in the tent when the people were encamped, always preceded them when they were on the march (Numbers 11³³⁻⁶, E; cf. Psalm 68⁷ (*Heb.* ⁸)). In P 'the ark of the testimony' reposed in the Most Holy Place, in the tent, or 'dwelling' (Hebrew: *mishkān*, R.V. 'tabernacle'), as the writer frequently prefers to call it, and when camp was struck the sacred furniture and appurtenances were conveyed by the Levites, who were preceded by six tribes and followed by the other six (Numbers 2¹⁷, 10²¹). Into the Most Holy Place, where the Most High was enthroned 'above the mercy seat . . . between the two cherubim which are upon the ark of the testimony' (Exodus 25²²), only the High Priest might enter, and that but once a year, on the Day of Atonement (Leviticus 16). Around the person of the High Priest were ranged, as in a series of concentric circles, the Aaronite priests, the Levites, and the Israelite laity, each with their respective rights of access to Yahweh in proportion to the degrees of holiness attaching to them. The symbolism of holiness concentrated in the Most Holy Place was

I

further expressed by the materials used in the construction of the tabernacle:

the three great metals of antiquity, bronze, silver, and gold, are used in a significant gradation as we proceed from the outer court to the innermost sanctuary. Of the last-named, two varieties are employed— the ordinary gold of commerce, and a superior quality in which the pure metal was more completely separated from its native alloys, hence known as refined or 'pure' gold.[a]

It hardly needs saying that such an elaborate 'tabernacle' as that of P never existed.[b] It is a composite and highly idealized structure embodying features from the Temple of Solomon, the sanctuary of Ezekiel's vision, and perhaps also the actual Temple of his own day. Ezekiel had represented God as saying,

My dwelling (*mishkān*) also shall be with them; and I will be their God, and they shall be my people. And the nations shall know that I Yahweh do sanctify Israel, when my sanctuary (*miqdāsh*) shall be in the midst of them for evermore (Ezekiel 37[27f.]).

The directions for the construction of the Priestly tabernacle say similarly: 'And I will dwell among the children of Israel, and will be their God' (Exodus 29[45]), and 'Let them make me a sanctuary; that I may dwell among them' (Exodus 25[8]). The aim of all priestly endeavour subsequent to Ezekiel was to 'implement' the vision that came to him. In what is perhaps a later supplement to that vision, the name of the holy city is to be 'Yahweh is there' (*Yahweh shāmmâh*, Ezekiel 48[35]). The authors of the Priestly Code no doubt found the attainment of their ideals conditioned by the practical possibilities of their time, a time which in many ways imposed severe restrictions upon them; but they did strive, within the limit of their means, to make their organization conform as nearly as possible to the pattern which, as they conceived, had been shown to Moses in the sacred mount (Exodus 25[9, 40], 26[30], 27[8]; Numbers 8[4]). In the temples of Zerubbabel and Herod the Most Holy Place appears to have been quite empty. This made it in some ways even more awesome and impressive than if it had

[a] A. R. S. Kennedy, art. 'Tabernacle', in *H.D.B.*, IV, p. 656a.

[b] Though see, to the contrary, W. F. Albright, *From the Stone Age to Christianity*, p. 203.

contained a visible symbol of the divine presence. On the other hand, had it been both empty and inaccessible,

men would have regarded the inner sanctuary as a place with which they had no concern, and would have ceased to think of it at all. But the admission of their highest representative in holy things on one solitary day in the year taught them that the most holy place was a place with which they had to do, and at the same time showed it to be a place very difficult of access.[a]

The Gentile world was outside the covenant, and proselytes were only admitted on the condition that they submitted to Jewish ordinances and kept the Law. Herod's Temple was provided with a large outer court, where buying and selling were carried on, and to which uncircumcized heathen were admitted; but they passed beyond that at the peril of their lives. Its inner court comprised, in ascending degrees of sanctity, the Women's Court, the Court of Israelites, the Court of the Priests, and the two compartments of the sanctuary proper, which were separated from one another by a costly veil. Such was the house which in Ezekiel's vision was to be filled with the glory of Yahweh, and of which the ineffable voice had said,

Son of man, this is the place of my throne, and the place of the soles of my feet, where I will dwell in the midst of the children of Israel for ever (Ezekiel 43[7]).

Holiness in the Priestly Code has a certain physical quality (cf. Leviticus 7[26ff.]), and what was conceived was a quasi-physical presence of the Most High in the midst of His holy congregation.

The symmetry of the conception, alike in its spacial proportions and in its relation to places and persons, is perfect. There is much in it that is very moving, and it certainly commanded the whole-souled devotion of the Jews themselves. Of this the Psalms almost everywhere bear witness.

> My soul longeth, yea, even fainteth
> For the courts of Yahweh;
> My heart and my flesh cry out
> Unto the living God (Psalm 84[2] (Heb. 3))

[a] A. B. Bruce, *Expositor*, December, 1889, quoted by McNeile, *Exodus*, p. lxxxv.

is typical. It has been very truly said that

> No just view of Jewish religion can be gained by anyone who does not
> see the Psalter written, so to speak, in parallel columns with the Book
> of Leviticus.[a]

Leviticus has to do with the sacrificial worship; it contains as it
were the rubrics to the liturgies embodied in Psalms. But Jewish
piety not only delighted in the sacrificial worship of the Temple;
it displayed equal enthusiasm for the Law as a whole, as Psalm
119 testifies. Of the godly man it could truly be said that

> His delight is in the law of Yahweh;
> And in his law doth he meditate day and night
> (Psalm 1[2]).

The Jew was not unhappy in his religion, and it would hardly be
fair to compare him with the exultant devotees of modern
dictatorships who have boasted that they despise and 'spit upon'
freedom. All the same, religion as the Priestly Code conceived it
was a matter of authority pure and simple. The God who at the
creation had said, 'Let there be', uttered His pronouncements as
and when it suited Him, and man's duty was simply to obey. The
primary purpose of the heavenly luminaries, even, had been to
determine the calendar of the sacred seasons (Genesis 1[14]).
Instead of religious institutions being the result of dynamic
historical processes, history was set in motion by their promulga-
tion. Everything had been delivered once for all in the far-of
past, and anything more that needed to be done was only in the
nature of more exact definition and commentary upon it.

II. CHRONICLES–EZRA–NEHEMIAH

The Chronicler does not add anything material to the priestly
interpretation of history. Wherein he differs from Samuel and
Kings, of which he made extensive use, is in his treatment of the
domestic history, rather than in the interpretation of history
as such.

If we exclude the genealogies in 1 Chronicles 1–9, which are
readily detachable, and may be later than the main work, the

[a] H. W. Robinson, *The Religious Ideas of the Old Testament*, p. 150.

Chronicler appears to have recognized no survivors of the house of Saul. He makes no mention of Eshbaal (Ishbosheth) and Merib-baal (Mephibosheth), who are named in 1 Chronicles $8^{33ff.}$, but says instead,

So Saul died, and his three sons (Jonathan, Abinadab, and Malchishua); and all his house died together (1, $10^{2, \ 6}$).

Accordingly, there was no interval of civil war between the partisans of the house of Saul in the North and those of David in the South; instead, 'all Israel' went, presumably immediately, to Hebron, and there anointed David king (1, 11^{1-3}). This tendentiously selective treatment of his sources is characteristic of the Chronicler's work. He passes over in silence the affair of Bathsheba. This might be because it had no bearing upon his main purpose, which was to glorify David as, in all but its actual building, the real founder of the Temple and its worship; but we get the impression also that he felt that the episode was too discreditable to his hero to be alluded to in such a splendid context. David not only purchased the site for the Temple (1, 21; cf. 1 Samuel 24), but gathered abundance of costly materials (1, $22^{3ff.}$, 29^{2-9}), assembled labourers (1, $22^{2, \ 15f.}$), organized its services and dedicated its officers (1, 23–6), and even delivered the 'pattern' (*tabhnîth*, 1, $28^{11f.}$), which he had received 'in writing from the hand of Yahweh' (28^{19}), much as Moses had received and delivered the *tabhnîth* of the tabernacle in the wilderness (Exodus $25^{9, \ 40}$). The only reason why David was not permitted to carry out the actual building was that the word of Yahweh came to him, saying,

Thou hast shed blood abundantly, and hast made great wars: thou shalt not build a house unto my name, because thou hast shed much blood upon the earth in my sight (1, 22^{8}).

We get not the slightest hint that Solomon was elevated to the throne by a palace intrigue. The disruption of the monarchy was an act of schism. The Northern Kingdom had no legal standing, and its history is only mentioned when it impinges upon that of Judah.

Overriding interest in the Temple is likewise largely responsible for the lacunæ and almost inextricable confusion manifest in

Ezra-Nehemiah. An abortive attempt to rebuild the *walls* of Jerusalem in the reign of Artaxerxes the First (464–424 B.C.), probably that reported to Nehemiah (Nehemiah 1³), has been placed in a context (Ezra 4⁷⁻²³) preceding the prophesying of Haggai and Zechariah (Ezra 5¹ᶠᶠ·), thus leaving upon the hasty reader the impression that it had to do with the rebuilding of the *Temple* (Ezra 4²⁴; cf. 5³). Also it seems fairly certain that the Chronicler's partiality for the priest-scribe Ezra led him to represent Ezra, and not the layman Nehemiah, as the prime mover in the revival of Judaism in the middle Persian period.

III. THE FINAL SYNTHESIS

The document P, though the latest component of the Pentateuch, is nevertheless the framework of the whole. It thus gives the impression that the constitution of Judaism was in its entirety the pronouncement of Moses. When a shell is fired from a gun its trajectory follows an ascending course until it reaches its zenith, after which it falls steeply. Such was roughly the actual course of the dynamic revelation initiated through Moses. But the priestly writers, as it were, turned the gun round, and fired it back in the direction of Moses. The consequence was that when the older historians wrote the history of Israel, four-fifths of their space was devoted to the pre-exilic period (including the patriarchal), and they had little to say of the post-exilic period. In this they were following the lead of the priestly historians, who, if another figure may be allowed, 'telescoped' the legislation, and made it appear that what was really the growth of many centuries, was actually the achievement of a single generation. Thus the true history of the Mosaic age was overlaid by the developments of the centuries which followed. P, which in its content has so much similarity to Ezekiel 40–8, differs from Ezekiel in an essential respect. Ezekiel's programme is priestly in its general outlook, but it is still prophetic in that it looks forward to the future, and not backward to the past, as P does. The total content of the Old Testament is, of course, the same as it has always been; the difference is that, if the critics are right, the sources must be distributed in very different chronological order, with consequently a very different presentation of the course of the history.

CHAPTER VII

ESCHATOLOGICAL AND APOCALYPTIC

THE VIEW taken in this lecture is that apocalyptic proper begins with the Book of Daniel, which is a product of the Maccabean revolt.[a] If that is so, Daniel is the only real apocalypse in the Old Testament. The section Isaiah 24–7 is frequently referred to as 'The Isaiah-Apocalypse', but that the chapters are an apocalypse in the true sense is emphatically denied by Joh. Lindblom, even though as a concession to convention he writes under that title.[b] Lindblom enumerates the characteristics of apocalyptic as follows:

transcendentalism, mythology, cosmological orientation; pessimistic estimate of history, dualism, division of time into periods, the doctrine of two ages, playing with numbers; and finally pseudo-ecstasy, artificial claims to inspiration, pseudonymity and mysteriousness.

Rowley[c] remarks that 'some of these are rather the accidents than the essence of apocalyptic', and prefers H. Wheeler Robinson's[d] definition of the marks of apocalyptic as:

(1) It is deliberately pseudonymous and not simply anonymous . . .;
(2) its view of history is deterministic, following the divine appointment and culminating in some crisis which is that of the writer's own age;
(3) its emphasis is thus on the future and tends more and more to become extra-mundane, in contrast with the prophetic conception of a Kingdom of God in this world (though this may be included);
(4) apocalyptic is literary, not oral, and is marked by the excessive use of symbolism, the use of animal figures being especially noticeable.

On either of these two definitions Isaiah 24–7 must be excluded from the category of apocalyptic proper. Still less have the Book

[a] cf. H. H. Rowley, *The Relevance of Apocalyptic*, p. 39; H. T. Andrews, art. 'Apocalyptic Literature', in *Peake's Commentary*, p. 432a.
[b] *Die Jesaja-Apokalypse, Jes. 24–27* (Lund, 1938), pp. 102f.
[c] op. cit., p. 23, note 2.
[d] In Manson's *Companion to the Bible* (1939), pp. 307f.

of Joel and Zechariah 12–14 a claim to be included, though they too are sometimes spoken of as apocalypses. Apocalyptic literature is a development from prophecy, and Isaiah 24–7, Joel, and Zechariah 12–14 are examples of literature in the intermediate stage between prophecy and apocalyptic rather than apocalyptic in the full sense.

The Book of Daniel, then, is the last as it is the first example of developed apocalyptic in the Old Testament. At the same time it is the precursor of a literature which, if not comparable in bulk with the Old Testament, is nevertheless considerable. To take account of the whole of this pseudepigraphic material would almost require a volume to itself, and to attempt it here would upset the balance of this lecture, which is on the *Old Testament* interpretation of history. The Book of Daniel is on any showing one of the latest books in the Old Testament, and its interpretation of history is in the nature of an appendix to that of the Old Testament as a whole rather than integral to it. Moreover, all the essentials of the apocalyptic interpretation of history are to be found in Daniel. The later apocalyptists, with their 'pseudo-ecstasy', were imitative rather than original writers. They modelled their work on that of the author of Daniel, and their inspiration is not, for the most part, on the level of his, let alone on that of the prophets. The instinct of the Church, both Jewish and Christian, was entirely sound when, out of the whole mass of apocalyptic, it admitted only Daniel to the Canon of the Old Testament. Daniel was written out of the fires of persecution. So also was the New Testament Apocalypse. For the rest, apocalyptic writings have all the character of lucubrations; they smell of the lamp, and while they are interesting enough and of considerable importance, especially to the student of eschatology, they lie outside the main stream of revelation.

It is important to define the marches between apocalyptic and eschatology, since the two are often confused, at least in the popular mind. Apocalypse is properly 'revelation' (Greek, ἀποκάλυψις); eschatology is the doctrine of 'the last things' (Greek, τὰ ἔσχατα). One of the main interests, perhaps the chief, interest, of the apocalyptists was eschatology, and the reason why Isaiah 24–7, Joel, and Zechariah 12–14 have so often been designated apocalypses is that they have such a high eschatological content. But apocalyptic and eschatology are not identical. There is an eschatology of prophecy, and eschatology occupied a much larger place in the outlook of the prophets than critics of the nineteenth century, who were inclined to regard them as social and moral reformers, generally gave them credit for. It used to be the fashion to assume that any passage in the Old Testament that savoured of eschatology was post-exilic, and probably late post-exilic at that. This judgement has had to be revised, even though it must be admitted that toward the end of the pre-Christian era a certain section of the Jews came to be more and more preoccupied with eschatological problems, and there is still a certain presumption in favour of developed eschatological conceptions being relatively late.

I. PRE-PROPHETIC ESCHATOLOGY (?)

Since the publication of Gressmann's work on the Origin of Israelite-Jewish Eschatology[a] scholars have had to take seriously his contention that there was even a pre-prophetic eschatology in ancient Israel. Gressmann laid stress among other things upon the conception of 'The Day of Yahweh', which seems to have been a popular expectation in the time of Amos (Amos 5[18ff.]). It had generally been assumed that 'the Day of Yahweh' was nothing more than a contemporary jingoistic-patriotic notion without real theological foundation or significance. Gressmann contended that it was more than that, and that the origin of these popular eschatological ideas was to be sought outside Israel, probably in Babylonia. Gunkel[b] had already, a decade earlier than Gressmann, put forward the theory that eschatology is primeval history, as originally conceived in Babylonian mythology, projected forward to the end of time, speculations about the beginning of the world being transferred to its end. More recently this general thesis has been elaborated by Sigmund Mowinckel[c] in connexion with his much-discussed theory that there was in pre-exilic Israel an annual festival of Yahweh's accession to His kingly throne (*Thronbesteigungsfest*). For a general picture of the 'myth and ritual pattern', as it has come to be called, of the Ancient East, the

[a] *Der Ursprung der israelitisch-jüdischen Eschatologie* (Göttingen, 1905).

[b] *Schöpfung und Chaos in Urzeit und Endzeit* (Göttingen, 1895).

[c] *Psalmenstudien II. Das Thronbesteigungsfest Jahwäs und der Ursprung der Eschatologie* (Kristiania, 1922); cf. Hans Schmidt, *Die Thronfahrt Jahwes* (Tübingen, 1927).

reader may consult the volume entitled *Myth and Ritual*, edited by S. H. Hooke.[a]

As Professor Hooke defines it,

the annual festival which was the centre and climax of all the religious activities of the year contained the following elements:

(a) The dramatic representation of the death and resurrection of the god.
(b) The recitation or symbolic representation of the myth of creation.
(c) The ritual combat, in which the triumph of the god over his enemies was depicted.
(d) The sacred marriage.
(e) The triumphal procession, in which the king played the part of the god followed by a train of lesser gods or visiting deities.

These elements might vary in different localities or at different periods, some being more strongly stressed than others, but they constitute the underlying skeleton, so to speak . . . of such seasonal rituals as the great New Year Festivals.[b]

According to Mowinckel, a drama very much on these lines was enacted yearly in Jerusalem at the autumn festival of the New Year. The evidence for this is chiefly adduced from the Psalms, especially Psalms 47, 93, 95–100, in which the phrase 'Yahweh reigneth' (*Yahweh mālākh*) is properly to be translated 'Yahweh is (now) become king'. These and other Psalms, it is claimed, presuppose an actual triumphal procession, a ritual combat in which Yahweh is victorious over rival gods, and they also extol Yahweh as creator. For Mowinckel these things are something more than broken literary fragments of an antique mythology; they are to be understood literally, and eschatological beliefs had their roots in this New Year ritual.[c]

Now whether Mowinckel and the 'myth and ritual' school are right is simply a matter of evidence. If that evidence is sufficient we need not be deterred from accepting it by any orthodox scruples. When we read that Josiah

---

[a] Oxford, 1933; cf. also S. H. Hooke, *The Origins of Early Semitic Ritual* (London, 1938).
[b] *Myth and Ritual*, p. 8.
[c] op. cit., pp. 226f.

broke down the houses of the (male) temple-prostitutes (Hebrew: qedhēshîm) which were in the house of Yahweh, where the women wove tunics[a] for the (goddess) Asherah (2 Kings 23[7]),

and of the bestialities, associated with Tammuz-worship, described by Ezekiel (Ezekiel 8), we can well believe that the weirdest rites were carried through even in the Temple itself. As Ezekiel pictures these things they may have been of the sort that flourish when a society is on the brink of collapse, and men take refuge in the grossest superstitions. But we hear of ritual-prostitution, needless to say at sacred shrines, at intervals during the history of Judah (1 Kings 14[24], 15[12], 22[46]; cf. Deuteronomy 23[17]). Such things belong to the 'sacred marriage' element in the myth and ritual pattern. Nevertheless, Hooke is right when he admits that

Old Testament scholars have been rather reluctant to accept Mowinckel's theory that the Processional Psalms imply the existence among the Hebrews of a New Year Festival of the enthronement of Jahweh.[b]

There is little evidence for the conception of 'the divinity of the king' in ancient Israel; indeed, such evidence as we have seems definitely to point against it.[c]

Moreover, if, as Mowinckel argues, the Enthronement festival flourished most in the period of the monarchy,[d] and was gradually discontinued after the exile, until the true meaning of any procession that may still have been held was forgotten, it is strange that, to judge from the evidence of theophorous proper names, the conception of Yahweh's kingship was not prominent during the monarchy, but did become so after the exile.[e] This evidence has not been given its due prominence in the discussion. The facts are these: during the periods of the settlement and early monarchy the only proper names compounded with *melek* ('king') are Abimelech (Judges 8[31]+), Elimelech (Ruth 1[2]+), Ahimelech

[a] So LXX Lucian.

[b] *Myth and Ritual*, p. 13.

[c] See my article 'The Religious Aspects of Hebrew Kingship, in *Zeitschrift für die alttestamentliche Wissenschaft*, 50 (1932), pp. 21–38; T. H. Robinson, in *Myth and Ritual*, p. 186; but cf., on the other side, A. R. Johnson, 'The Rôle of the King in the Jerusalem Cultus', in *The Labyrinth*, edited by S. H. Hooke (London, 1935), pp. 73–111.

[d] op. cit., p. 206.

[e] cf. O. Eissfeldt, 'Jahwe als König', in *Zeitschrift für die alttestamentliche Wissenschaft*, 46 (1928), pp. 81–105.

(1 Samuel 21^2+), and Malchishua (1 Samuel 14^{49}). Of these, the only one that is without parallel in the cognate languages is Malchishua, which is probably a genuinely Hebrew name. Ahimelech is still attested on Samaritan ostraka in the middle period of the monarchy,[a] but there is no coining of new names, as we should expect if the idea of Yahweh's kingship had had any great vitality. It is not until the seventh century that we again meet with names compounded with *melek*. Then only do we find the name Malchijah ('Yah is King'). Gray[b] pointed out that it differs from all other names in *melek* in that 'it affirms something not of *melek* but of *Yah*'. It is the first proper name which unambiguously ascribes kingship to Yahweh, and it was evidently widely popular, being the name of quite a number of individuals well into post-exilic times (Jeremiah 21^1, 38^6; Ezra 10$^{25(bis)}$, 31; Nehemiah 3$^{14,\ 31}$, 8^4; 10$^{3\ (Heb.\ 4)}$, 12^{42}). Had the case been as Mowinckel imagines, the history of names compounded with *melek* would surely have been in reverse. The Processional Psalms are not, as Mowinckel argued, earlier than Deutero-Isaiah, who imitated their style. Their style is modelled upon his, even if we concede that they may be adaptations of cruder originals dating from the time of the monarchy.

But the question whether there was a festival of Yahweh's Enthronement in ancient Israel is of little importance for the theology proper of the Old Testament. If there was, it is clear that the post-exilic editors of the Old Testament did their best to expunge all recollection of it, doubtless because they regarded it as heathenish and foreign to the true Yahwistic tradition. As, indeed, it was. The whole myth and ritual pattern was based upon the conception of the dying and rising god, and its purpose was to ensure that the universe was a going concern. It was sympathetic magic. The system of nature needed to be wound up once every year, or it would run down and the world be faced with starvation. It is true that the yearly act of recreation was related to an original act, or series of acts, of 'creation', in which the god triumphed over the original chaos. But the myth and ritual pattern is bound up with the conception of cyclic recurrence which is of the very essence of all nature religions, and it is questionable whether it produced, or was capable of producing, any

---

[a] G. B. Gray, in *Expository Times* (November, 1915), p. 60.
[b] *Hebrew Proper Names*, p. 119.

genuine eschatology. It may be argued that nowhere in the Old Testament, not even in Genesis 1, is the thought of creation *ex nihilo* reached. That is perfectly true; nevertheless, there is a profound difference between Yahwism and the whole complex of ideas underlying the myth of ritual pattern. Those ideas were essentially those of Baal-worship, and with the Baal-principle true Yahwism knew no compromise. The myth and ritual school are fain to admit that the prophets, beginning with Moses himself, were hostile to all that the ritual pattern stood for.[a] It may be that some elements of it were temporarily grafted even into the official worship of Yahweh. We do not know for certain, nor do we know to what lengths such syncretism went. Eissfeldt[b] seems prepared to grant that in some passages which speak of Yahweh as King what he calls a *kultisch-mythisch* interpretation is not altogether impossible; but on examination he cannot find that in any single one it is probable, let alone necessary. On the contrary, the ascription of Kingship to Yahweh is *relativ-sozial*, and above all *absolut-hymnisch*; Yahweh is King because He leads and protects His people, and His is a majesty that is absolute. That is to say, genuine Yahwism starts from Yahweh's mighty acts in history. Mowinckel, to be sure, admits that 'the myth came to be related to the events of history' (*historifiziert worden*, 'became historicized'); that in this development of it the equivalent of the creation is the Exodus from Egypt, that the counterpart of the primeval chaos (*Urmeer*) is the Red Sea, and that Rahab is Pharaoh.[c] But for the Hebrews the relative order of the two conceptions, both in their intrinsic importance and the time of their apprehension, is the other way round. The conception of Yahweh as Creator is secondary in importance to that of him as Redeemer. The order of thought is Redeemer=Creator, and that too is the order in which the two ideas Redeemer-Creator came to expression. Great psalms like the *Venite* are not historicized mythology; they are pæans in which 'the helpers of Rahab' (Job 9[13]) are led captive to grace the triumph of the almighty Lord of history.

[a] cf. Hooke, in *Myth and Ritual*, pp. 10ff.
[b] op. cit., pp. 97–103.
[c] op. cit., p. 214.

II. THE ESCHATOLOGY OF THE PROPHETS

(a) 'The Day of Yahweh.' The protagonists for the Festival of
Yahweh's accession are divided on the question whether the
conjectured festival had any relation to 'the Day of Yahweh' of
Amos's contemporaries. Mowinckel does not seem to enlist
Amos 5[18ff.] in support of his thesis; but Hans Schmidt[a] does,
though naturally as evidence of a similar festival in North Israel
to that in Jerusalem. But whatever eschatological content the
idea may have had for the people at large, Amos was emphatic
that the real Day of Yahweh would be exactly the opposite of
what they anticipated.

> Ah! You who long for the Day of Yahweh!
> What should you want with the Day of Yahweh?
> It is darkness, the very reverse of light:
> As if a man should flee before a lion,
>   And a bear meet him!
> And then enter his house and lean his hand against the wall,
>   And a serpent bite him!
> Shall not the day of Yahweh be darkness, and not light?
>   Yea, deep darkness with no brightness in it at all!
>   (Amos 5[18ff.]).

So far from the Day of Yahweh being a day of salvation and
victory, it is to be a day of annihilating judgement. Further,
what Amos appears to anticipate is something more world-
shaking than the military defeat and political extinction of Israel.

> For this shall not the earth tremble,
> And everyone mourn that dwelleth in it?
> And it shall rise up like the Nile, all of it,
> And sink down again like the River of Egypt.
> And it shall come to pass in that day,
> 'Tis the oracle of the Lord Yahweh—
> That I will cause the sun to go down at noon,
> And I will darken the earth in the clear day (Amos 8[8f.]).

This is not to be dismissed as poetic exuberance. What Amos
seems to envisage is convulsions of nature on something like a

[a] Die Thronfahrt Jahves, pp. 45f.

cosmic scale. It is genuine eschatology; Yahweh is 'Lord of the End of Things'.[a] It goes without saying, too, that the eschatology of Amos, like everything else in his thinking, is conditioned by his moralized conception of Yahweh's nature.

But even if the eschatology of Amos may have been concerned only with the fate of Israel, that of Isaiah certainly has a wider range.

> Enter into the rocks,
> And hide thyself in the dust,
> Away from the terror of Yahweh,
> And away from his dread majesty!
> For Yahweh of Hosts has a day,
> Against all that is proud and haughty,
> And against all that is lifted up and exalted;
> And against all cedars of Lebanon,
> And against all oaks of Bashan;
> And against all high mountains,
> And against all uplifted hills;
> And against every lofty tower,
> And against every fenced wall;
> And against all deep-sea ships,
> And against all luxury craft:
> And human pride shall be brought low,
> And the loftiness of men shall be abased,
> And Yahweh alone shall be exalted in that day
> (Isaiah 2[10, 12-17]).

Isaiah announced that judgement was coming upon Judah, but it would come with at least equal decisiveness upon Assyria (Isaiah 10[12]), and the passage just quoted must be interpreted as meaning that it would be world-wide. To assert that Yahweh is Lord of History is to assert that He is Lord of all history. Idols are 'nonentities' ('*elîlîm*). As the conception of God becomes monotheistic, so must the scope of eschatology become commensurate with universal history and nature. The judgement begins at Jerusalem, but from there it passes outward and even gathers momentum as it reaches the confines of the world.

The next prophet to speak of the Day of Yahweh is Zephaniah. His conception of it is very similar to that of Amos:

[a] For the phrase see Oesterley and Robinson, *Hebrew Religion: Its Origin and Development* (Second Edition), p. 227.

> Near is the great Day of Yahweh,
> Near, and hasteth greatly;
> Swifter is the Day of Yahweh than a runner,
> Speeding faster than a warrior:
> A day of wrath is that day,
> A day of distress and anguish,
> A day of ruin and desolation,
> A day of darkness and gloom,
> A day of cloud and deep darkness,
> A day of the trumpet and alarm,
> Against the fenced cities,
> And against the high battlements
>   (Zephaniah 1^{14-16}).

Zephaniah pictures the Day of Yahweh as a storm sweeping over Judah and Jerusalem, thence over the Philistine sea-board to Egypt and Ethiopia (2^{1-12}), while another arm of it passes north to Assyria, engulfing Nineveh ($2^{13ff.}$). Everywhere in its wake shall be ruin and desolation.

The general opinion is that the immediate occasion of Zephaniah's prophecy was an irruption of Scythian barbarians from beyond the northern confines of Assyria, and that these marauders are the 'guests' whom Yahweh has 'sanctified' and for whom He has 'prepared a sacrifice' (Zephaniah 1^7). The same applies to the so-called 'Scythian Songs' embodied in Jeremiah 4–6. Neither in Zephaniah nor in Jeremiah are the Scythians actually named, and the only external evidence for the theory is a story of Herodotus[a] to the effect that some time prior to the fall of Nineveh a host of Scythians made a raid toward Egypt, and that they were only persuaded to retrace their steps by the bribes and prayers of the Pharaoh Psammetichus. The story as Herodotus tells it is not without its difficulties, and one or two scholars, most recently A. C. Welch,[b] deny that it has any historical foundation at all. According to Welch, the 'Scythian Songs' of Jeremiah were not prompted by any historical event; they have the character of pure apocalyptic, and are the original or the Gog and Magog prophecy in Ezekiel (Ezekiel 38–9). It has generally been assumed that one element that went to focus the mind of a prophet upon his life's task was the imminence of some threatened

[a] i, 103–7.
[b] *Jeremiah: His Time and His Work* (London, 1928), Chapter VI.

catastrophe. Welch appears to deny this utterly: all that was
needed to make a man a prophet was the consciousness of God in
his own soul; no contributory cause of a mundane kind was
needed. In principle he is right: the prophets did not argue from
the threatened invasion of Assyrians, Scythians, or Babylonians
that Israel was sinful and would therefore be punished;

the prophets always predict a judgement on Israel, not because Israel
was weak, but because it was sinful. . . . They did not therefore begin
from a casual event in history, like the emergence of Assyria or the
growing power of Babylonia. They began from Yahweh, whose character and whose standards they knew, and whose perfect will could
not fail to bring about His end.[a]

This is perfectly true, but it need not detract from the dignity and
inspiration of prophecy if it is closely related to actual history.
One broad difference between prophecy and apocalyptic is that
the latter is frequently quite unrelated to history, and sometimes
even presumes to write history on the basis of *a priori* principles.

In what is probably a later addition to the original prophecy
of Zephaniah the faithful people of Yahweh are bidden to wait
for Him against the day when He shall rise up as a 'witness'[b]
(Zephaniah 3⁸):

> For it is my purpose to gather the nations,
>> To assemble the kingdoms,
> To pour out upon them my indignation,
>> All my burning anger;
> For in the fire of my jealousy
>> Shall all the earth be devoured.
> For then will I restore to the peoples
>> A pure speech,
> That all of them may invoke Yahweh,
>> And serve him as one man (Zephaniah 3⁸ᶠ·).

These verses are typical of the Day of Yahweh as it came to be
conceived in exilic and post-exilic prophecy. Instead of being
primarily directed against Israel, 'the Day' comes to be pictured
as a day of judgement against Israel's enemies and oppressors,
sometimes with reference to a particular people, as for example

---

[a] op. cit., p. 119.   [a] So LXX, Syr.

K

Babylon in Isaiah 13–14. Sometimes the judgement is with a view to the ultimate conversion of the heathen, as in the Zephaniah passage above; but too often this note is lacking (e.g. Joel 3 9–21 (*Heb.* 4 9–21)), or, if the heathen are thought of as turning to Yahweh, it is under duress (e.g. Zechariah 14 16–19), and their position in the theocratic community is to be a distinctly subordinate and even menial one (e.g. Isaiah 14 1f., 60 10–14, 61 5f.).

These later descriptions of the Day of Yahweh come increasingly to approximate to those of apocalyptic proper. Yahweh acts directly, without physical or human intermediary. Gone are the days when the faithful expected Him to accomplish His purpose even through enlightened rulers like Nebuchadrezzar or Cyrus.

> And he saw that there was no man,
> And was astonished that there was none to interpose:
> Therefore his own arm wrought salvation for him,
> And his righteousness, it upheld him.
> And he put on righteousness as a breastplate,
> And salvation for a helmet;
> And he clothed himself with garments of vengeance,
> And was clad with zeal as a cloke
>
> (Isaiah 59 16f., cf. 63 5).

Neither does Yahweh require the armed assistance of His own people. In some *midrashim* of the Priestly Code (Numbers 31) and Chronicles (2 Chronicles 20) whole armies of aliens were slain without the Israelites suffering a single casualty, and, as we have seen, the tendency grew to think of the conquest of Canaan as Yahweh's sole act, and of his people's part therein as little more than that of gatherers of the spoils. Similarly, in the pictures of the blood-stained Hero emerging from Edom (Isaiah 63 1–6) and the judgement in the valley of Jehoshaphat (Joel 3 9–21 (*Heb.* 4 9–21), cf. Zechariah 14 1–15), Israel's rôle is an entirely passive one. Of the first of these passages Skinner[a] says:

The image presented is one of the most impressive and awe-inspiring in the Old Testament, and it is difficult to say which is most to be admired, the dramatic vividness of the vision, or the reticence which conceals the actual work of slaughter and concentrates the attention on the divine Hero as he emerges victorious from the conflict.

[a] 'Isaiah', *Cambridge Bible*, II, p. 214.

The Joel and Zechariah passages have not this superb literary quality. They quote (Joel 3 (*Heb.* 4) ¹⁶; cf. Amos 1²), or modify (Joel 3 (*Heb.* 4) ¹⁰; cf. Isaiah 2⁴), phrases from the creative masters of prophecy, and the miraculous stream which issues from the Temple, which is common to them both (Joel 3 (*Heb.* 4) ¹⁸, Zechariah 14⁸), is borrowed from Ezekiel 47¹⁻¹². In this respect also they approximate to apocalyptic, which, besides being literary in character, is consciously modelled upon literary originals.

(*b*) *The Messiah.* There is in some quarters a tendency to describe as 'eschatological' any conception that relates to the future, and if the Wellhausen school were wrong in their assumption that eschatological beliefs were not earlier than the third century B.C., the followers of Gressmann may be giving to eschatology a wider connotation than it should properly bear. Dr. Sidney Smith[a] says of Gressmann that

he was able to show that much in the earlier books foreshadowed, or might lead to, the later eschatological scheme; but his definition of eschatology is so loose that the term becomes unscientific.

It is questionable whether Gressmann's pre-prophetic 'Day of Yahweh' had any relation to 'the last things', and even though we regard the 'Day of Yahweh' of the prophets, with its commotions in heaven and earth, as coming within the definition of eschatology, we must consider that the farthest horizons of their vision of the future were very much closer at hand than ours commonly are. They might speak of 'new heavens and a new earth' (Isaiah 65¹⁷, 66²²), meaning a world transformed, without any serious thought of a termination of the universe.

The messianic hope relates, of course, to the future; but it need not be, in the strict sense, an eschatological conception, even as the Old Testament conceived of eschatology. It is not, for example, in Jeremiah. Although Jeremiah was the very reverse of a chauvinist, he nevertheless found a place, albeit a subordinate one, for the ideal king of the future. His Messiah is 'an ordinary good king',[b] a Scion of the house of David, who shall

[a] *Isaiah, Chapters XL-LV: Literary Criticism and History* (1944), p. 18.
[b] Skinner, *Prophecy and Religion*, p. 319.

reign as king and prosper, and execute judgement and justice in the land. In his days shall Judah be saved, and Israel shall dwell in security; and this is the name by which he shall be called, 'Yahweh is our righteousness' (Jeremiah 23[5f.]).

That is all, a modest enough expectation. Haggai's and Zechariah's expectations of Zerubbabel are associated with shakings of the heavens and the earth, and the sea and the dry land, and the overthrow of kingdoms (Haggai 2[6], [21f.]; cf. Zechariah 4[7]), but all that was soberly anticipated appears to have been the divinely appointed downfall of Persia and the re-establishment of the Davidic dynasty in all its first prosperity. Isaiah's vision, assuming, what there is no real reason to doubt, that Isaiah 9[5f.] and 11[1-9] are his, is wider and more supernatural in character. For him

the Messiah is a semi-divine personage, the radiant source of supernatural powers which regenerate nature and human society.[a]

It shall be as if the primeval paradise were come again. Associated with this general conception, though without explicit mention of a personal Messiah, is the expectation that in the new heavens and new earth which Yahweh will create, there will be a return of the longevity that was customary when the world was young, so that the man who has lived a century will still be considered young, while anyone who dies less than a hundred years old will be reckoned accursed (Isaiah 65[20]). Messiah's reign shall be one of universal peace (Isaiah 9[7]; cf. 2[4], Micah 4[3ff.]). But it is not until we come to the Enochic Son of Man that the Messiah is thought of as an extra-mundane figure, divine in any strict sense of the word.

III. APOCALYPTIC. THE BOOK OF DANIEL

The circumstances in which the Book of Daniel was written were very different from those which had produced the Priestly Code. The Persian Empire, notwithstanding that it was a despotism, was, by comparison with previous empires, a benevolent despotism, with some concern for the welfare of its subjects. Cyrus,

[a] Skinner, loc. cit.

Darius, Artaxerxes the First and Second, were enlightened rulers who befriended the Jews. It was no longer simply a case of the central government sending armies to the outlying provinces to extort the annual tribute, and doing nothing for them in return. The Jews had been free in the exercise of their religion so long as they made no bid for political autonomy. Their attitude to the state may be compared with that of St. Paul to the imperial power in Romans 13^{1-7}. To the Seleucid and Ptolemaic successors of Alexander the Great, who with their titles Soter and Epiphanes kept up the pretensions to divine kingship which he had revived, and who in the person of Antiochus Epiphanes tried to stamp out their religion, that attitude of contented submission changed to one very like that of the New Testament Apocalypse to the harlot Babylon.

Of the constant characteristics of apocalypse already enumerated, four are of the utmost relevance for the interpretation of history, and all are present in Daniel. They are (a) Transcendentalism, (b) Historical Determinism, (c) Historical Pessimism, and (d) Historical Dualism.

(a) *Transcendentalism*. By transcendentalism here is meant simply the conception of God as transcendent, not 'the investigation of what is *a priori* in human knowledge, or independent of experience', still less pantheistic mysticism of the kind associated with the name of Emerson, which would have been utterly unintelligible and even repugnant to the Hebrews. The conception of the divine transcendence did not, of course, originate with the apocalyptists; it is a presupposition of the Priestly Code, and even of the great monotheistic prophets. It is, indeed, an inevitable corollary of true monotheism. The doctrine of the sovereign omnipotence of God, therefore, was not first formulated by the apocalyptists; it is the point of departure of all their thinking about the world. If we except Daniel 9^{4-20}, Daniel's prayer, which according to Charles[a] did not originally belong to the text, the tetragrammaton YHWH is found nowhere else in Daniel except in 9^2, where it might be retained on the ground that the writer is using a citation from Jeremiah, though Charles himself, on the basis of the LXX, thinks the original reading was *'adonai* ('Lord'). The usual expressions for God are 'God' simply (*hā'elôhîm*, always with the article), 'the God of heaven', 'the heavens

[a] See either of his *Commentaries* on Daniel, *in loc.*

(4^{26} *(Aram.* 23*)*), 'the Most High God', 'the Most High'. The sentence pronounced upon Nebuchadnezzar is

to the intent that the living may know that the Most High ruleth in the kingdom of men, and giveth it to whomsoever he will (4^{17} *(Aram.* 14*)*).

The phrases 'God of heaven' (Genesis 24^7, J) and 'Most High' (Hebrew, *'elyôn*, Numbers 24^{16}; Deuteronomy 32^8) are found occasionally before the Exile, and they were becoming increasingly frequent before Daniel was written. (For 'the God of heaven' see Ezra 1^2, $5^{11, 12}$, 6^9; Nehemiah $1^{4, 5}$, $2^{4, 20}$.)

The emphasis upon heaven as the dwelling-place of the Most High almost necessitated the conception of angelic intermediaries between God and the world. It is long since Yahweh had appeared *in propria persona* as 'The Angel of Yahweh' (*mal'akh Yahweh*) or theophanic angel; it is now of angels, in the plural, that we must speak. Nebuchadnezzar in his vision sees 'a watcher and a holy one', that is 'a holy watcher', coming down from heaven ($4^{13, 23}$ *(Aram.* 10, 20*)*), and the sentence passed upon him is 'by the decree of the watchers' (4^{17} *(Aram.* 14*)*). In Daniel 8^{13} the seer overhears a dialogue between two angels ('holy ones'), and in what follows (verses 15–19) Gabriel is bidden to communicate to him the meaning of the vision he has just seen (similarly 9^{21-3}). This conception of angelic interpreters is already found in Proto-Zechariah (Zechariah 1^7–6^8), and becomes normal in later apocalyptic. But the most remarkable development of angelology in the Book of Daniel, though it again has its roots in the earlier literature, is in the conception of angelic patrons of the nations. In $10^{5ff.}$ Daniel is visited by a resplendent angel who tells him that he would have come to him sooner, had it not been that

the prince (Hebrew, *śar*) of the kingdom of Persia withstood me one and twenty days; but, lo, Michael, one of the chief princes, came to help me: and I left him there with the prince of the kings of Persia (10^{13}, emended after LXX and Theodotion).

After these explanations the angel announces that he is 'returning to fight with the prince of Persia: and when I go forth, lo, the prince of Greece shall come' (10^{20}). Michael, who is his only ally against the princes of Persia and Greece, is the prince of the Jews (10²¹, 12¹; cf. Jude⁹, Revelation 12⁷). Apparently, each nation has its own patron angel. The idea is already adumbrated in Deuteronomy 32⁸, where for 'Israel' we should read 'El' ('God'), with LXX and Old Latin, and render:

When the Most High gave to the nations their inheritance,
When he separated the children of men,
He set the bounds of the peoples
According to the number of the sons of God.

'The sons of God' are supra-mundane beings, members of the heavenly council of Yahweh.[a] It is this 'divine assembly' ("*dhath 'ēl*) which is the theme of Psalm 82:

God standeth in the divine assembly;
Among the gods he judges.
How long will ye judge unjustly,
And respect the persons of the wicked?
Judge the weak and fatherless:
Do justice to the afflicted and destitute.
Rescue the poor and needy:
From the hand of the wicked deliver them.
They know not neither do they understand;
They walk to and fro in darkness,
So that all the foundations of the earth are moved.
I said, Ye are gods,
And sons of the Most High, all of you.
Yet surely ye shall die like men,
And fall like one of the princes (*śārîm*).

(b) *Deterministic Conception of History*. It has never been easy to reconcile the sovereign omnipotence of God with human freedom. Even when we have conceded a measure of freedom to the individual, he seems very much at the mercy of world forces which he has not created and which he cannot control, and there does appear to be a certain inevitability about the great movements of history. How is this to be accounted for? Speaking of 'mechanical elements in the theology of Daniel', Charles[b] remarks that

[a] See H. W. Robinson, 'The Council of Yahweh', *Journal of Theological Studies*, xlv (1944), pp. 151–7.
[b] *A Critical Commentary on the Book of Daniel*, p. cxv.

it could not well be otherwise, since the prophetic era had passed and apocalyptic had begun its attempt to grapple with the world problems which confronted it—a struggle for which it was not sufficiently equipped.

According to the conception of angelic patrons of the nations, the issue of any conflict upon earth is predetermined by the conflict between the princes in the heavenly places. That nation is victorious on earth whose 'prince' has already defeated his rivals. The visions of the four world-empires are presented to Nebuchadnezzar and Daniel ostensibly as intimations beforehand of what is to happen in the future, the point of departure being the sixth century in which they are assumed to be living. In reality, of course, they are retrospective summaries of history from the sixth century, to the writer's own time. Even so, his conception of history is deterministic. What has happened is presented in the form of what is to happen, and there is no reason to doubt that he believed that what had happened was what had to happen. His four world-empires have their counterpart in the scheme of four world-eras, already noted, of the Priestly Code. For him dates are fixed: there is to be a 'consummation, and that determined' (9^{27}).

(c) *Pessimistic Interpretation of History*. The words 'optimist' and 'pessimist' have worn so threadbare in recent years that one hesitates to use them at all. Fundamentally, the apocalyptists were anything but pessimists; their ultimate philosophy was splendidly optimistic. They believed in the near-approaching triumph of the kingdom of God, but they believed in spite of, we may even say because of, the parlous plight into which the world, as they saw it, had fallen. It was as though they snatched faith out of the very jaws of despair. Apocalyptic, indeed, was born of despair of the prospects of the present world-order. The world was going down the steep, at an ever accelerating pace, into the abyss of moral corruption and consequent destruction. Its end would be catastrophic. The present world-order was incapable of amendment; a complete end of it would have to be made.

This idea of a world in process of deterioration may be illustrated from the four world-empires of Nebuchadnezzar's vision. The Babylonian empire of Nebuchadnezzar himself is of gold:

'thou art the head of gold' (Daniel 2³⁸). The Median empire is
inferior to it, of silver (2³⁹);[a] the Persian is of brass (2³⁹); while
the fourth, the Greek, is partly iron and partly clay (2⁴⁰ff.). The
decreasing preciousness of the metals of which the empires are
composed may partly signify a progressive decline in power: the
Median empire manifestly has not the splendour of the Babylonian, and the mixed iron and clay of the Greek signifies that 'the
kingdom shall be partly strong, and partly broken' (2⁴²). But in
the parallel vision of Daniel the fourth kingdom is not only
bestial; it has a robot-like quality which gives it a capacity for
evil which none of its predecessors had possessed:

a fourth beast, terrible and dreadful, and strong exceedingly; and it
had great iron teeth: it devoured and brake in pieces, and stamped
the residue with its feet: and it was diverse from all the beasts that were
before it (7⁷).

In the final vision (Chapter 11) the description becomes more
detailed as we approach the crisis of the writer's own day. This
is not to be accounted for simply from the fact that his knowledge
of recent events was fuller and more accurate than that of times
more remote. His description of Antiochus Epiphanes (11 ³⁶⁻⁹),
who was to 'prosper till the indignation be accomplished', is
such that we can only suppose that in his view the climax of
wickedness had been reached.

How is this pessimistic view of world history to be reconciled
with the writer's faith in the divine transcendence? That God
was supreme he did not doubt. On the other hand, it was plain
to him that the world was in the grip of demonic powers. He
accepted both facts. The solution he offered, for want of a better,
was to transfer the antinomy to the heavenly places, where the
patron angels fought out their conflicts apparently with the
permission of the Most High. Why they should have been allowed
to do this he nowhere hints. But he had inherited a conception
of the divine assembly in which the erstwhile gods of the heathen
had a place, if now subordinate and only on sufferance, and in
which 'the satan' (lit. 'adversary') of the Prologue to the Book of
Job and the vision of Zechariah (Zechariah 3²) had an official
standing. In 1 Chronicles 21¹ Satan, now without the article,

---

[a] For the interpretation of the four world-empires see H. H. Rowley, *Darius the
Mede and the Four World Empires in the Book of Daniel* (Cardiff, 1935).

has become a proper name. We may perhaps see here the influence of Persian dualism, the conflict of Ahura Mazdah (Ormuzd) and Angra Mainyu (Ahriman).

(d) *Historical Dualism.* The apocalyptic philosophy of history is essentially dualistic. The same is true in germ of earlier Old Testament conceptions, and has its origin in the doctrine of Yahweh's 'choice' of Israel. With the reconstruction of Judaism after the Exile the policy of 'separatism' (*habhdālâh*) was vigorously pursued by Nehemiah and Ezra, and the Priestly Code is an attempt to legislate for a 'holy people' living in an enclave surrounded by heathenism. The contrast between secular and 'holy' history[a] is already apparent. But the circumstances of the time did not call for embittered hostility. The created world had been pronounced by God 'very good'. The peculiar position of the Jews in it was due to the fact that a series of special revelations had been vouchsafed to them. In some ways the conflict was less tense than it had been in the days before the Exile, when the question of one God had been a living issue. If the Jews by keeping themselves free from the contamination of heathenism or semi-heathenism could worship God in peace, they were content. It was only when the secular power took the initiative by trying to stamp out their religion, and Antiochus Epiphanes brought matters to a climax by setting up 'the abomination of desolation' in the Temple, that they were goaded into revolt. Such an action by the blasphemer could not be accounted for simply by the fact that he belonged to a people that had not shared in the divine revelation. It could only be due—though the writer of Daniel does not say so explicitly—to the fact that he had been instigated to it by 'the prince of Greece'. Evil had its origin in demonic, supramundane powers. The dualism apparent in world-history was carried up into the very heavens.

Not that the apocalyptists ever adopted the thoroughgoing dualism of Persia. They were saved from that peril by their robust monotheism. There is therefore a certain inconsistency in their thinking. At the appointed time God would act, and when He did so it would be as though the prince of Greece and his minions did not even exist, much less hamper His sovereign freedom. A stone 'cut out (from a mountain)[b] without hands',

[a] cf. Otto Piper, *God in History* (New York), pp. 67 *et passim.*
[b] So LXX, Theodotion; cf. verse 45.

upon which no human tool had been used, would smite upon the iron and clay feet of the image, and break them in pieces (2[34]). This stone would become a great mountain, and would fill the whole earth (2[35]). All would be entirely of God's doing, and the phrase 'they shall be holpen with a little help' (11[34]) is generally understood to mean that the author had a certain contempt for human resource and effort. The stone cut out without hands represents the kingdom of God, which would belong to a different order from the kingdoms of this world. It would, however, be established in this world, and the righteous dead would be raised up to participate in the blessings of it (12[2]). The conception of a final kingdom of God outside the order of time and space is still beyond the horizons of the Book of Daniel, and was only developed in subsequent apocalyptic writings. Nevertheless, the Danielic philosophy of history is fundamentally dualistic, and the logical consequent of it was a kingdom altogether heavenly.

It has been said[a] that

Apocalyptic arose out of prophecy by developing and universalizing the conception of the day of the Lord. Its chief interest lay in the questions and problems connected with this idea. . . . What would happen when the 'great day' came? What would be its antecedents? What would be the character of 'the judgement' and the punishment meted out to the guilty? What would be the nature of the new kingdom that was to be set up? Would it be composed of Israelites only, or would Gentiles be admitted to it? Would it be permanent or only temporary, and, if the latter, what would be its duration? Would the pious dead have any lot in it, and, if so, what would be the nature of their resurrection? Would the wicked also be raised for punishment? What was the nature of the unseen world and heaven and hell? These and many other difficult questions naturally arose, and it was the task of Apocalyptic to attempt to find the answers.

The Book of Daniel is only a preliminary exploration into this vast and hitherto uncharted territory, and many of the prolific speculations about heaven and the hereafter which followed in the next two centuries were superseded almost as fast as they were adumbrated, and were never accorded canonical authority. It was not until the very end of the pre-Christian era that a coherent doctrine began to emerge from all this welter of opinion,

[a] H. T. Andrews, art. 'Apocalyptic Literature', in Peake's *Commentary*, p. 432ab.

and the aristocratic Sadducees, with their assertion that 'there is no resurrection' (Mark 12^{18}), came to be regarded as rather singular. One of the unresolved tensions of Old Testament religion arises from the fact that, except in one or two isolated passages, it attempted to justify the ways of God to men entirely upon the plane of this world.[a] History was indeed the stage, but it was the only stage, on which God had dealings with men. In Daniel we see the beginnings of an attempt to transcend history, but the impetus that could only come from a fresh creative revelation was lacking, and even so Daniel is by way of being an afterthought to the interpretation of history already contained in the Prophets and the Law.

[a] cf. C. H. Dodd, *The Authority of the Bible*, pp. 182–5.

CHAPTER VIII

GOD IN HISTORY

C AN WE AFFIRM that God has revealed Himself in history? Hardly, if we are pantheists, nor yet if we are deists. But the Old Testament conception of God is neither pantheistic nor deistic. Lessing's famous dictum that 'contingent truths of history can never be made the proof for necessary truths of reason' has, of course, deism for its background; and deism is dead. Pantheism, on the other hand, with its denial of divine personality, is still very much alive, and many who would stoutly deny that they are pantheists would nevertheless confess that their thinking is tinged with it. Dr. H. H. Farmer, indeed, has gone so far as to assert that 'the modern man, seemingly, has a certain inhibition in his spirit from experiencing, and thinking of, God as personal',[a] and that this prevailing temper of modern thought has 'soaked into the minds of those professing to be earnest participants in the Christian tradition and experience'.[b] But whatever hesitations the average thoughtful laymen, even Christian layman, may have about thinking of God as personal, and therefore, it is to be presumed, active in history, the responsible Christian theologian has no option in the matter. As Dr. C. H. Dodd has put it[c]

Christianity is thoroughly committed to the view that God reveals Himself in and through history. It is no doubt paradoxical to affirm that our knowledge of eternal and necessary truths of religion depends upon contingent truths of history. Christianity accepts the paradox.

According to Nicolas Berdyaev,[d]

The historical in the real sense of the word brings with it the revelation of essential being, of the inner spiritual nature of the world and of the inner spiritual essence of man, and not merely of the external phenomena. The 'historical' is by its nature not phenomenal but deeply

---

[a] *The World and God*, p. 2.   [b] ibid., p. 4.
[c] *The Authority of the Bible* (Second Edition), p. ix.
[d] *The Meaning of History*, p. 16.

ontological. It has its roots in some deep primal foundation of being which it makes available for our communion and understanding. The 'historical' is a sort of revelation of the deepest essence of universal reality, of the destiny of the world focused in that of man. It is a revelation of noumenal reality.

Quotations from contemporary theologians might be multiplied almost indefinitely; but these will suffice.

Can we, however, take the conclusion for granted? And what light, if any, has the Old Testament to throw on the problem?

As to Deism, the Old Testament knows nothing of what Tennyson's Lucretius describes as

> The Gods, who haunt
> The lucid interspace of world and world,
> Where never creeps a cloud, or moves a wind,
> Nor ever falls the least white star of snow,
> Nor ever lowest roll of thunder moans,
> Nor sound of human sorrow mounts to mar
> Their sacred everlasting calm!

Rather does it say:

> Yahweh shall go forth as a warrior-hero,
> Like a man of war he shall stir up zeal:
> He shall raise a shout, he shall utter a war-cry;
> Against his enemies he shall show himself a mighty one.
> Far too long have I held my peace,
> Keeping silence and restraining myself:
> Like a woman in travail will I groan;
> I will gasp and pant together.
> I will lay waste mountains and hills,
> And all their herbage will I dry up;
> And I will turn rivers into desert-wastes,
> And the standing pools I will dry up.
> And I will guide the blind by a well-trodden path,
> Along raised highways will I lead them:
> I will turn darkness into light before them,
> And the rough places into a level plain.
> These are the things I will do,
> Nor will I leave them undone.
> They are turned backwards, they are greatly ashamed,
> That trust in a carved idol,
> That say to molten images,
> Ye are our gods (Isaiah 42¹³⁻¹⁷).

All this, it goes without saying, not by way of wanton destructiveness, but by contrast with the inanition of heathen idols. The language may no longer be crudely anthropomorphic, but it is nothing if not strongly anthropopathic. And, being anthropopathic, it accords very well with the contemporary theological outlook. It is the veriest commonplace of present-day preaching that God suffers, and that a God incapable of suffering, or who declined to suffer, would be unworthy of our worship. We have reacted to the other extreme from deism. We no longer believe in, indeed we heartily repudiate, the doctrine of divine impassibility. Preachers and congregations alike are ready to applaud Browning's lines:

> I think this is the authentic sign and seal
> Of Godship; that it ever waxes glad,
> And more glad, until gladness blossoms, bursts,
> Into a rage to suffer for mankind.

That is our more refined way of saying what the Second Isaiah said, with no attempt at fastidiousness, three thousand years ago. But it is possible to quote Browning and the Second Isaiah, and really mean something very different from what either of them meant. I can use anthropopathic language about God, and my presuppositions may be fundamentally pantheistic. I may conceive of God as Process, Something to which the universe is striving to give birth; the Life-force which finds expression in man, and also, conceivably, in higher forms of being than man; and all manifestations of reality, from the lowliest to the highest, may be bound up together in a common struggle in which suffering is inevitable, and from which it is inseparable. That is emphatically not the standpoint of the Bible, whether of the Old Testament or the New. Equally emphatically, that is not what the Old Testament means when it speaks of God revealing Himself in history.

The root problem at the heart of the concept of God in history is the problem of divine personality. The most serious difficulty that confronts many readers of the Old Testament is the very strong emphasis upon Yahweh as personal. On this the Old Testament is uncompromising; it makes not the slightest attempt to remove the stumblingblock.

The personality of Yahweh is sharply and vividly conceived—so vividly that it would hardly be an exaggeration to say that He is the most clearly drawn figure in the portraiture of the Old Testament.[a]

This is to say that, at least in the early narratives, He is anthropomorphically portrayed, often naïvely so. And although, speaking generally, the conception of Yahweh is gradually freed from grosser anthropomorphisms, He retains to the end his individual character. He is always a personal God.

This at once raises the age-long philosophical problem, How can personality be ascribed to God without limiting the Being who is, by hypothesis, infinite? I remember the late Dr. Claude Montefiore[b] once testifying to what a comfort it was to him to turn, from the intellectual perplexities of modern philosophy, to the Old Testament, which seems so utterly unaware of any such perplexities. The comfort he received was despite, nay even, because of the fact that the Old Testament is so completely unself-conscious in the matter. Was he just burying his head in the sand?

It will be remembered how Richard Jefferies prayed that he 'might touch to the unutterable existence infinitely higher than deity'. Europeans who come under the spell of the pantheistic mysticism of the East generally make some such assumption as that

Personality already implies some degree of limitation: every specification must always be sharply distinguished from the unspecifiable Infinite. So long as it is accepted that Personality occupies a lesser degree of universality than the Infinite, the Supreme Principle of All—there is no objection to admitting it as one among possible determinations. The enemy to be shunned at all costs is a permanently dualistic conception, an immutable persistence of pairs of contraries, such as Creator-Creature, or Worshipped-Worshipper.[c]

I quote this not because it is particularly profound, but because it is typical of a widespread attitude of superiority to the concep

---

[a] H. Wheeler Robinson, *Record and Revelation*, p. 308.

[b] In a presidential address to the Society for Old Testament Study, subsequently published under the title 'The Achievement of the Old Testament', in *The London Quarterly and Holborn Review* (April, 1930).

[c] Marco Pallis, *Peaks and Lamas* (1939), pp. 176f.

of divine personality. On the issue it raises, the prophets would have been uncompromising; they would have denounced such a conception as a species of Baal-worship. From a somewhat different angle, scientific humanists like Dr. Julian Huxley view the ascription of personality to God as patent anthropomorphism, even though no obviously anthropomorphic language is used. Huxley pleads for 'the release of God from the anthropomorphic disguise of personality',[a] and speaks of 'reclaiming from the idea of God that garment of personality which we have put upon it'.[b] He declines to be put off with such pleas as that God alone is fully personal, or by 'the supra-personal nature (whatever that may imply) of God'.[c] Apparently it is not quite intellectually respectable to credit God with personality.

Now if it be a fatal objection to the Old Testament that Yahweh is a person, the same objection applies—notwithstanding that it is less pronouncedly anthropomorphic—to the New Testament as well, and indeed to any theistic interpretation of the universe. It is not the special responsibility of the Old Testament scholar to vindicate belief in a personal God. Nevertheless, although we cannot pretend to solve the problem of divine personality simply by appeal to the Old Testament, it may yet be that the Old Testament can help to clarify the issue as between theism and pantheism.

It is a matter of historical fact that the only religions which conceive of a revelation of God in history are the three great monotheistic religions, Judaism, Christianity, and Islam. These religions all derive from the Old Testament. Insofar as early Zoroastrianism was monotheistic, this was because Zarathushtra was a prophet, with presuppositions substantially identical with those of the Old Testament prophets. There are, it is true, personal gods in Hinduism, and some of the Bhakti-cults are for all practical purposes monotheistic. But there is a fundamental difference between them and the religion of the Bible. H. Kraemer[d] points out that

despite all . . . theological and psychological similarities, the spiritual climate and the really dominant urge in this deeply sincere and fervid religion of deliverance are radically different from the prophetic

---

[a] *Religion without Revelation*, p. 18.
[b] ibid., p. 14.   [c] ibid., p. 13.
[d] *The Christian Message in a Non-Christian World*, pp. 170f.

L.

religion of Biblical realism. . . . The all-pervading naturalistic-monistic spirit with which these authorities—[he means the Hindu sacred writings]—are imbued keeps his [Ramanuja's] conception of God, *notwithstanding his religious intention to the contrary*, in principle monistic. The world is not God's creation but evolves out of Him. . . . The relative independence and reality of the world is in Ramanuja's thinking necessary because it is needed for the sake of the primitive soteriological drive in his thinking. The same is the case with the conception of a real, personal God. The religious demand of the heart for a real deliverance makes a real, personal God necessary, and in order to emphasize the reality of this Saviour-God the world gets a relative independence and reality.

Nevertheless, he goes on:

bhakti-theology and *bhakti*-religion are, despite the moving praises of God who forgives and is the exclusive cause of salvation, not theocentric, but fundamentally anthropocentric, as all good monistic, mystic Hindu religion is. The whole range of *bhakti* experience and thinking is set in motion by the need of the soul for deliverance.

In other words, God is a projection on to the universe from man's religious need, somewhat like a Brocken spectre, if the illustration be not too irreverent. All religions and philosophies, except that of the Bible and its derivative, Islam, begin with the universe as they find it, and then seek to discover the principle of reality within it. This is as true of modern scientific humanism as it is of Chinese Taoism and the Hindu Upanishads. Only the Bible, as Kraemer further reminds us, can use such language as 'Hear, O heavens, and give ear, O earth, for Yahweh hath spoken' (Isaiah 1²). If to set God and the world over against one another as Creator-Creature is to limit God, I have never been able to understand why it should be more reasonable to begin with the world as something given and uncaused, and suppose that intelligence somehow emerged out of it, than to begin with Creative Intelligence. All things considered, it would seem more reasonable to begin with God than to begin with the world. Dr. Huxley appears to suppose that monotheism was a result of 'the fading of the several gods into one God'.[a] This is surely a misreading of the facts. Such a 'fading' invariably and inevitably results in pantheism. Hinduism is the classical example of it. The gods of the Rig-Veda that finally became merged in Brahman are patently

[a] op. cit., p. 37.

personifications of natural phenomena. They are both anthropomorphically described, and anthropomorphically conceived.
Yahweh, on the other hand, is frequently anthropomorphically
described, but it is not really correct to say that He is anthropomorphically conceived. He stands over against man. He confronts man as absolute demand. We can speak of Him as being
Other without being extravagantly Barthian in our emphasis.

Most readers, I imagine, will agree with me thus far. Indeed,
we seem to be committed to it, if we make any honest subscription
to Christian beliefs. We are neither pantheistic monists nor
scientific humanists. We neither believe that the world is evolving
out of God, nor that Something to which we may for convenience
give the name God is evolving out of the world. We believe that
God created the world. We have no objection, either on intellectual or on moral grounds, to conceiving of God as personal.
If, further, we believe that God is love, we can hardly imagine
otherwise than that He is active in the world for its salvation. We
believe wholeheartedly in the Incarnation.

Nevertheless, many of us find ourselves in difficulty when we
are asked to believe that stories of divine activity in history at
the stage prior to the 'emergence' of monotheism are of anything
more than local and temporary significance. We no longer place
the emphasis upon the Old Testament as a divine revelation, but
upon the history and religion of the Hebrews, upon their 'upward
striving' after God. We look upon it from the human rather than
from the divine side, from below rather than from above. It may
be little more than the story of how the Hebrews 'discovered'
God. Let us suppose that 'revelation' and 'discovery' are correlative terms, and that none of us, even if he places the emphasis
upon discovery, quite has the hardihood to banish the word
'revelation' from his theological vocabulary. But it is always
'progressive revelation'.

Now I have no wish to pillory 'progressive revelation'. It is a
valid concept. The Epistle to the Hebrews has it that God spake
'unto the fathers in the prophets by divers portions and in divers
manners'. But 'progressive revelation' has become for many
'a blessed word'. They seem to infer from it that when the
revelation has progressed beyond any given point, what was
previously revealed is now of little more than historical and
antiquarian interest. They tacitly invoke 'progressive revelation'

to justify them in ignoring, or even regarding as now positively
untrue, anything in the earlier Scriptures that jars upon their
conscience, concepts of the 'wrath' or 'jealousy' of God, and the
like, or anything that may appear to justify war. For example,
the Israelites took possession of Canaan by force, though criticism
may now warrant us in saying that force was not their only means,
thus to some extent alleviating the moral difficulty. The Canaanites were not all slaughtered; moreover, as we have seen,[a] the
later historians of the Conquest were not really so ferocious as
they sound. All the same, it is indisputable that the Hebrews did
gain their initial entry into Canaan by force. No doubt they did
so without any qualms of conscience, and so it was 'justified', in
the circumstances of three thousand years ago. But, it may be
pleaded, we cannot suppose that any occupation of Canaan by
force was strictly the will or the act of God, since it was really
'unprovoked aggression'. But what would we have? If God was
to make anything of the Hebrews, it would seem that He had to
take hold of them while they were still nomads, innocent of the
degradations inseparable from religion at the naturalistic agricultural stage of society. On the other hand, it is difficult to see
where He could have got with them if He had kept them permanently isolated in the wilderness. The beginnings of the true
religion, from all we can make out, had to be learned in the
wilderness. But when they had been learned there, their validity
had to be tested and demonstrated in the more complex *milieu* of
agricultural and urban civilization. The Hebrews, then, had to
enter Canaan if the divine purpose in and through them was to
be fulfilled. How, then, we may well ask, were they to get there?
It is inconceivable that any Canaanites, either then or now, would
give them amicable entry. And if their entry was only possible by
rough and tumble means, or, to speak plainly, by force, are we to
say that that particular series of episodes in their history lay outside God's covenant with them? Surely we must face facts. We
cannot bowdlerize the story whenever it jars upon our conscience. I am not saying that the ethical standards of Joshua and
his paladins were Christian; I am not saying that they should be
ours. I am only pleading that we are not at liberty to cut the
story about in essential particulars, and say, This was included in
the purpose of God, but that was not.

[a] *Supra* pp. 93.

Some Christians go so far as to cut the Gordian Knot of the Old Testament problem by practically ignoring the Old Testament altogether. They assume that the New Testament contains all truth necessary for salvation, and that the Old Testament, because it presents us with formidable critical and moral difficulties, may therefore to all intents and purposes be neglected. The presupposition underlying this attitude is similar to that in the story —said now to be apocryphal—of how the Caliph Omar justified the burning of the library at Alexandria:

If these books contain doctrine contrary to that of the Quran, they are false; if their doctrine is in agreement with that of the Quran, they are unnecessary; therefore, in any case, they may be destroyed.

We cannot honestly, *pace* Mr. A. G. Hebert,[a] allegorize the Old Testament, as earlier generations did, since we have been taught that interpretation must be literal, and must concern itself with what the text originally meant, not with what may be read into it in the light of the Christian revelation. The consequence is that many well-meaning Christians are to all intents and purposes Marcionite in their attitude to the Old Testament. Their Bible consists of the New Testament—sometimes not even all of that— and some purple passages from the Old, which they pick and choose at their discretion.

At this point it is worth considering in some further detail the fundamental difference between Yahweh and the gods of a typical pantheon. Yahweh, it is true, is a personal name. To call God by some such name was natural enough, and even necessary, in the days before a fully monotheistic faith was reached, when Yahweh was as yet only one among many gods whose existence was acknowledged. Any one among several Elohim must have a personal name if he is to be accorded character and individuality. Only the one God can be called Elohim without qualification. What the original meaning of the name Yahweh may have been is uncertain. Even if He was originally a personification of some natural force—'He who causes to fall', or the like, a personification of storm phenomena—such a meaning had already been forgotten or transcended by the time Exodus 3 (E) was written. That the name meant 'He who causes to fall' is a permissible conjecture

[a] *The Throne of David.*

of the philologists, and may find some support in descriptions of storm phenomena such as we have in Psalm 29; it is hardly an inference from the Old Testament as a whole. No doubt Yahweh is Lord of nature, but He is in an altogether different category from the nature-gods of the Rig-Veda. Even if He was originally a personification like Aghi ('Fire'), He differs from Agni in that Agni was only one of a number of gods, Indra, Soma, and the rest, that were legitimate objects of worship among the Indo-Iranians. Yahweh alone might be worshipped by the Hebrews. This, of course, is not to say that they worshipped no other. The prophets, and the Elephantine Papyri, make it clear that they did; but it was precisely for this that the prophets denounced them. Again, even if Yahweh was originally a personification of some natural force—and this, I repeat, is by no means certain—it is with the Yahweh of Hebrew worship in historical times that we are concerned, and our earliest sources appear to dwell upon His actions, particularly upon His deliverance of Israel from Egypt. That deliverance may have been accompanied by abnormal meteorological phenomena, but the real emphasis is not upon the accompanying phenomena, but upon the act of deliverance itself. Popular Hebrew religion, in the days following the settlement, may have confused Yahweh with Baal, even to calling Him Baal. But in the genuine Hebrew tradition Yahweh was emphatically not a Baal. The gods of the Rig-Veda and of other such polytheisms as finally dissolve into pantheism are, on the other hand, personifications, not persons, and as such are of the Baal type. All such pantheisms are, as Kraemer argues,[a] radically anthropocentric. Old Testament religion is from first to last theocentric. It was theocentric long before it was monotheistic. Hebert is quite right in his insistence[b] that the dogma of 'the Reality of God' must be distinguished from 'monotheism'. Yahweh, as the Hebrews encountered Him, was never a departmental god, a personification, like the gods of the Rig-Veda; nor was He a hypostatization of the spirit of the nation, like Chemosh of Moab. He was, even in the days when the existence of other gods was freely acknowledged, an all-purposes God, and therefore of necessity strongly personal.

We are faced, then, with the fact that the only true monotheism the world knows had its origin in monolatry, not in any polytheistic

[a] op. cit., p. 167.   [b] op. cit., p. 26.

naturalism. Yahweh was once a tribal God, and some of the accounts of Him may even be objectionable to us. But again, what would we have? For it would appear, not only that monotheism originated in what may have been a rather crude monolatry, but that monolatry alone is capable of being the parent of monotheism. Why, then, should we fall foul of what are sometimes naïve descriptions of Yahweh in the early narratives of the Old Testament? They may look grossly anthropomorphic; but the anthropomorphism is more apparent than real, a necessary accompaniment, at an early stage of reflection, of any conception of God as truly personal. As Dr. C. H. Dodd has put it:[a]

Crude enough indeed is the early conception of the character of this mighty God of Israel. Yet it is a great thing that He *has* a character, in a true sense. . . . Crudely anthropomorphic; and yet it is upon such a conception of the Deity that a truly ethical monotheism can be built, not upon a remote heavenly 'Creator-god' (*Urhebergott*) like the Chinese Shang-ti, or a metaphysical abstraction like Brahma, beyond good and evil.

All attempts to discover the riddle of the universe from within itself result, in ancient times, in some form of pantheism, and in modern times in some form of scientific agnosticism. When man is left to begin with the universe as he finds it he never, so long as he repudiates the Hebrew revelation and the Christian tradition that succeeded it, gets much farther than to think of God as the Principle that animates, or emanates from, what he sees. It is a commonplace that the cosmological and teleological arguments fall short of proving the existence of God. Monotheism is not obvious. It is not a necessary conclusion from human reasoning. Its cradle was in Palestine, amongst a fourth-rate people, as the historian, from every point of view but one, may justly account them. Paradoxically, it would appear that it is only among a small people like the Hebrews, living in a country compact and more or less isolated, and small enough to enable them to make do with an all-purposes God, that monotheism becomes possible. Over a wide area like North India, with few physical barriers, it is almost inevitable that there should be a pantheon of gods, each of whom is a personification of some natural phenomenon, with

[a] *The Authority of the Bible*, Second Edition, p. 46.

specialized functions. Similarly, in wide empires like the Assyro-
Babylonian, the local gods come to be members of a pantheon,
and any development in the direction of belief in one God tends
toward pantheism, due to the 'fading' of the several gods, as
Huxley terms it, into one. Palestine, in the providence of God,
was not capable of becoming the centre of an empire. It had not
the resources for such an adventure, and any attempt of a David
or a Solomon to make it more than a compact little kingdom of
the second class was foredoomed to failure. That Yahweh became
the sole Creator of the world was not due to any Semitic genius
for monotheism, as Renan supposed. The Semitic peoples contemporary with the Hebrews show no disposition toward monotheism. Nor, if we are to judge from the denunciations of the
prophets, were the great majority of the Hebrews monotheistically
inclined. That they became monotheists was due in no small
measure to the peculiar geographical situation of Palestine. But
the final explanation of a faith so apparently contrary to that of
the natural man would seem to be that God spake by the
prophets.

Yet another paradox awaits us: the Hebrews may have been
a fourth-rate people, but they had an eventful history, far more
eventful than that of neighbours like the Moabites and Edomites.
From all we can glean of the character of Chemosh from the
Mesha inscription, it is likely that the popular religion of Israel
in the ninth century B.C. did not differ greatly from that of the
Moabites. But so far as we know, or can imagine, the Moabites
never had such a romantic introduction to Chemosh as the
Hebrews had to Yahweh. Their relation to Chemosh was a
natural relation: they were the 'sons and daughters of Chemosh'
(Numbers 21²⁹; cf. Malachi 2¹¹); Chemosh was their ancestor,
no doubt in a physical or quasi-physical sense. The more enlightened Hebrews, those who stood in the prophetic tradition,
would never speak so of Yahweh. They might call their sons by
the name Abijah—meaning 'Yah(weh) is father'; but, even if for
some the name implied the physical paternity of Yahweh, there
was current in Israel an entirely different tradition of their
relation to Him. That relation was the covenant-relation. Israel's
sonship to Yahweh was adoptive, not natural. All through their
history the Hebrews retained a vivid recollection of a time when
Yahweh was unknown to their fathers, when, indeed, He *began*

to be their God. This was at the Exodus, when He delivered
them from the Egyptians. Accordingly they laid the emphasis
upon Yahweh as the 'God of battles', not as their eponymous
ancestor.

When the Hebrews established themselves in Palestine they
advanced beyond the semi-nomadic stage of culture, a thing
which contemporary monolatrous peoples like the Moabites and
Edomites, who remained in the steppe-land east and south of the
Dead Sea, never had a chance of doing. The Baal-controversy
served to sharpen the contrast between the God of history, and,
therefore, at that early stage of history, of battles, and the Baal-
principle rooted in the soil. The fundamental issue in Old Testament religion is not between monotheism and monolatry, but
between the Reality of Yahweh and the Baal-principle. That
takes us back beyond the eighth-century prophets to Elijah, to
Moses, and even, it may be, to Abraham. When, therefore, we
say that Yahweh, the Lord of heaven and earth, was once a God
of battles, and that the God of battles, and He alone, finally
became recognized as the Almighty Creator and Lord of heaven
and earth, it would almost seem as though none but the God of
battles could ever have become the Almighty Lord of heaven and
earth.

The underlying reason for the modern Marcionite attitude to
the Old Testament, and likewise the error in it, is that we unconsciously tend to lay the emphasis upon certain *ideas about* God,
which we assume to be true, or untrue, independently of
history. It is a concession we make, quite needlessly, to Lessing.
We grant that the ideas have been mediated through history, and
we are scrupulously careful, when we expound them, to place
them in their historical setting. We fail to see that the historical
circumstances are an integral part of the revelation. Instead, we
are inclined to treat them as so much husk to the pure grain of
truth. The historical occasion, once it is past, is more or less
irrelevant except for purposes of illustration. It has served its
purpose as a matrix for the truth, and may now, without much
loss, be ignored. In point of fact, the historical occasion is an
essential element in the revelation. To say that God is loving, or
righteous, or holy, or jealous, or wrathful, is to announce pro-
positions which, in themselves, are abstract. But Christianity,
and for that matter Judaism, does not lay the emphasis upon

doctrines, announced in the abstract. The Bible does not describe what God *is*, but what He has *done*.

As soon as we try to abstract the values from their concrete embodiment, we evacuate them of all reality and become sentimentalists.[a]

The Bible is the story of redemption, not a description of what God is like. It may say 'God is love' (1 John 4[16]), but only after it has first insisted,

Herein was the love of God manifested in us, that God hath sent his only begotten Son into the world, that we might live through him (1 John 4[9]).

Our present preference for 'God is love' rather than for

God so loved the world, that He gave His only begotten Son, that whosoever believeth on Him should not perish, but have eternal life (John 3[16])

marks a certain decline in evangelical conviction and emphasis. 'The revelation consists in a redemption, not the redemption in a revelation.'[b] Primitive Christianity recognized this with unerring insight, as almost any page of the New Testament testifies. But as the creative age receded, the emphasis came to be laid more and more upon God's attributes, instead of upon His mighty acts. This was nowhere more evident than in Protestant scholasticism, with its impossible doctrine of verbal inspiration. Criticism, with its rediscovery of the historical context, gave us a chance to get back to the realism of the Bible. But too many of us, so far, have not taken full advantage of it. Our method of interpretation is historical, but we are still largely dominated by the precritical concept of a revelation consisting in doctrines. We unconsciously tend to think of the divine purpose as educative rather than redemptive. That is not the attitude of the Old Testament. Nor were God's dealings with the Hebrews so much educative preparation for the redemption that was to be wrought in Christ. They were an essential part of the world's redemption, and as such their significance was not local or temporary merely, but eternal.

[a] H. W. Robinson, *Redemption and Revelation*, p. xliv.
[b] H. W. Robinson, op. cit., p. 88.

Berdyaev, in the first chapter of *The Meaning of History*, makes what he calls 'a digression on the essential nature of the "historical" '.[a] As he sees it, there are three periods in relation to the historical. The first is 'one of direct integral and organic experience in some settled historical order'. Such a period is of great interest to historical science, though the latter has as yet no function within it. Thought is static: man is in the historical order without being intellectually aware that he is, or even that there is any such thing as a historical order; much less does he speculate upon it.

The second period is that in which there is

fateful and menacing schism and disruption, when the foundations of an established order are tottering. It is in this collapse of organic structure and vital rhythm that the historical process originates, with its train of catastrophes and calamities of varying intensity. The result of this schism and disruption is that the knowing subject no longer feels himself directly and wholly a part of the historical object; and this gives birth to the speculations of historical science. But this does not favour either a real elaboration of a philosophy of history or a real definition of the historical process, because it involves a divorce between subject and object, and the withdrawal of the speculating subject from the life in which he had hitherto directly participated. He is separated from the innermost life, from the 'historical' itself. An antithesis is set up between the 'historical' and the knowing subject, now divorced from the inner essence of the former.[b]

This second period is an inevitable and necessary stage in the building up of a true philosophy of history. It does succeed in relating, collecting, amassing and partially apprehending very much. But it is impotent to grasp the very essence of the 'historical'.

The known object itself gradually recedes, is lost sight of and ceases to exist as that primal reality which constitutes its only claim to be called historical and its only means of revealing the sources of history. This process is particularly flagrant in the sphere of historical criticism.[c]

Attempts are indeed made to build up philosophies of history, but they are always fatally wanting in depth and in penetration into the mysteries of history.

[a] op. cit., p. 3.   [b] ibid., p. 3.   [c] ibid., pp. 7f.

The third period, which alone is capable of building up a valid philosophy of history, is that in which the knowing subject returns to the 'historical', there to 'rediscover the mysterious sources of historical life, its inner significance and the inner soul of history'.[a] This rediscovery is likely to follow

those catastrophes when the human spirit, having experienced the collapse of a given historical order and the moment of schism and disintegration, is able to appose and oppose these two moments—that of the direct participation in an historical order and that of the divorce from it—in order to arrive at a third spiritual state which induces a particularly acute consciousness, a particular aptitude for speculation and a corresponding aspiration toward the mysteries of the 'historical'.[b]

Accordingly, the 'historical' is not something toward which the historian can assume an attitude of aloofness or detachment. So long as he looks upon the materials with which he is dealing as something external and objective to himself, he can never appreciate their true inwardness.

In order to grasp the mystery of the 'historical' [Berdyaev argues], I must have a sense of it and history as something that is deeply *mine*, that is deeply *my* history, that is deeply *my* destiny. I must situate myself within historical destiny and it within my own human destiny. . . . All historical epochs, from the earliest to that at the topmost peak of modern history, represent my historical destiny; they are all mine.[c]

I have quoted Berdyaev at such length because his style, and the nature of the subject, make it difficult to summarize or paraphrase him without misrepresenting him. His scheme may seem open to objection as conforming too closely to the Hegelian conception of thesis, antithesis and synthesis. But there is an obvious parallel between his three periods in relation to the 'historical', and three attitudes toward the Bible, and particularly toward the Old Testament. The parallel is the more close because biblical criticism is essentially historical criticism, and also because it was in the *Aufklärung* of the eighteenth century that biblical criticism, like historical criticism generally, originated. Biblical criticism is only one department of modern historical criticism. Until very near the close of the eighteenth century no Christian

[a] ibid., p. 4.   [b] ibid., pp. 4f.   [c] ibid., p. 16.

had any doubts about the historical accuracy, or indeed the verbal inspiration of the Bible. This long period of unquestioning acceptance corresponds to Berdyaev's first period in relation to the historical. Then came criticism, with its minute analyses of documents and its rewriting of the history and religion of the Hebrews from the standpoint of the Graf-Wellhausen hypothesis. It would hardly be right to call this criticism negative, though it may fairly be described as entirely dispassionate and even somewhat aloof. Its attitude to the Old Testament was altogether objective, and a great deal of what had once been precious to an unquestioning faith was to all intents and purposes consigned to the waste-paper basket. It corresponds to Berdyaev's second period or attitude in relation to the historical, an attitude which, he insists, however inevitable and even valuable it may have been, is yet inadequate. Many students of the Old Testament, it is not too much to say, never get beyond this second stage. Before they have mastered the technique of criticism, a discipline which may take them well into middle life, they have lost all interest in the subject, and turn to some one of the other studies which nowadays clamour for the attention of the working minister. They have not the time, even if they ever heard of it, to put to the test what, according to Dr. John Baillie,[a]

Mr. Aldous Huxley has somewhere observed [namely that] the course of every intellectual, if he pursues his journey long and unflinchingly enough, ends in the obvious from which the non-intellectuals have never stirred.

Were it not better, it may be asked, to have remained a 'fundamentalist', if the end of a toilsome journey is, after all, only another kind of fundamentalism? 'But alas! It is too late for that now', and few teachers as yet seem to have learned how to short-circuit the process for their students, even if it were wise to attempt it.

I have ventured to insert the foregoing summary of Berdyaev's 'digression on the essential nature of the "historical" ' because it seems to me so extraordinarily relevant to the problem that confronts the well-meaning but perplexed student of the Old Testament today. But when Berdyaev speaks of my having 'a

[a] *Our Knowledge of God*, p. 250.

sense of . . . history as something that is deeply *mine*, that is deeply *my* history, that is deeply *my* destiny', is he just being esoteric? Surely not. Does not what Dr. John Baillie has written of his own experience,[a] awaken memories in us all, memories which have perhaps been overlaid by our toilsome wrestlings with the minutiæ of J, E, D, and P?

The story told me how God had spoken to Abraham and Moses and the prophets and apostles, but what gave the story its power over my mind and imagination and conscience was the knowledge that 'in, with, and under' this speaking to these others of long ago He was also now speaking to myself. . . . What is it to me that God should have commanded David to do this or that, or called Paul to such and such a task? It is nothing at all, unless it should happen that, as I read of His calling and commanding them, I at the same time found Him calling and commanding me. . . . God reveals Himself to me only through others who went before, yet in so doing reveals Himself to me now.

He quotes Dr. F. Gogarten:[b]

However one may try to solve it, and however one may alter its form in so doing, the problem of history is fundamentally the problem of the presentness of the past. Were the past merely past, as it is in the case of all natural events, there would be no such thing as history but only an unhistorical present—and indeed not even that. For there can be a real present only where there is something past that becomes present. History is something that happens in the present.

Baillie's conclusion is:

Such, surely, is the right way of it. *It is only in the conception of history as something that happens in the present that the apparent contradiction in our doctrine of a mediated immediacy can be reasonably resolved.*[c]

This power of bringing the past to life in the present is not, of course, confined to the Bible. But no literature can compare with the Bible for the consistency and intensity with which it exercises it. No history so speaks to the conscience or so directly confronts man with God as the history recorded in the Bible. Imaginative literature, plays, poems, and novels are also capable of doing

[a] op. cit., pp. 181–9.   [b] *Ich Glaube an den Dreieinigen Gott*, pp. 71f., 83.
[c] op. cit., p. 189.

this; but they have not the universality of appeal of the Bible, and, even so, the best of them are, more often than not, directly or indirectly inspired by the Bible, or deal with problems which the Bible has already handled in a creatively-original way. Even Bible stories which we may hesitate to claim as 'historical' in the literal sense, such as Abraham's offering of Isaac (Genesis 22), or Moses' vision of Yahweh (Exodus 33$^{17-23}$), speak to the soul as urgently and insistently as others whose historical accuracy is entirely above suspicion. They might have done this in any case, if we can imagine their having been written; but can we imagine their being written except by men whose faith was anchored in the concept of revelation in history? They are, if we like to put it so, imaginative descriptions by individuals who, being heirs of the historic tradition, had re-experienced the presence of God in their own souls, and who then proceeded to relate their experiences in the form of stories about the heroes of old. They are thus woven into the texture of the historical revelation, and as such they are far more psychologically convincing than (say) the communications of Krishna to Arjuna in the Bhagavadgita.

There is, even for the newcomer to criticism, if he is intellectually honest, no going back to 'fundamentalism'. He has tasted of the fruit of the tree of knowledge, and been driven out of the garden. The way back to the Eden of his pre-critical innocence is for ever barred against him by the Cherubim with their swords of whirling flame. What, then, is he to do? He may either wander for a while in the wilderness, until he decides that some study other than that of the Old Testament offers him more competence for exercising his ministry in this very modern world. He will then take refuge in talking vaguely about 'progressive revelation', while really he has thrown in his lot with the Marcionites. Better, he will exercise patience, all the while listening for the Voice that still speaks through even the most ancient Scriptures, until he reaches, not by describing a circle, but by mounting a spiral, the vantage ground of a higher certainty. And I venture to assert that no theological discipline is more rewarding. There are those who defend the Old Testament mainly on the ground that without a knowledge of it no man is capable of understanding the New, that without its Old Testament foundation the New Testament is left suspended in mid-air. That is something, but it is not enough. The unity of the Testaments is pregnant with a much deeper meaning. The Old Testament was not written in order that the modern theologian might have a point of departure for his study of the New. Together with the New it tells the story of God's redemption of mankind. That story is one and indivisible. It is, on any showing, unique in history. The Old Testament is not so much prolegomena, it is an integral part of the story of redemption. Without it the New Testament is but a torso, magnificent indeed, but nevertheless incomplete. We cannot think of the world's redemption beginning in the reign of Herod the Great; it goes back to the call of Moses, to the call of Abraham, and indeed to man's first disobedience. Of course there was progressive revelation. There had to be. God had some very intractable material to deal with. The measure and method of his approach to man were conditioned by the fact that man was not only ignorant; he was a fallen being. If we have to call in the doctrine of Kenosis to help us to understand the Incarnation, much more do we need to employ a similar concept in dealing with the Old Testament part of the story. But if we accept the doctrine of the indivisibility of the Testaments, the remedy for dealing with the much advertised 'moral difficulties' of the Old Testament does not lie in a wholesale revival of the principle of allegorizing. By all means, let us allegorize occasionally, if it helps us in our private devotions, and even in our pulpit ministrations, provided we are frank with ourselves and honest with our congregations. But the Old Testament part of the history of redemption was history before ever it lent itself to being allegorized. And if David was not the impeccable saint we once made him out to be, does that exclude him from a rightful place in the majestic unfolding story? On the roll of the heroes of faith in the Epistle to the Hebrews there appear the names of Gideon, Barak, Samson, and Jephthah. I once heard Bishop Lunt liken Gideon to Mr. Winston Churchill; Barak to a typical country squire—or was it the other way about? it does not greatly matter—Samson, with all his strength and weakness, to the average sergeant-major; and Jephthah to Lawrence of Arabia. Such men had, and still have, their part to play in a divine purpose of which they may apprehend but little. There was even 'Rahab the harlot' (Hebrews 11[31])! Whether she really played just the part that is credited to her in the story of the Conquest is not of great importance so long as the main features of Old Testament history are as clear as scholarship has established them to be. She fits perfectly· into the picture as archæology helps us to reconstruct it.[a]

I fear I may have descended in this chapter from the high places of philosophy to something like homiletics. If so I have done it deliberately. In these days when there is a wide gulf fixed between the specialist and the average general-practitioner minister, to relate the two is necessary if the Old Testament is to recover the place it once had in our esteem and reverence; and I have tried to bear in mind that in the terms of the original Fernley Trust this lecture was intended to meet the needs of Methodist ordinands.

[a] cf. Millar Burrows, *What Mean These Stories?* (New Haven, Connecticut, 1941), p. 139.

M

CHAPTER IX

ISRAEL THE SERVANT OF YAHWEH

D ID GOD really make choice of Israel, as the Old Testament writers claim? Or was it only their national pride that emboldened them to say that He had? Professor Gilbert Murray has written:[a] 'History in every country is to a great extent a *fable convenue*, a version of events suited to the local taste.' This is undeniable, and to some extent it is inevitable: we laid it down at the beginning that there are no 'bare' facts for the historian, that every historian is obliged, whether he will or no, to put some interpretation upon the events with which he is dealing. In a critique of the film, *The Hitler Gang*, Mr. Edgar Anstey wrote:[b]

It may well be that *The Hitler Gang*, in seeking to reproduce rather than to interpret a piece of history, is attempting the impossible.

If that is true today of an attempt to give an accurate representation of a contemporary movement extending over little more than a decade, we can hardly censure the ancient Jews if they put a generous measure of interpretation upon the events of their national history extending over a millennium. They lived before the age of scientific history. The question is, did their national pride and religious enthusiasm, when they asserted that they were the chosen people, lead them beyond the bounds whither we can follow them?

The modern historian of the religion of Israel describes how a monolatrous people, who believed themselves to have a proprietory right in one god out of many that were worshipped by their contemporaries, came to believe that their own particular god was actually the one and only God of the whole world. If their final faith was justified—and most sympathetic historians are prepared to agree that it was—it was entirely natural, even if it was illogical, that they should continue to believe that God was

[a] *The Spectator*, No. 6,063 (8th September 1944), p. 214.
[b] *The Spectator*, No. 6,067 (6th October 1944), p. 311.

in a unique sense their own. The obvious paradox, how the one God could continue to be the God of a particular people, was one which they were hardly in a position to resolve. Their view of the case, as it finds expression in the post-exilic Priestly Code, was that the God of the whole world had deliberately chosen them out of all the nations. Which of the two accounts of the matter, that of the modern historian, or that of the Priestly Code, if either, is the true one? Is there any real need to set them over against one another as contraries? May we not accept the critical account of how the Jews became monotheists, and still believe that the interpretation of the Priestly Code was, viewed *sub specie æternitatis*, perfectly valid? How otherwise are we to explain the story as the modern historian disengages it from its superincumbent layer of legend? The legend, as well as the story, may very well be true.

That the story is remarkable, nay, unique, is obvious on the face of it. Consider, first, the physical factors. Palestine occupied a geographically central position in the ancient world. It lay between the two great river-basins, the Nile and the Euphrates-Tigris. Since the political decline of Islam the cultural and religious affinities of Egypt and Mesopotamia have been with the East rather than with the West. But in ancient times their outlook, though naturally restricted, was on the whole toward the West. There may have been correspondences between the civilization of Sumeria and that of Mohenjo-daro, in the Indus basin; but after the Semitic conquest of Sumer and Akkad contacts were mainly with the Mediterranean seaboard. Not until the empire of Alexander was there again much contact with India. Nowadays we speak of anywhere east of Benghazi as the 'Middle East', and the 'Near East' seems to have disappeared from the map. Properly, the Middle East has its centre in India, and the Far East is beyond Singapore. The Near East should lie between Egypt and Iraq inclusive, with perhaps—now that North Africa is Muslim—one margin along the southern shores of the Mediterranean, and another into Persia. The civilizations of the Middle and Far East may conceivably be as old as those of Egypt and Babylonia, but so far they have lain outside the main stream of 'Western' civilization, which properly had its rise in the Near East, and which now, for good or ill, the East is doing its utmost to copy. In ancient times there was some mutual borrowing between Egypt and Greece, by way of the Aegean civilization, the usual direction being from south to north rather than vice versa. Western civilization is the result of the confluence of two main streams, one Semitic-Hamitic and specifically Hebrew, the other Hellenic. The Semitic-Hamitic is older than the Hellenic; the two great river basins, the Nile and the Euphrates-Tigris, are the cradles of Western Christian civilization.

Not only did Palestine lie between the Nile and the Euphrates-Tigris; it lay right across the only convenient line of communication between them. Merchants, and armies, on their way from the one to the other, had to pass through it. It was thus, from very early times, open to influences from both sides. If we are to look anywhere in the ancient world for a measure of cultural and religious syncretism amounting to saturation, it is to the eastern Mediterranean seaboard, of which Palestine occupied the southern half. Then there were the Indo-European Hittites, who broke in from the north, and who, it is now widely thought, contributed something to the characteristic Jewish physiognomy (cf. Ezekiel 16[3]). The historical background to the birth and development of Israel is largely the story of the three-cornered contest between Egyptian, Assyro-Babylonian, and Hittite, each of whom left his impress upon the country. Nevertheless, the land succeeded in preserving its individuality. This individuality, as Mr. J. N. Schofield remarks,[a]

may be, in part, due to the fact that for much of its history the land formed the boundary, rather than an integral part, of neighbouring kingdoms.

Now Egypt would hold it, less for its own sake than as a protective margin against Hyksos or Hittite; and now Assyria would seize it as a base for operations against Egypt. Until late in Old Testament times it was, when not independent, always a precariously held outlying province of whatever power happened to be in the ascendant.

On its eastern side Palestine lay open to nomadic tribes closely related to the Aramæans from which Israel had sprung. T. H. Robinson[b] stresses this point. By the second millennium B.C., when the Aramæans began to seek entrance into the Fertile

<hr />

[a] *The Religious Background of the Bible*, p. 33.
[b] Oesterley and Robinson, *A History of Israel*, Vol. I, pp. 48ff.

Crescent, most of the desirable localities were already firmly occupied, and many poor kinsmen of the Israelites had perforce to make do on its fringe. The result was that centuries might go by, but the receding past never seemed very far distant; there was constant reminder of it just beyond the Jordan, whence an Elijah might suddenly appear from Tishbe of Gilead. Not less significant, as T. H. Robinson has more than once reminded us, is the fact that Amos, the first of the great eighth-century prophets, came from the wilderness of Tekoa, in the uplands of Judah. The main highway between Egypt and Mesopotamia passed through Northern Israel, but not through Judah, which lay outside the main stream of the world's life. Bounded on the east by the Dead Sea, on the South by the Negeb, on the west by the Philistine plain, and on the north by Israel, Judah was comparatively isolated, and economically much poorer than her sister kingdom. Jerusalem is little more than thirty miles distant from Samaria, and only ten from Bethel. True, it was a strong fortress, but the Assyrians could no doubt have reduced it after their capture of Samaria had they considered it worth their while. But Judah was no more a military than it was an economic prize, and it was sufficient that an Assyrian army marching against Egypt should mask the capital as a protection from attack on its flank. This is probably all that Sennacherib intended in 701 B.C.[a] As Hebrew historians let their memories dwell on the resplendent reigns of David and Solomon, their wounded pride and religious zeal led them to mourn the division of the kingdom as an unmitigated disaster. In reality it was a blessing in disguise.[b] It was thereafter vain for either of the two petty kingdoms to think of setting out on a career of world-empire, the inevitable result of which, had it even been barely possible, would have been to stifle a religious promise as yet hardly begun, besides inviting the hostility of some power which in the nature of things had far greater resources. North and South would have gone down in one common ruin, as likely as not when Samaria fell. As it was, Judah was able to take over the best of the religious heritage of the North, and retained at least a nominal independence for another century and a half, during which time Yahwism became sufficiently established to survive the Exile. Moreover Judah,

[a] cf. Oesterley and Robinson, *A History of Israel*, I, pp. 395, 398f.
[b] A. S. Peake, *The People and the Book*, p. 259.

from the nature of its soil, was predominantly pastoral rather than agricultural, and therefore not so exposed as Israel had been to the subtle allurements of Baal-worship.

So much for the geographical factors. What, now, is to be said of the nature-miracles which, according to the Old Testament, accompanied and assisted the fortunes of the chosen people?[a] These fall mainly into two groups, one connected with the Exodus and the subsequent Conquest of Palestine, the other with the ministries of Elijah and Elisha. It is convenient to deal with this latter group first. Marvellous things are related of Elijah, and even more marvellous things of his disciple. Some of the stories told of Elisha represent him as a thaumaturge (2 Kings 2^{19-22}, 4^{38-41}, 6^{1-7}); they have all the characteristics of folk-story, and are readily capable of natural explanation. Elijah was much the greater of the two men, and the wonders related of him have more semblance of moral justification than have those told of his disciple. Other stories related of Elisha look like doublets of Elijah stories (2 Kings 4^{1-7} / 1 Kings 17^{14-16}; 2 Kings 4^{18-37} / 1 Kings 17^{17-23}), and although they are still well told they are, as we should expect, more prolix than their originals. On the whole it seems vain and unimaginative to attempt to rationalize the Elijah miracles, and in particular the rationalizing explanation[b] that the 'water' which Elijah poured over the sacrifice on Mount Carmel was really naphtha seems a desperate expedient. That something extraordinary happened is certain, but what it was we do not know. That the stories are of North Israelitish provenance, and therefore comparatively early, is no guarantee that they do not contain legendary elements. It is a well-recognized fact that legend can surround the figure of a saint even during his lifetime, and it seems best to agree with Wellhausen[c] that 'legend, and not history, could alone preserve the memory of Elijah's figure'. To say that it is foolish to try to rationalize the Elijah miracles is not to say that if we had a straightforward account of Elijah's ministry we should not find even the most wonderful events in it capable of scientific explanation. We probably should, without much difficulty. The likelihood is that it contained no 'miracle'

[a] The most recent treatment of this subject is an article by H. Wheeler Robinson: 'The Nature-Miracles of the Old Testament', in *Journal of Theological Studies*, XLV (1944), pp. 1–12.

[b] R. H. Kennett, *Old Testament Essays*, pp. 103f.

[c] *Religion of Israel and Judah*, English Translation, p. 65.

in what is still the popular meaning of that ambiguous word. The real miracle, if that is not a burking of the issue—though of that below—is the towering personality of Elijah himself. He appeared at a time of crisis, and if he had not appeared when he did, or had acted otherwise than as he did, the situation would have taken some retrieving, for Israel would certainly have gone 'limping' (cf. 1 Kings 18[21] *Heb.*) on the wrong opinion.

The miracles told of the Exodus and its sequel are not only more important in themselves; they are more integrally related to the history. It is obvious that the Plagues have a close similarity to natural conditions in Egypt,[a] and it is generally agreed that they have an historical basis. There seems no reason to doubt that prior to the Exodus there was in Egypt an unusually severe series of epidemics and pestilences. We have already noted[b] that the miraculous element, alike in the Plagues and in the crossing of the Red Sea, is heightened as we proceed from J, through E, to P.

The divine power worked in Egypt by means of a wonderful series of natural phenomena; and the religious instinct of the Hebrew narrators seized upon these as signs of God's favour to the Israelites and of punishment to their oppressors. The religious conviction led, as time went on, to accretions and amplifications; and the stories in the course of frequent and triumphant repetitions, acquired more and more of what is popularly called miracle.[c]

P's account of how the waters stood as walls on either side of the advancing Israelites may, therefore, be accounted legend; the story as we have it in J may be given a natural explanation, either by the more usual theory that the tide was delayed by wind, or by the seismic-volcanic theory of Phythian-Adams.[d] Both theories are able to adduce in their support similar, though of course by no means frequent, phenomena, either in what must have been the approximate locality of the actual crossing, or, on the volcanic theory, elsewhere in the world. The crossing of the Jordan at Adam (cf. Joshua 3[16]) was made possible by a landslide similar to several which have been observed at Ed-Damieh—almost certainly the actual site—in modern times. The fall of the walls of

[a] See any modern commentary on Exodus.   [b] *Supra*, p. 29.
[c] McNeile, *Exodus*, pp. 43f.   [d] *The Call of Israel*; cf. *supra*, p. 3.

Jericho is confidently said on archæological grounds to have been due to earthquake.[a] The two accounts of the manna (Numbers 11 6-9, JE; Exodus 16 14-35, P) are related to one another in much the same way as the earlier and later accounts of the crossing of the Red Sea. There is nothing in Numbers 11 to suggest that the manna was either supernatural or that it was miraculously provided.

The writer speaks of it as a natural product of the desert; and it is probable that he had in mind some of the 'mannas' described by modern travellers in Sinai and Arabia.[b]

The supernatural element in the story—this is heightened in the Exodus account—is that the quantity of manna must have been greater than anything we can conceive possible by natural means. There is no natural explanation why the slaughter in the last plague should have been confined to the firstborn of Egypt, nor why it should have passed by none of them. It must therefore be conceded that even in the earliest stories an element of 'what is popularly called miracle' is intended. But if we had an unexaggerated account of what actually happened at the Exodus it is fairly safe to say that it would include nothing of miracle in the dictionary definition of

a marvellous event exceeding the known powers of nature, and therefore supposed to be due to the special intervention of the Deity or of some supernatural agency.[c]

All the same, the series of events, so far as we can recover it, was sufficiently remarkable. Is it to be explained as due simply to coincidence? Such a chain of pure coincidence is, of course, perfectly possible, once in a way. Or is McNeile justified in writing that 'the divine power worked in Egypt by means of a wonderful series of natural phenomena'? That would seem to imply, to put it plainly, that God took a hand in directly controlling the weather. The Hebrews never doubted that He could,

[a] J. Garstang, *Joshua-Judges* (1931), p. 404; J. Garstang and J. B. E. Garstang, *The Story of Jericho* (1940), pp. 133–6.

[b] G. B. Gray, *Numbers, I.C.C.*, p. 105.

[c] *Shorter Oxford English Dictionary*, s.v.

and did, do that.[a] Modern opinion is sceptical, even though we still speak of 'Acts of God', and though prayers for fair weather are included in the *Prayer Book*, and are still, occasionally, used. We have learned to think of the world of nature as existing and functioning independently of the Creator, who has delegated control of its processes to what we call 'natural laws'. But if we go so far as to say that God never 'interferes' with the natural order, and never has done, we seem shut up to the conclusion that every day's weather, everywhere in the world, always has been, always is, and always will be determined by the configuration of the original nebula. And that is pure deism. It is agreed that man, with the tools now at his disposal, can affect the climate of a locality by ruthlessly cutting down primeval forest and expecting to grow corn there in perpetuity. Without 'breaking' any natural law he finds himself in danger of reducing fertile land to a desert. Without breaking any natural law I can pick up a stone from the ground, where by all the laws of nature it ought to continue to lie, and throw it into the air.[b] Do we seriously propose that man has freedom of direct action in the world of nature, and that God has not? Whatever it was that happened at the Exodus, God could have initiated and contrived it, without necessarily doing anything 'contrary to the laws of nature'. From all we can make out, nothing happened at the Exodus, or perhaps has ever happened, exceeding the powers of nature, though much may have happened that exceeds the *known* powers of nature, even as those powers are '"known" to-day. For the Hebrews, all nature was supernatural, though on some occasions its supernatural content was greater, or more obvious, than at others. During the period between the ancient and the modern age some happenings were labelled natural, and others supernatural. That distinction has gone, and with it has gone 'miracle' in the medieval connotation of the word. For us nature is just natural. But 'the known powers of nature', as contemporary scientists are coming to know and exploit them, are such that the world is in a state of anxious foreboding. What are 'the laws of nature' but generalizations based upon our observations of the ways in which nature

---

[a] cf. *supra*, p. 69.

[b] See H. H. Farmer, *The World and God*, p. 146. Farmer's two chapters (IX-X) on 'Miracle and the Laws of Nature' are very relevant in this connexion; they conclude with an illustration from the miracle stories with which we are dealing.

behaves? They are abstractions, and if we had to make a choice it is at least arguable that the Hebrew way of looking at the world as a sphere within which God can at any time act directly is truer to reality than our negative assumption that He never acts directly at all.

Whether or not there was a special providence at work in the events of the Exodus, the Hebrews certainly believed there was, and we seem justified in concluding that they were right rather than that their faith was based upon what was really illusion. Or we might conceivably account for the situation by saying that although even God could not interfere with the predestined meteorological or seismic phenomena, He could so act upon the mind of Moses that Moses and his Israelites were on the spot just at the opportune moment. If God cannot deflect the course of a bullet that is aimed at me, He can conceivably put into my mind some thought which will cause me to get out of the way of the bullet. That, however, seems casuistical. Should we not rather think of God as fully in control of all the elements in the situation, both physical and psychical? The physical 'event', as we have seen, is nothing in itself, apart from the prophetic interpretation put upon it. Such an interpretation Moses promptly put, and a religious 'fact' emerged which altered the whole course of history.

> Thou didst blow with thy wind, the sea covered them:
> They sank as lead in the mighty waters (Exodus 15^10).

The Elizabethans were equally quick to see the hand of God in the destruction of the Spanish Armada. We are more self-conscious and hesitant. 'Dunkirk weather' is a subject for newspaper debate. But if ever there were 'miracles' they have not ceased, and if 'miracles' do not happen now they probably never did. The difference between the Old Testament age and our own is that it was an age of prophecy while ours is not. The outstanding miracle of the Old Testament is the prophetic consciousness.

I have spoken in the preceding paragraph as if Moses was a prophet. So, in fact, he was, even though he lived in what we are accustomed to regard as the pre-prophetic era. The Hebrew estimate of him was that he was a prophet, indeed the greatest of the prophets (Deuteronomy 34^10; cf. 18^15, 18). If the function of the prophet was to act as interpreter between Yahweh and his people,[a] that estimate does not seem exaggerated. We may know more about later prophets and their messages than we do about Moses; the contents of their messages may have been fuller than his; but as the first of 'the goodly fellowship of the prophets' his work was creative, unique.

Skinner[b] pointed out that

the higher prophecy of the Old Testament represents a transitional phase in the development of religion from a nationalistic basis, on which history is the chief medium of divine revelation, to an individual and universal basis, on which God enters into immediate fellowship with the human soul.

Prophecy, as we meet it in the Old Testament, is a temporary phenomenon; it is only possible where the nation is the unit for religion. To quote Skinner again:[c]

In this limitation of religion to the national consciousness of Israel we can see a reason for the existence of a special order of men through whom God makes known His will to the nation at large.

Skinner called Jeremiah 'the last of the prophets . . . the first of the psalmists'.[d] This, as he recognized, must not be taken too literally. Nevertheless, the New Covenant oracle of Jeremiah (Jeremiah 31$^{31-4}$) marked the beginning of the end of prophecy; henceforth every man was to be his own prophet.

Now, if prophecy in the true sense is only possible at the stage of religious nationalism, it is equally, at that stage, necessary, if the religion is to make any progress. But where, elsewhere than among the ancient Hebrews, do we find anything like it? In Zoroastrianism perhaps. But Zarathushtra had no successor, with the result that when he died many of the superstitions against which he had fulminated, revived, and found permanent lodgement in the religion he had founded. That would doubtless have been the fate of Mosaism if Moses had not been followed by Elijah, Elijah by Amos, Amos by Hosea, Hosea by Isaiah, Isaiah by Jeremiah, Jeremiah by Ezekiel, and Ezekiel by the Second Isaiah. Nor were these all. What nation so small as Israel has ever given birth in so short a time to a more astonishing succession

[a] cf. supra, p. 40.   [b] Prophecy and Religion, p. 14.
[c] ibid., p. 7.   [d] ibid., p. 222.

of geniuses of any kind, let alone religious geniuses? The only medium of expression that lay open to their use was a language that lent itself to the utterance of superb religious poetry. But the prophets were more than great religious poets. Their genius did not run to poetry for lack of other media. God had called them, so they claimed, and what they uttered was what He had bidden them utter.

The question whether the prophets are to be taken at their word when they assert that God called them must surely be answered in the affirmative. That answer depends, ultimately, upon the intrinsic value of what they had to say. The broad truth of that message has commended itself to the mind and conscience of Jew and Christian alike. There has been much discussion in recent years as to whether the canonical prophets, Amos and his successors, were 'ecstatics', as, there seems little doubt, the early *nebhî 'îm* were. This question need not detain us;[a] what is important is what the prophets said, not the manner of their saying it.[b] I do not, therefore, propose either to repeat, or to attempt to add to, the already sufficiently voluminous discussions on the psychology of prophecy.

There is, however, one aspect of the subject which is very relevant to our purpose. We have seen that the 'I' of the prophetic oracle is not the prophet himself; it is Yahweh. The prophet not only speaks for, he speaks, for the time being, *as* Yahweh. He is Yahweh's plenipotentiary. What he speaks is Yahweh's word, and what he does, when he enacts some piece of symbolism, is Yahweh's act. When he speaks and acts he becomes, in some sort, identified with the God who has commissioned him. At the same time it is obvious that the word

---

[a] The leading protagonist for the ecstatic theory is Gustav Hölscher: *Die Profeten* (Leipzig, 1914). For a similar view by a British scholar see T. H. Robinson: *Prophecy and the Prophets in Ancient Israel* (1923); 'Neuere Propheten-Forschung', in *Theologische Rundschau*, Neue Folge, iii (1931), pp. 75–103. For more cautious or negative views see W. F. Lofthouse: 'Thus hath Jahveh said', in *American Journal of Semitic Languages*, xl (1923–4), pp. 231–51; N. Micklem: *Prophecy and Eschatology* (1926); S. Mowinckel: 'Ecstatic Experience and Rational Elaboration in Old Testament Prophecy', in *Acta Orientalia*, xiii (1935), pp. 264–91; A. Heschel: *Die Prophetie* (Krakow, 1936); N. W. Porteous: 'Prophecy', in *Record and Revelation*, ed. H. W. Robinson (1938), pp. 216–49; H. H. Rowley: 'The Nature of Prophecy in the Light of Recent Study', in *The Harvard Theological Review*, xxxviii (1945), pp. 1–38. On the whole, opinion seems to be hardening against extremer forms of the ecstatic theory.

[b] This is implicitly conceded even by Hölscher: *Die Profeten*, p. 197.

or deed is in an equally real sense his own. Amos does not speak, nor does he act, in the manner of Hosea. His language is different, his metaphors are different, his conceptions are different. Each prophet is his individual self, and yet each, in his own peculiar way, reflects the mind of God. Abraham Heschel[a] has attempted to explain this by speaking of the prophet's 'sympathy' with the divine 'pathos' (in the sense of the Greek πάθος). This sympathy is the prophetic answer, the human correlative to the divine initiative in revelation. Sometimes the divine 'pathos' takes the form of utter abhorrence:

> Yahweh hath sworn by himself:
> I abhor the pride of Jacob,
> And his palaces I hate (Amos 6[8]).

> What use is the multitude of your sacrifices to me,
>   Saith Yahweh:
> I am satiated with burnt-offerings of rams,
>   And with the fat of well-fed beasts;
> And in the blood of bulls and he-goats
>   I take no pleasure.
> When you come to see my face,
> Who hath required this at your hand?
> Trample my courts shall ye no more;
> The bringing of offerings is vanity;
> Sacrificial smoke is abhorrent to me:
> New moon and sabbath, the calling of convocations—
> I cannot endure fastings and sacred assemblies!
> Your new moons and your appointed feasts
>   I do hate:
> They are a burden to me;
>   I am weary of bearing them (Isaiah 1[11-14]).

At other times it finds expression in a passion of unrequited love, almost regret:

> How am I to give thee up, O Ephraim?
>   To deliver thee over, O Israel?
> How am I to make thee as Admah?
>   To set thee as Zeboim?
> My heart is turned within me,
>   My compassions are kindled together
>   (Hosea 11[8]).

[a] *Die Prophetie,* p. 70.

Or of deep yearning:

> Is Ephraim a very precious son to me?
> Or a child in whom I delight?
> That as often as I speak against him,
> I do earnestly remember him still:
> Therefore my bowels are stirred for him;
> I will surely have compassion upon him
>   (Jeremiah 31[20]).

Illustrations could, of course, be multiplied indefinitely.

To say that the prophets sympathized with the divine pathos, and thus far identified themselves with God, is, however, a very different thing from saying that they aimed at achieving mystical union with God. The Old Testament knows nothing of any such thing. The prophets were poles removed from the Hindu Yogi or the Sufi devotee. They were not concerned with their own souls, nor to escape from the world. They experienced the reality of the divine pathos with the same immediacy as they did their own feelings. But the direction of the movement was from God to themselves, not from themselves to God. We are to speak in terms of unity of will and feeling with the divine, not of a union of being; of a *unio sympathetica*, not a *unio mystica*.[a] The prophets could never for long lose sight of their relation as fellow-members of the body, of the nation whose destruction they were bidden to announce, whose sufferings they themselves must share even while they shared the pathos of God. Theirs must have been a soul-shattering experience; they were in a strait betwixt two, belonging in a measure to both. (It may not be altogether impertinent to remark that the servant of God in any age must know something of this if he is to do any good.) What they endured can best be illustrated from the story of Moses' behaviour when he descended from the sacred mountain with the tables of the testimony in his hand, and saw the people rollicking round the golden calf (Exodus 32[15-35]).[b]

And Moses' anger waxed hot, and he cast the tables out of his hands, and brake them beneath the mount. And he took the calf which they

---

[a] Heschel, op. cit., p. 176.

[b] The passage is generally assigned to a late hand of E, and may therefore have been influenced by prophecy.

had made, and burnt it with fire, and ground it to powder, and strewed it upon the water, and made the children of Israel drink of it . . . And Moses returned unto Yahweh, and said, Oh, this people have sinned a great sin, and have made them gods of gold. Yet now, if thou wilt forgive their sin—; and if not, blot me, I pray thee, out of thy book which thou hast written.

And what a depth of pathos lies in Jeremiah's agonized cry!

> If I say, I will not make mention of him,
> Nor speak any more in his name,
> Then there is in my heart as it were a burning fire,
>   Shut up in my bones,
>   And I am weary with restraining,
>   And I cannot contain (Jeremiah 20⁸).

In the early days the ability to prophesy was spasmodic, conditioned by the descent of the spirit upon the prophet.

And Yahweh came down in the cloud, and spake unto Moses, and he took of the spirit which was upon him, and put it upon the seventy elders; and it came to pass that when the spirit rested upon them, they prophesied, but they did so no more (Numbers 11²⁵).

That is to say, the prophetic frenzy was only of temporary duration. Even Jeremiah would not trust himself to deliver an oracle on demand. When the 'false' prophet Hananiah broke from off his neck the bar he had been wearing as a symbol of long submission to Babylon, 'the prophet Jeremiah went his way', almost as though he was for the moment nonplussed by Hananiah's confidence.

Then [so the story proceeds], the word of Yahweh came unto Jeremiah, . . . saying, Go, and tell Hananiah, saying, Thus saith Yahweh: Thou hast broken the bars of wood; but thou shalt make in their stead bars of iron (Jeremiah 28¹¹ff.).

On another occasion, when Johanan ben-Kareah and his companions wanted to decamp into Egypt, and approached Jeremiah to know whether their purpose was in accord with the divine will, it was only 'after ten days, that the word of Yahweh came to Jeremiah' (Jeremiah 42¹⁻⁷). It is as though a prophet hesitated to give a positive 'word' on the instant, as a modern pastor may—

without impiety—be expected to do out of the garnered wisdom of his Christian experience. We, as it might seem, spread over a lifetime's ministry less than might come to a prophet in a dozen crises of blinding insight. No wonder our butter is very thinly spread, if the metaphor be not irreverent! We may, therefore, perhaps, be pardoned if we are not as positive or unanimous in our interpretations of phenomena like 'Dunkirk weather' as the prophets were. Besides, we are not geniuses, and there are so many of us, and we have to preach according to the exigencies of 'the circuit plan', whether we have anything vital to say or not. We cannot announce, 'There will be no sermon this morning, because the Lord has given me nothing to say'. If we did, we should quite properly be convicted of sloth. We live under the Christian dispensation, in which the Spirit is given to quite ordinary men and women, if they study to be faithful, as an abiding possession. What we have to account for, then, if we can, is the fact that the prophets were so few in number and so outstanding, and at the same time, considering the poverty of the human resources of the nation which produced them, so astonishingly many. In view of their positive achievement, and of the New Testament sequel, I see no alternative but to take them at their word, and to say that the Lord God called them. To repeat, the outstanding and really astounding miracle of the Old Testament is the prophetic consciousness. In the prophetic sympathy with the divine pathos we have something which it is no exaggeration to call an earnest of the Incarnation. I use the word miracle advisedly, and with no attempt at begging the question. A miracle I take to be an occurrence, or series of occurrences, which, without exceeding the powers of nature, is nevertheless due to immediate divine initiative. If we believe in providence we can hardly disbelieve in miracle.

Now, if the prophets were 'called' of God, by that same token was the nation called of which they were members. That it was a major part of the prophets' commission to announce that God had rejected the nation makes no difference in the long run. Amos, Micah, and Zephaniah—assuming that Amos 9^{8b-15}, Micah 4–7, Zephaniah 3^{8-20} are later additions—may have been wholly prophets of judgement; but the others either looked beyond chastisement to restoration, or were, like Deutero-Isaiah, messengers of comfort. And if later generations added to the genuine

oracles of Amos, Micah, and Zephaniah, it was because in the
light of what other and even greater prophets had said, and also
in the light of the sequel, their messages were felt to be incomplete.
For there is no denying that there was a restoration, a restoration
which presumably had its place in the divine purpose. That
purpose may be defined as the missionary vocation of Israel.
Israel had its prophets, men who addressed the nation on behalf
of Yahweh; Israel in its turn was to be the prophet-nation,
Yahweh's spokesman to the peoples. We may wish that this had
been more clearly enunciated in the Old Testament. We could
wish that the Old Testament contained more passages of the
clarity and charity of Jonah and Ruth, of Isaiah 2$^{1-4}$ / Micah
4$^{1-4}$, Isaiah 19$^{18-25}$, and Malachi 1^{11}. Jonah, indeed, appears
to have been a protest against a widespread attitude of sour
exclusiveness. Even Deutero-Isaiah, with his

> Turn unto me, and be ye saved,
> All ye ends of the earth
>   (Isaiah 45^{22}),

seems to have assigned to Israel not only a primacy among the
nations, but a primacy that carried with it privilege (Isaiah 45^{14},
49$^{22-6}$, cf. 60^{10}). That Deutero-Isaiah did look forward to the
conversion of the Gentiles is clear from the second Servant-Song
(49^{6}), if we may assume that the Servant-Songs are his.[a] Nor
is there anything in the Songs to suggest that the Gentiles are to
be accepted on sufferance. But it must not be taken for granted
that the Servant, who is to be 'a light to the Gentiles', is the
empirical Israel.[b] The most we can say positively is that in
Deutero- (and Trito-) Isaiah the Gentiles are to come to Israel's
light (60^{2}), rather than that Israel is to carry the light to the
Gentiles. Nevertheless, the title of this chapter, 'Israel the
Servant of Yahweh', has the authority of Deutero-Isaiah (41^{8},
44$^{1f.}$) behind it. The Servant of the Songs may not be Israel, but
it is upon the basis of the equation the Servant=Israel that the
conception of the individual Servant is raised, by way of further

---

[a] My opinion is that they are, though the question cannot be argued here.

[b] See my articles, 'Who was the Servant of the Lord in Isaiah 53?' in *Expository
Times*, 52 (1940–1), pp. 181–4, 219–21. The phrase 'a light of the Gentiles'
occurs also in 42^{6}, but there are good reasons for thinking that it is not original in
that context.

N

and narrower definition. Israel as Servant may have been an inadequate instrument for the complete fulfilment of the divine purpose, but it was an instrument nevertheless.

It is not to be wondered at that the Jews were unable to shake themselves entirely free from the principle of nationalism in religion. Even Jeremiah, for all his New Covenant oracle, did not succeed in doing that. He conceived of the future kingdom of God as somehow bound up with the restoration of His own people.

This concentration of interest on the new Israel [says Skinner], is due to a limitation inherent in the Old Testament point of view which even Jeremiah was unable to transcend. The limitation springs from a fundamental truth of religion, that religion has a social aspect, and cannot unfold its full powers except in a community; and nationality was the only form of religious community known to the men of the Old Testament. The idea of a new community created by the spirit of religion itself and founded on a relation to God common to all its members, was beyond their grasp, because the conditions for the formation of such a community did not yet exist.[a]

The Persian empire was a much more humane and civilized affair than any empire the world had yet seen, but a truly international religious community had to wait for the spread of Greek language and culture under the aegis of imperial Rome. Not without reason did St. Paul say that 'when the fullness of the time came, God sent forth his Son' (Galatians 4[4]). Had Christ come earlier than He did the conditions would have been unripe for His coming. Yet He came not a year too soon, for by the time He came the need was urgent. He came as soon as He usefully could, and as late as it was safe to do if morality and religion were not to disintegrate utterly. In this coincidence of the *terminus a quo* with the *terminus ad quem* of His coming the hand of God is signally manifest.

If further apology for the Jews is needed, it may be found in the fact that the treasure which had been committed to them was so infinitely precious that they would have been guilty of culpable negligence if they had not guarded it jealously. Therein lies the justification for the policy, so often condemned, of *habhdālâh*, or separation. What were men like Nehemiah and Ezra to do, in

a Prophecy and Religion, p. 309.

the situation in which they found themselves? It is easy enough
to dub them fanatics, but when the attempt had to be made to
translate the principles of prophetic religion into means whereby
the average unregenerate Israelite might direct his steps, the
result was a plant of such tender growth that it needed to be
protected against the semi-heathenism of Sanballat and his like.
No more splendid utterance than Jeremiah's New Covenant
oracle is to be found in the Old Testament; but if Jeremiah's
successors had forthwith taken the line that every man now knew
Yahweh, and that religious instruction was therefore no longer
necessary, in the course of a very few generations there would
have been no tale left to be told. Even under the Christian
dispensation, and amongst the strictest sect of Quakers, too literal
an application of the New Covenant oracle would speedily lead
to anarchy. It would be possible to write a very lively imaginary
conversation between Nehemiah and the author of Jonah; but
when each had explained himself we should doubtless be constrained to say that both are to be commended as faithful servants.
Each of them has his honoured place in the hospitable pages of
the Old Testament.

It may further be objected that the Jews laid undue stress upon
promises of material prosperity, thus mistaking their calling for
one of privilege rather than service. But again, what were they
to do? Or, if they ought to have known better, is it surprising that
their insight was defective? It was not until the end of the Old
Testament period that faith in a blessed future life began to dawn
at all clearly. Such a faith only becomes possible with the discovery of the religious significance and value of the individual.
So long as the nation is the unit for religion, as it was until almost
the end of the prophetic period, the question of the destiny of the
individual does not arise. A nation can only live on in the fortunes
of its succeeding generations, and until bitter experience had
corrected their natural optimism it is difficult to imagine how the
ancient Hebrews could anticipate otherwise than that the divine
blessing would be evidenced by a modest plenty of the good
things of the world which God had pronounced very good. They
were not ascetics. Nor, when they drew pictures of abundance
and prosperity, were they hedonists. There was, as they saw it,
something sacramental in the blessings of corn and wine. These
things were the outward and visible signs of the inward and

spiritual grace that should rest upon the people of God's possession.
A nation may conceivably be called to martyrdom, but no nation
can be expected to embrace martyrdom willingly or as its first
choice.

It almost looks as if Israel was called to martyrdom, or, what is
much the same thing, to a service of which martyrdom was the
inevitable outcome. With the suffering of the Jews in Christian
times, a good deal of it, especially in the middle ages, deliberately
inflicted on the charge that they had rejected and crucified Christ,
we are not here concerned. On the Christian view—which I hope
will not be thought uncharitable—that the main mission of the
Jews was accomplished by the beginning of the Christian era, we
are still left with the problem of a relatively righteous nation
receiving far more than its fair share of tribulation. So far as the
average Israelite was concerned, he probably endured no more
of actual physical suffering than his Ammonite or Moabite cousin.
The difference between him and them was that they, it may be
safely assumed, accepted their fate as a matter of course, without
moralizing upon it. They had no prophets to tell them that they
thoroughly deserved it, thus adding mental and moral anguish
to physical pain. All the little principalities of Syria and Palestine
were between the hammer of Assyro-Babylonia and the anvil of
Egypt. By all the canons of secular history from that day to this
they were foredoomed to destruction. But as if to make their lot
more hard, the Israelites alone had a succession of prophets who
constantly dinned into their ears that the fate which awaited them
was a divine judgement upon their sins. They were, perhaps,
neither better nor worse than their contemporaries. They may
have been rather better. They ought to have been, it may be
argued, with the Exodus tradition as an inheritance from the past,
and the prophets as mentors in the present. Or they may have
been rather worse. There are, indeed, indications that social and
moral standards had deteriorated in the years immediately
preceding the appearance of Amos. But the prophets were not
concerned with nice relative distinctions of better or worse. For
them the fundamental consideration was not whether the Israelites
were so much better or worse than their neighbours, or so much
better or worse than they had been in the decades preceding. Such
considerations were entirely irrelevant. It was by the absolute
righteousness and holiness of Yahweh that Israel stood to be

judged. 'You only do I know . . . therefore will I visit upon you all your iniquities' (Amos 3²). Theirs must have been an un-enviable lot; the prophets must have been an intolerable nuisance. Take everything into consideration, the weakness of average human nature, the entail of Canaanitish Baalism, so difficult to cut off, and no moral philosopher will have the heart to denounce the Israelites with the violence that their own prophets did. As a people they were very much what we should expect them to have been. And their misfortune was to be judged by standards impossible of attainment. In any case, whether they were righteous or unrighteous, their doom was only a matter of time. How are we to explain it? Once more it is the prophets who cannot be fitted without remainder into any purely naturalistic interpretation of history. Their interpretation of history was supernatural—and it was essentially true.

Whatever hopes the Jews may have had of material prosperity were transmuted into something of more lasting promise for good. They demonstrated that suffering, when it is loyally accepted, can itself become a blessing far greater than riches. We have already observed that whereas Persia had only one prophet, Israel had many. By this means the truth was continually reinforced and error gradually weakened. Another advantage that Judaism had over Zoroastrianism was that the Jews went into exile. They were removed from the associations of Baal-worship, given time to reflect upon their situation, and when at length they returned to the homeland they were able to make a fresh start. On the whole they accepted their lot with a good grace. The strictures of the prophets seemed to be justified by the sequel, and the exiles took them to heart. They found it true, as Jeremiah had promised (Jeremiah 29¹²ᶠ·), that if they had access to Yahweh in prayer, they had all of essential religion that mattered. The Exile thus became the beginning of the Diaspora. As the centuries passed Jews went of their own free will to other lands besides Babylonia, especially to Egypt, where they were accorded special privileges, so that by the beginning of the Christian era there were well-established synagogues in all the strategic centres of the Graeco-Roman world. Partly to meet their own needs, as they ceased themselves to understand Hebrew, and partly to explain and commend their faith to Gentiles, they translated their Scriptures into Greek. Proselytes were received, and even welcomed and sought, so that St. Paul could depend upon finding, wherever he travelled, communities of liberal-minded Jews and other 'devout persons', Gentile adherents, to whom he could address his message. If, instead of letting our minds dwell upon the more fiercely nationalistic passages of the Old Testament, we remember with reasonable charity the limitations of a people whose faith was of necessity cradled in nationalism, we shall need to confess that the Jews did their work of preparation for Christianity astonishingly well. They may through force of circumstances have exceeded their own intentions; if so, by so doing they sufficiently fulfilled the intention of God. The Old Testament was the essential and indispensable preparation for the New. In no other milieu could Christ have been even remotely understood, and even though His own people rejected Him we cannot conceive of His having come to any other. It seems safe to anticipate that in no country that waits to receive the Christian faith will the Old Testament that we know be permanently set aside in favour of any other *præparatio evangelica.*

a cf. G. E. Phillips, *The Old Testament in the World Church* (London, 1942).

CHAPTER X

ZION CITY OF GOD

THERE HAS been much discussion in recent years on the question whether the prophets of the eighth and seventh centuries repudiated sacrifice altogether. In his posthumously published work on Old Testament Sacrifice, Buchanan Gray expressed himself with caution:

Whether they (the prophets) actually set themselves absolutely against all sacrifice, we need not here determine. What we have to observe, however, is this: in repudiating the popular theory of sacrifice as gifts, the prophets never made the slightest attempt to recall or establish the claims of any other theory of sacrifice in its place . . . their attitude towards sacrifice, even unabused sacrifice, is at best one of indifference. . . . In brief we may say the tenor of their teaching was, not gifts but fellowship; but the way to fellowship which they pointed out was not through the existing sacrificial system re-interpreted, but through conduct.[a] [And later on:] We cannot safely infer, therefore, that generally speaking they demanded sacrifice as well as well-doing.[b]

Notwithstanding Gray's caution, however, it did begin to look, twenty years ago, as if the opinion that the prophets repudiated sacrifice altogether was going to become general. More recently caution has operated in the other direction, presumably from two motives. First, no one wishes, if he can avoid it, to see in the Old Testament two utterly irreconcilable traditions, the prophetic and the priestly; and second, the present tendency to move away from purely moral influence theories of the Atonement is more likely to commend itself if the validity of the sacrificial principle is not dismissed out of hand on the ground of a supposedly negative attitude to sacrifice on the part of the prophets.

That the prophets did condemn sacrifice in forthright terms is indisputable (cf. Amos 4^4, 5^{21-5}; Hosea 6^{4-6}; Isaiah 1^{10-17}; Micah 6^{6-8}; Jeremiah $7^{21f.}$). But that they even considered the

---

[a] *Sacrifice in the Old Testament: Its Theory and Practice* (1925), pp. 43f.
[b] ibid., p. 89.

question which has so much exercised their modern interpreters, namely whether their condemnation extended to sacrifice as such, or only to the abuse of it, is extremely unlikely. They might perhaps have found it difficult to answer the question if it had been put to them. Sacrifice as they knew it they condemned outright, without staying to consider the theological or practical consequences of what they said. Even if that should mean that they denounced sacrifice as such, we are not obliged, in deference to their great prestige, to say that theirs is the last word on the subject. We have no right to demand of them logical or theological consistency. How to reconcile Isaiah's two attitudes to Jerusalem with one another has always been a puzzle to his commentators.[a] Jeremiah, to judge from the main tenor of his teaching, ought not to have concerned himself about a return from exile; but he did so nevertheless. It is possible to take the view that the pre-exilic prophets' condemnation of sacrifice was absolute, and still believe that if they had known the sin-conscious sacrificial system of post-exilic times they could quite conscientiously have come to terms with it. It is therefore open to us to believe that certain prophets repudiated sacrifice altogether, without setting the prophetic and priestly approaches to religion over against one another as absolute contraries, and also without prejudice to modern discussions of the doctrine of the Atonement.

Let us imagine that the extreme view, that the prophets were opposed to sacrifice as such, is the right one. That would not alter the fact that the priestly religion of post-exilic times was based, speaking broadly, upon the teaching of the prophets. It was an entirely praiseworthy and necessary attempt to make the religious postulates of prophecy available for the daily life of the chastened and restored community. We make a mistake if we think of the prophetic and priestly traditions as parallel streams which develop quite independently of one another without ever making any confluence. They obviously did meet in Deuteronomy, which is both prophetic and priestly in its emphasis. They meet in Ezekiel; if not—so some recent writers have suggested[b]—in the person of Ezekiel himself, then at least in the

[a] cf. George Adam Smith in *H.D.B.*, II, pp. 489f., and G. B. Gray, *Isaiah*, *I.C.C.*, p. xciv.

[b] cf. G. Hölscher, *Hesekiel, der Dichter und das Buch* (Giessen, 1924); V. Herntrich, *Ezechielprobleme* (Giessen, 1932); J. B. Harford, *Studies in the Book of Ezekiel* (1935); W. A. Irwin, *The Problem of Ezekiel* (Chicago, 1943).

book that bears his name. They meet in the Law of Holiness (Leviticus 17–26), which obviously originated in priestly circles, and yet contains a summary of ancient Hebrew ethics at its best (Leviticus 19$^{9-18}$). Even the Priestly Code is not just a throwback to antique conceptions, now revived and elaborated by cultic/specialists. It is, to be sure, now generally agreed that P contains much ancient material, which is not the free invention of its post-exilic authors. Examples of such antique conceptions are the ritual of 'the goat for Azazel' (Leviticus 16), the semiphysical qualities of 'holiness' and 'uncleanness' (Leviticus 6$^{24-30}$ (*Heb.* 17-22)), the laws relating to 'leprosy' (Leviticus 14), the ordeal for a woman accused of marital unfaithfulness (Numbers 5$^{11-31}$). It has often been remarked that these matters have no place in the Deuteronomic programme, for the obvious reason that they were too closely related to the heathenism which Deuteronomy was striving to extirpate; but that by the time the Priestly Code was written the battle against paganism had been so decisively won that they could be given official recognition without seriously compromising the people's loyalty to Yahweh. And if faith in the one God was now securely established it was because the prophets had spoken. The situation, then, is that the Judaism of post-exilic times was directly derived from the genuine Yahwistic tradition as expounded by the prophets, with some survival of antique conceptions and rituals. It was not an independent and parallel development. Much the same thing happened in the Christian Church in the early centuries; many survivals of Mediterranean paganism were permitted in popular faith and practice, but few would wish to deny that the total result was still recognizably Christian.

To say that the Deuteronomic reformers gave no sanction to semi-magical rituals is not to say that such rituals were therefore in abeyance, or that they could easily have been suppressed. On the contrary, it is antecedently probable that they were very much in evidence, and this probability is confirmed by the vigour of the Deuteronomic polemic against heathenism of every kind. There is little doubt that, notwithstanding the Deuteronomic protest, antique conceptions of holiness and the like persisted right down to the exile. Haggai 2$^{10-13}$ is sure evidence, if evidence were needed, that they continued throughout the period of the exile, at any rate in Palestine. It is only for the exiles themselves that we can imagine that such ideas were out of sight and therefore out of mind. Nor can they, even for the Babylonian Jews, ever have been far out of mind. We may well ask how the Babylonian legislators, when the time came to formulate programmes for the reconstitution of religion in the homeland, could have avoided making concessions to popular superstition, if that is what we should call it, even if they had been entirely free from such 'superstition' themselves. No religious reform has ever been carried through without some compromise with average human capacity to embody its principles in community life. That is as true of the prophetic reformation as it has been of any other in history. The initial creative event in Old Testament revelation, the Exodus, lay nearly a thousand years in the past. How were post-exilic legislators to make out of it, together with purely ethical demands of the prophets, a system and ritual regulative of the life of a community, without calling in as aids such ancient institutions as sacrifice? Besides, the prophets, even Jeremiah, had spoken of a return from exile. A return from exile meant—whatever Jeremiah may have contemplated—Jerusalem as a religious centre, and within Jerusalem the Temple as its visible sanctuary, and within the Temple precincts the altar of sacrifice, and with sacrifice 'clean' and 'unclean' and much else. Anything better, if anything better was possible, had to await the impetus of a fresh series of creative events, the birth of Christ, His Cross and Resurrection, and the gift of the Holy Spirit. What was, served very well in the interim, and deserves to be regarded sympathetically.

It may perhaps be remarked, in parenthesis, that there is an aspect of truth in the Jewish view that the place of the prophets in the revelation was secondary. The orthodox Jewish view is that the prophets were sent because Israel had forsaken the Law, and that their mission was to recall the nation to its true obedience. That is not quite the way we should put it; yet, notwithstanding the immense importance of the prophets, it is at least arguable that the prophets were sent to recall Israel to the Exodus tradition, a tradition which, in the first instance, enshrined the memory of a divine act of deliverance. Later on, through its association with the giving of the Law, the Exodus proper tended to be obscured by the precepts of the Law; but during the age of the prophets the Law had not grown to the proportions it afterwards assumed.

We speak of the prophets as creative geniuses, as indeed they were. They set the religion upon a higher plane of development than had hitherto been possible for it. But that is not exactly how they would have defined their mission to themselves. The very prominence of the Exodus tradition in their utterances is evidence that they gave the primary importance to what happened in the age of Moses rather than to anything fresh that they themselves had to say. There are two decisive and culminating events in the history of revelation, one in the Old Testament and the other in the New. Moreover—and this is a striking fact—each initiates rather than comes at the end of the process. In the Old Testament it is the Exodus and the passage of the Red Sea; in the New it is the Cross and Resurrection, which have the centrality in Christian faith that the Exodus had in Jewish.[a] In the one, Moses is the central figure, in the other Jesus. The parallel is the more striking if, as seems probable, elements from the same general stock of folklore have coloured the nativity stories of both.[b] The interpreters of the Exodus were the prophets; of the Cross and Resurrection the apostles, supremely St. Paul.

To return: if sacrifice and other primitive rituals were accorded a place in the Priestly Code, that is not to say that they were already, at that stage in history, nothing more than fossilized remains from an antique past. The Ras Shamra materials have, it is true, proved that much that the original Wellhausen school took to be innovations of P was really very ancient.[c] Nevertheless, this inheritance from the past was still sufficiently 'alive' to lend itself to enthusiastic elaboration and development. The priests did not incorporate into their system ancient rites in exactly the forms in which they inherited them, as so much padding. They believed in them wholeheartedly. Ever since the destruction of the second Temple the Jews have been obliged to worship without sacrifice; but, officially at least, the sacrificial system is only in abeyance. No doubt, if we can imagine Jew and Arab so far

---

[a] cf. John Mason Neale's hymn: 'The foe behind, the deep before,' *M.H.B.*, 218.

[b] See W. J. Gruffydd, 'Moses in the Light of Comparative Folklore', in *Zeitschrift für die alttestamentliche Wissenschaft*, 46 (1928), pp. 260–70. Professor Gruffydd does not mention the Christian nativity story in this article, but he does in his *Math vab Mathonwy* (Cardiff, 1928), pp. 373ff. I am indebted to Mr. T. Parry, of the Department of Welsh Language and Literature, University College of North Wales, for this last reference.

[c] cf. J. W. Jack, *The Ras Shamra Tablets*, pp. 29f.

composing their differences as that the Arabs should present the
Jews with the freehold of the original Temple site, the Jews would
be in a serious dilemma. Would they, or would they not, reinstate
the system of animal sacrifices? Could they reinstate it, and face
the conscience of the world, or the conscience of their own most
spiritually-minded teachers? They were able to adjust themselves
to the tragedy of A.D. 70 because their synagogue worship had
prepared the way. They have since come to be reasonably
satisfied with forms of worship from which animal sacrifice is
excluded. And it might well be that, if they were entirely free to
please themselves, they would prefer to go on as they have been
doing for well-nigh two thousand years. But if they did—if they
were put in the position that they had to decide that their non-
sacrificial worship was a matter of choice, not of necessity—
something would have gone which is still capable of giving an
imaginative background of colour and vividness to worship that
would otherwise be rather austere. Christians of the strictest
evangelical persuasion are able to regard animal sacrifice with
indifference and even revulsion, but that is largely because for
them the whole conception of sacrifice has been transfigured and
consummated in the Cross. Even so, other Christians with a richer
liturgical tradition feel that worship without some element of
pageantry is too severely and predominantly ethical to be quite
ideal.[a] In some ways the Jews are fortunate that the question, to
sacrifice or not to sacrifice, is not for them a matter of urgent
debate. If it were, and they deliberately elected not to sacrifice,
something would have gone which has saved Judaism from
becoming only a form of barren intellectual or ethical monotheism.

Our conclusion thus far, then, is that the distinctive ritual of
P was of something more than antiquarian interest to the framers
of the code. It met a real need. More than that: there was much
more in it that was positively good than Christians commonly
recognize. I have spoken more than once in the course of this
lecture of the sharp antagonism between the Yahweh and Baal
principles, the one anchored in history and the other rooted in the
soil. That remains true, and nothing that I have said needs now
to be unsaid. Nevertheless, it might be pleaded that there is a
certain similarity—let us for the moment call it a superficial
similarity—between the two principles. For example, both were

[a] cf. W. J. Phythian-Adams, *The People and the Presence* (1942), Chapter VI.

capable of conceiving of God's relation to man in terms of the father-son and even of the husband-wife relationship. Such language was at home in the Baal cults; it was also used by the prophets who denounced Baal-worship and all that it stood for. Both figures are employed by Hosea. This leads us to ask whether superficial is quite an adequate word to use of the similarity between the two principles. May it not be that something more fundamental underlay the similarity, and that the antagonism of the prophets to Baalism was all the more bitter just because the difference between themselves and their opponents was at bottom sufficiently subtle for the world's salvation to depend upon a correct definition of the difference? The *homoiousios* versus *homoousios* controversy is a similar case. Why should Hosea sail so close to the wind as to use language that could easily be misinterpreted in a sense that he loathed with his whole soul? Why did he not renounce the sex-metaphor altogether? Perhaps he had a 'sex-complex'.[a] But other prophets, Jeremiah (chapter 2), Ezekiel (chapter 16), and Deutero-Isaiah (Isaiah 54[1-8]), did not hesitate to employ the same figure. The difference between the conception of the prophets and that of their opponents was, of course, the difference between a relation proceeding from grace and one subsisting in nature. But to say that would seem to imply that nature is prevenient to grace. There is a certain parallelism between the two kingdoms, the higher kingdom of grace and the lower world of nature; and every now and again in history there is a downward thrust from the realm of grace into the realm of nature. By this means, even under the old covenant the creation itself was being 'delivered from the bondage of corruption', to use the Pauline phrase (Romans 8[21]). That which was by nature earthy was caught up some way to meet the heavenly, as the heavenly condescended to it. To speak as though animal sacrifice is, and always was, neither here nor there so far as true religion is concerned is, therefore, a hasty over-simplification. The instinct to sacrifice is too deeply rooted in the human heart to be accounted simply as error. It met a need that was only fully satisfied when that which was perfect was come. Or take the 'myth and ritual pattern', and all the other pagan ideas which may be

[a] cf. A. Allwohn, *Die Ehe des Propheten Hosea in psychoanalytischer Beleuchtung* (Giessen, 1926), p. 60; Oesterley and Robinson, *An Introduction to the Books of the Old Testament* (1934), p. 351.

subsumed under the conception of the dying and rising god. The superficial resemblance between the myth of the dying and rising god and the Cross and Resurrection of the Son of God is so close that earlier generations might readily, had they known of it, have concluded that the Devil was parodying the truth in advance in order to discredit it. It cannot be too strongly insisted that there is *no historical connexion* between the Tammuz myth and the Cross and Resurrection of Christ. Nor is the higher religion of the Old Testament to be accounted for as a development from any myth and ritual pattern under the influence of the prophets. We may, however, call it a sublimation of the myth, if we use the language of psycho-analysis. The God-implanted but obstructed and perverted instinct of the ancients was in some sort a *præparatio evangelica*, and the gospel of the Resurrection was able to win its widening way because there was already in the human heart that to which it could directly appeal. The decisive reason why Christianity was able to triumph over the Mystery Religions was that it was able to assert beyond a peradventure that what they had only blindly groped after had now become actualized in history.

We have seen that the legislation of the Priestly Code was an attempt to make actual a quasi-physical presence of the Most High God in the midst of Israel His holy congregation.[a] Zion is the City of God, His localized dwelling-place on earth. This ideal goes back to a prophet, Isaiah, and the priestly legislators at least partially succeeded in making it real. The highest Old Testament anticipation of the Incarnation is to be found in the prophetic consciousness, and specifically in the prophets' sympathy with the divine pathos.[b] Human personality, culminating in Jesus Christ, is the highest of God's revelatory media, as Wheeler Robinson used to say. But on another, and, as most would admit, lower level than that of psychical mediation through the prophets, there is in the Old Testament another road, that of physical mediation as set forth in the priestly conception of Zion the City of God. Along this road we have a second bridge to the Incarnation, so Wheeler Robinson wrote me not long before his death. The two roads are not exactly parallel, since we have argued that the prophetic and priestly conceptions are not interminable parallels, but that the priestly is broadly derived

[a] See *supra*, Chapter VI.   [b] See *supra*, p. 176.

from the prophetic. The prophetic consciousness of God is immediate; that of the Jewish, or, indeed, of any other community, is mediate. I therefore prefer to put it that the relation of the priestly to the prophetic in the Old Testament is similar to that in the New Testament of the Church, the body of Christ, the extension of the Incarnation, to Christ Himself. The Church, declared St. Paul, was the body of Christ, notwithstanding that its membership included many who, like some of the Corinthians, had but recently been gathered in from the populace of a not very reputable city. Zion likewise was the City of God, notwithstanding that some even of the high-priests, like some of the late medieval popes, were rascals.

Frankly to admit the imperfections of the Church, whether Jewish or Christian, is not to deny that the Church is of divine institution. St. Paul knew the seamy side of human life, and the unedifying side of Church life, better than any of his contemporaries; yet he did not hesitate to call the Church, even at Corinth, the body of Christ (1 Corinthians 12²⁷). And we are less than fair to the Jewish Church of post-exilic times if we look only upon its imperfections. That it had its imperfections is obvious. Some of them were not simply accountable to the human failings of its members; they were inherent in its very constitution. The Old Testament was an imperfect revelation. It needed to be supplemented by the New, and indeed many of its passages, notably those we call messianic, seem to look forward beyond itself. 'Judaism', writes Dr. H. G. Wood,[a] 'is an attempt to systematize an incomplete revelation, and such attempts however worth while have their inevitable limitations.' He is summarizing what Dr. C. H. Dodd says in his masterly chapter on 'The Inconclusiveness of the Old Testament Religion' in *The Authority of the Bible* (Chapter VI). Since Dodd wrote on this subject little remains to be said, and yet I have no option but to follow Wood's example, even at the risk of repeating some of the things that Dodd has so finely said, though I will try to put the matter in my own way, avoiding mere paraphrase.

According to Dodd,

there are evidences of strain and tension within the accepted system (of post-exilic Judaism), as various unsolved questions are brought into

[a] *Christianity and the Nature of History*, p. 99.

prominence by the pressure of changing conditions. Partly they are
due to insufficient assimilation or application of prophetic ideas, partly
to defects or gaps in the prophetic teaching itself. But some such tension
there must be wherever a high type of religion like that of the prophets
is taken seriously by a community of ordinary men and women who
try to make it the guide of an active social life in a complex and
civilized world.[a]

The first of the 'tensions' of which Dodd speaks is the one which
has engaged our attention so much in the preceding paragraphs,
namely that 'between the priestly conception of religion as cultus
and the prophetic conception of it as spiritual and ethical life'.[b]
No corporate religion can entirely dispense with cultus, though it
be only the simple worship of the Methodist village chapel, or
even of a Quaker meeting. And there is always a danger that the
form, originally intended to enshrine and preserve the initial
inspiration, may take the place of the inspiration itself as that
gradually lessens in intensity. That is not always nor altogether
a bad thing: there is always the possibility, if so much as the form
is preserved, that the initial inspiration may be recaptured;
whereas if it had not been canalized at all it might have been lost
altogether. Forms can serve to tide over times when there is 'no
open vision'. But the more elaborate the cultus the greater the
temptation to be content with it or to keep adding to it, instead
of seeking for true spiritual renewal, until the organization
becomes so complex that it smothers the spirit which once gave it
birth. That was the peril in post-exilic Judaism. What the
original motives underlying sacrifice may have been it is difficult
to say. It is probable that they were complex, and that no one
theory, such as the totemistic theory of Robertson Smith[c] is
sufficient to account for all the facts. Buchanan Gray[d] seems
to have established that in Old Testament historical times the
dominant conception was that sacrifice was a gift to God, and
that all sacrifices, even the 'sin-offering' (Leviticus 4[23f.], 2[8f.]),
came to be included within the category of gifts to the Deity. But
if, as it would appear, in the Priestly Code the festivals came to be

---

[a] op. cit., pp. 171f.
[b] ibid., pp. 172ff.
[c] See *The Religion of the Semites*, especially the third edition, with S. A. Cook's valuable
Additional Notes.
[d] *Sacrifice in the Old Testament, passim.*

divorced from their original connexion with the agricultural year,[a] until the *raison d'être* of sacrifice was reduced to the fact that God had simply ordered it; and if, further, sacrifices could be extensively commuted for money payments;[b] it is obvious that this 'points to the absence or waning of any idea of communion' through sacrifice, and that the whole economy was in grave peril of becoming commercialized.

It is therefore not surprising that individual voices began to be heard suggesting that sacrifice was, to say the least, a unideal expression of religious devotion. The psalmists who spoke so (Psalm 40[6ff.] (*Heb.* [7ff.]), 50[9-15], 51[16f.] (*Heb.* [18f.])) are not polemical as the eighth- and seventh-century prophets had been. They show no impatient loathing of sacrifice. It is rather that they have followed the conception of sacrifices as gifts to its true spiritual conclusion, and have come to see that the proper sacrificial gift to offer to God is the gift of one's self, the sacrifice of 'a broken and a contrite heart'. Much the same thought came to gather round the altar of incense, the description of which (Exodus 30[1-10]), by general consent, belongs to a late stratum of P. The altar of incense was a miniature replica of the altar of burnt-offering, but it was of costlier materials, acacia wood overlaid with pure gold. Unlike the larger altar, which stood outside the Temple proper, it stood under cover, within the Holy Place, before the veil that screened the Holy of Holies. It was called an altar (*mizbēaḥ*='place of slaughter'), but the only offering that was ever kindled upon it was incense. The fire wherewith the incense was kindled was conveyed to the smaller from the larger altar in the outer court. The altar of incense, therefore, had no independent existence, which is presumably a reason why the Jews have never constructed similar altars to serve in their synagogue worship. That the symbolism attaching to the altar of incense was suggestive of the ascending prayers of the faithful is obvious. The Old Testament does not say this in so many words—though cf. Psalm 141[2]—but by New Testament times it would seem that the inference was clearly drawn (Luke 1[9f.]; cf. Revelation 5[8], 8[3f.]). Philo, too, is quite explicit:

Whence it is plain that God regards even the smallest offering of incense from a holy man of more worth than a thousand beasts sacrificed by

---

[a] See *supra*, p. 89.   [b] Gray, op. cit., pp. 33–40.

o

any one who is not altogether nice (ἀστεῖος). For, I suppose, as gold is better than useless (εἰκαίων) stones, whatever is within is holier than that which is without the fane, by so much is thanksgiving offered by means of incense better than that offered by victims of blood. . . . All which is a symbol only of the fact that with God it is not the number of things slain in sacrifice that is of value, but the entire purity of the rational soul of him that sacrifices.[a]

But whatever individuals like Philo may have felt, it is clear that the Jewish Church could not voluntarily do away with the altar of burnt-offering without abolishing the altar of incense, since the one was served from the other. Nor could it deliberately abolish sacrifice without flouting major ordinances of the Law, and that was unthinkable. For the Jews it was necessity, not choice, that settled the matter, and it was left to a Christian convert from Judaism to discern that the sacrificial system was but the shadow of something very far better (Hebrews 9^1–10^{25}).

Dodd's second 'acute tension' is that 'between the idea of religion as essentially universal (since God is one), and the sectarian nationalism of the Jewish system'.[b] With this I have already dealt at some length in the preceding chapter.[c] We have seen that the situation is perfectly intelligible, and that it was in some measure inevitable, in the circumstances of Old Testament times. Nevertheless, when all is said, there is, as H. G. Wood puts it,[d] an inherent contradiction in any national monotheism.

A similar contradiction is inherent in any attempt to localize the God whom 'heaven and the heaven of heavens cannot contain'. This is frankly recognized in the Old Testament (1 Kings 8^{27}; 2 Chronicles 2^6, 6^{18}), and indeed, as Dodd points out, 'a certain tension between the aloofness and the nearness of God is inseparable from religion'.[e] We should not, therefore, lay it to the sole charge of post-exilic Judaism. We must all depend, if our religion is not to be diffused into a platitudinous vagueness, to some extent upon sacred places with hallowed associations. Nevertheless, it can hardly be denied that Judaism succeeded very inadequately in reconciling the transcendence of God with His immanence. 'Immanence', perhaps, is not quite the right word to use of any Old Testament conception. But whatever the

---

[a] *De Vict. Off. 4*, quoted by Gray, op. cit., p. 146.   [b] op. cit., p. 174.
[c] See *supra*, pp. 178 f.   [d] op. cit., p. 100.   [e] op. cit., p. 176.

right word may be, it would seem that for all their zeal to locate Him in Zion, God came for the majority of Jews to recede ever farther and farther away, both spacially and in time. It was a far cry back to the age of Moses, and the piety of the scribes took the form of inceasingly minute definition and commentary on what had already been given, not upon anything new or creative. There was, indeed, nothing very new to be said, since prophecy, alike *ex hypothesi* and in the experience of the community, had not survived the passing of Ezra. There is a wealth of suggestiveness in the story of how Judas Maccabaeus purified the Temple after his victory over Lysias at Bethsura:

And they pulled down the altar, and laid up the stones in the mountain of the house in a convenient place, until there should come a prophet to give an answer concerning them (1 Maccabees 4[46]).

There we have, hardly articulate, a keen sense of loss, coupled with a hope far less robust and confident than the Messianic certainty of an Isaiah. As to God seeming distant in space, it is difficult to say whether, as the centuries passed, the meticulous ceremonial of the Temple had become an attempt to persuade the God of heaven to condescend to earth, or to dissuade a God who had once seemed near from reascending to His proper abode in heaven. The gap was only inadequately bridged by an elaborate angelology, which was, significantly, more Persian than native Hebrew.

Most poignant of all, perhaps, was the ever-growing conviction that the theodicy of the prophets was inadequate to lift the burthen of the mystery of all this weary, unintelligible world. The prophets, as we have seen,[a] did not hesitate to apply their doctrine of retribution with extreme rigour, even to threatening individual kings for their conduct of public affairs. Ezekiel, with his atomic conception of personal responsibility, stated the case with such relentless logic that sooner or later an impasse was unavoidable. So long as the nation was the religious unit the theory of exact moral retribution could easily be defended, since the evils present in any community can always be represented as sufficient, if viewed in contrast with the divine holiness, to account for any calamity that may overtake it. Moreover, as we have seen,[b] a community is capable of turning necessity to glorious gain. It

[a] cf. *supra*, pp. 66 ff.   [b] *Supra*, p. 181.

can face adversity with a good grace, and be ennobled in the process, as the Jews undoubtedly were. A community, too, is in some sort immortal, since it lives on in succeeding generations, of whose better fortune hope, if not quite imperishable, dies hard. But how justify the ways of God to the individual, if the end is a cavernous Sheol? An occasional saint may accept his situation with pious resignation; but that is not to say that his friends will acquiesce in it without protest. All that Job, or the author who portrays him so understandingly, can do, is to show the inadequacy of the current orthodoxy; they have nothing convincingly positive to put in its place. The most that Job appears to contemplate is that he will be recalled for a fleeting moment from the world of shades to hear that God has justified him (Job 19[25f.]). One or two Psalmists go farther (Psalms 16[9ff.], 49[15] [(Heb. 16)], 73[23-6]), but their testimony is not so explicit that we have not to interpret it from the vantage ground of a higher certainty. One of the most appealing passages in the Psalms is one which is not very frequently quoted in this connexion:

> Hear my prayer, O Yahweh,
>   And give ear unto my cry;
>   Hold not thy peace at my tears:
> For I am a stranger with thee,
>   A sojourner like all my fathers.
> Look away from me, that I may brighten up,
>   Before I go hence, and be no more
>   (Psalm 39[12f.] [(Heb. 13f.)]).

The psalmist has been a guest-stranger (Hebrew, gēr, 'resident alien') in the land of the living, where God, the God who everywhere exhorts to compassion toward the stranger, must Himself be the soul of compassion. Communion with God has been something more precious to him than life itself, and has awakened in him longings for which the cold comfort of Sheol will be no sort of fulfilment. If only God will look away from him, instead of by His presence encouraging hopes which are doomed to disappointment, he will contrive to meet death, if not with enthusiasm, at least with patient resignation. We are in a position to draw the inevitable inference, but for the Old Testament saint it was by no means so clear.

There are two avenues of approach to the hope of a blessed future life. The one starts from present communion of the soul with God, a communion so real that, for him who truly experiences it, it is unthinkable that even the dissolution of the body can terminate it. Such was the hope of the writer of Psalm 73, once he had got the better of his embittered feelings and won through to peace of soul. But it needs the assurance that One has risen from the dead (cf. 1 Corinthians 15$^{14-18}$) before assurance can become doubly sure. The other approach is by the way of appeal from the inequalities and injustices of this present life. The wicked prosper, the righteous suffer; therefore, since God is beyond question just, there must be a final reckoning in which all accounts shall be squared. This, in its more defiant forms, can come near to presenting a demand note to the Almighty; it is perhaps ethically grounded, but it lacks the highest religious sanction. Not the sorrows of life, but its highest joys, are the real earnest of the life to come. That the lower approach to the problem lends itself to more precise definition than the higher, a comparison of Isaiah 26^{19}, Daniel 12^2 with Psalm 73$^{23-6}$ will show; but it easily lends itself to vain and even contradictory speculations. It is, on the whole, the apocalyptic approach to the problem.

Apocalyptic theology is a theology of crisis, and like every theology of crisis it is radically dualistic in its emphasis. And being dualistic it tends to make even more acute the tension between the nearness and the remoteness, the immanence and transcendence of God, between history and that which is supra-historical. There is something flushed and hectic about it, and from all we know of him a cool-headed sceptic like the author of Ecclesiastes would probably have been mildly amused by its bizarreries. Dodd says of Ecclesiastes that 'a religion that could tolerate his book in its sacred Canon must have been very sure of itself'.[a] It must indeed. It may be argued that at least the last two tensions we have been considering, the problem of immanence and transcendence, and the problem of individual survival, are still with us to disturb the minds of men. That is both true and not true. It is not true within the Christian Church, despite the fact that the average Christian makes no pretence to being a philosophical theologian, and that even the most learned and saintly are not without their perplexities. If so many of our

[a] op. cit., p. 185.

intellectuals decide to contract out from the Christian revelation
that is their own affair. And if we do not dream of adding their
negations to our Christian Scriptures it is not because we are
afraid to meet them in the open forum of discussion; it is because
for the Christian the tensions of life have been adequately resolved
in the Incarnation, the Cross and Resurrection, and in the abiding
ministry of the Holy Spirit.

What was lacking in Judaism may be stated in any one of
several ways, each of which comes in the end to much the same
thing. As I see it, the incompleteness of Old Testament religion
is most manifest in its lack of any really vital doctrine of the Holy
Spirit. We may call this the cause, or we may call it the effect, of
the incompleteness; but whichever it be, cause or effect, it is here,
more than in any other single particular, that the incompleteness
is obvious. Naturally, the Old Testament knows nothing of the
Incarnation in the full sense of the word. The last Servant Song
(Isaiah 52^{13}–53^{12}) knows something of a cross and resurrection;
but it is like some solitary piece of sea-wrack cast up on the flood
tide of prophetic inspiration, and left stranded on the oblivious
shore to tease the beholder with speculations as to what it is and
whence it came. On the other hand, the Old Testament might
have been expected to develop the very ancient conception of the
spirit of Yahweh (cf. Judges 11^{29}, 13^{25}, 14$^{6,\ 19}$, 15^{14}, etc.). Not
that the conception never advanced beyond that of the crude
demonic energy that 'clothed itself with Gideon' (Judges 6^{34},
R.V. margin) and 'rushed upon Saul' (1 Samuel 11^6). It did.
As the conception of God became moralized that of the 'spirit'
became moralized also, and in three—though in only three—passages we read of the 'holy spirit' of Yahweh (Psalm 51$^{11\ (Heb.\ 13)}$;
Isaiah 63$^{10f.}$). One of these (Isaiah 63^{10}) says of the Israelites
in the wilderness that they 'grieved' the holy spirit of Yahweh,
and it is often remarked that here we have a semi-hyposta-
tization of the spirit, since none can 'grieve' an impersonal force
or influence. But much as the 'Servant' remained an enigma
until Christ came and, as Wheeler Robinson put it, 'served
Himself heir' to the conception, so it would appear as if Judaism
had not the strength to bring a dynamic conception of the
Holy Spirit fully to birth. Even in the New Testament it is
recorded of certain disciples whom St. Paul found at Ephesus,
and who had been baptized into John's baptism, that they had

not been informed whether they might expect to receive the Holy Spirit when they were baptized. Only when they were 'baptized into the name of the Lord Jesus' did the Spirit come upon them (Acts 19[1-6]). Jesus had assured His disciples in the Upper Room that He would not leave them orphans:

I have yet many things to say unto you, but ye cannot bear them now. Howbeit when he, the spirit of truth, is come, he shall guide you into all the truth: for he shall not speak from himself; but what things soever he shall hear, these shall he speak: and he shall declare unto you the things that are to come. He shall glorify me: for he shall take of mine, and shall declare it unto you (John 16[12ff.]).

Whatever view we may take of the verbal fidelity of the Fourth Evangelist's reports of the words of Jesus, there is no doubt that what Jesus is reported to have promised in the Upper Room was fulfilled in the experience of the apostolic Church. Nor has the guidance of the Holy Spirit ever been entirely lacking in the life of the Church, though naturally enough the Church has been more conscious of it, and given itself more readily to receive it, at some times than at others. The 'development' of Christian theology, worship, and practice, has not, on the whole, been by means of syllogistic and analogical deductions from the sayings and actions of its Founder, as, speaking generally, Jewish development has been from the Torah, and Muslim from the Quran and *Hadith*. I do not, of course, wish to imply that everything that has eventuated in the course of Christian history has been prompted by the Holy Spirit, nor, on the other hand, that there has been no organic development, no 'life of the Spirit', in Judaism and Islam. There has. But on the whole, Christianity is characterized by development, Judaism and Islam by deduction. Moses is dead, and Muhammad is dead, and neither of them promised that his 'spirit' would come and abide with his people for ever. Moses is reported to have said, 'Yahweh thy God will raise up unto thee a prophet from the midst of thee, of thy brethren, like unto me' (Deuteronomy 18[15]). No prophet had so accredited himself to Israel by the time the last chapter of Deuteronomy was written (Deuteronomy 34[10]). Nor had he in the time of the Maccabees (1 Maccabees 4[46], 9[27], 14[41]). Nor has he yet, not even in the second Moses, Moses Maimonides. But until he comes, if ever he does come, Judaism must continue to find its inspiration in the past to a degree that is foreign to the genius of Christianity.

What shall we say of the concept of Wisdom? Christian theologians have usually related Wisdom to the Logos conception, and so seen in it yet another bridge to the Incarnation. But in itself the Wisdom conception has perhaps more affinity with the doctrine of the Holy Spirit. Of Bezalel Yahweh spake unto Moses, saying, 'I have filled him with the spirit (*rûaḥ*) of God, in wisdom (*ḥokhmâh*), and in understanding, and in knowledge, and in all manner of workmanship' (Exodus 31²). And when the book of Proverbs makes Wisdom say:

> Yahweh possessed me as the beginning of his ways,
>   The first of his works.
> I was set up from everlasting,
>   At the very beginning of the world.
> When as yet there were no deeps (*tᵉhômôth*) I was brought forth;
> When there were yet no fountains abounding in water.
> Before the mountains were yet settled,
>   Yea, before the hills was I brought forth:
>   Before he made the earth and its fields,
>   And the sum of the dust of the world.
> When he established the heavens, there was I:
> When he set a circle upon the face of the deep (*tᵉhôm*):
> When he made firm the skies above:
> When the fountains of the deep (*tᵉhôm*) became strong:
> When he gave to the sea its bound,
> That its waters should not transgress his command:
> When he marked out the foundations of the earth:
> Then I was by him, a master-workman:
> And I was his delight day by day,
> Rejoicing before him at all times (Proverbs 8²²⁻³⁰),

we are reminded of the beginning of creation, when 'darkness was upon the face of the deep (*tᵉhôm*), and the spirit of God was brooding upon the face of the waters' (Genesis 1²). May we not then supplement the comparatively feeble doctrine of the Holy Spirit in post-exilic Judaism by calling in the semi-hypostatized concept of Wisdom? It would seem that we may. But when we have done so, we begin to move away from a genuinely Hebrew conception to a kind of cosmic force or world-soul, as the Wisdom of Solomon describes it, doubtless under the influence of Egyptian mysticism and Greek philosophy.

For wisdom is more mobile than any motion;
Yea, she pervadeth and penetrateth all things by reason of her pureness.
For she is the breath of the power of God,
And a clear effluence of the glory of the Almighty;
Therefore can nothing defiled find entrance into her.
For she is an effulgence from everlasting light,
And an unspotted mirror of the working of God,
And an image of his goodness.
And she, being one, hath power to do all things;
And remaining in herself, reneweth all things:
And from generation to generation passing into holy souls
She maketh men friends of God and prophets (Wisdom 7^{24-7}).

Yet in this lovely and attractive guise the doctrine of Wisdom was, as Dodd remarks,

at once too intellectualist and too nearly mystical to strike deep root in Judaism, except in so far as Wisdom could be kept strictly identified with the concrete Torah as the form of a national religion.[a]

In which case we are back where we were. In Christianity the Holy Spirit is no cosmic force or world-soul; He is the Spirit of JESUS, and we look in vain for any dynamic conception of the Spirit in Judaism unless and until Messiah shall come. As indeed He has.

[a] op. cit., p. 180.

AUTHORS QUOTED

ALBRIGHT, W. F.... 26, 114
Allwohn, A.... 189
Andrews, H. T.... 119, 139
Anstey, E.... 162

BAENTSCH, B.... 30, 31, 35
Baillie, J.... 157, 158
Berdyaev, N.... 141, 155, 156, 157
Browning, Robert... 143
Bruce, A. B.... 115
Budde, K.... 36
Burrows, M.... 161

CHARLES, R. H.... 19, 133, 135
Cook, S. A.... 72, 192
Cooke, G. A.... 70
Cornill, C. H.... 36
Cunliffe-Jones, H.... vii

DE WETTE, W. M. L. ... 85
Dodd, C. H.... 140, 141, 151, 191, 192, 194, 197, 201
Driver, S. R.... 28, 29, 30, 31, 35, 37, 92

EISSFELDT, O. 17, 21, 22, 23, 25, 28, 30, 36, 85, 123, 125
Emerson, R. W.... 133
Erbt, W.... 51

FARMER, H. H.... 141, 169
Froude, J. A.... 67

GALLING, K.... 43, 53
Garstang, J.... 168
Gogarten, F.... 158
Gray, G. B.... 18, 124, 168, 183, 184, 192, 193, 194
Gruffydd, W. J.... 187
Gressmann, H.... 3, 121, 131
Gunkel, H.... 121

HARFORD, J. B.... 184
Harper, W. R.... 56
Hebert, A. G.... 149, 150
Herntrich, V.... 184
Herodotus... 128
Heschel, A.... 172, 173, 174
Hölscher, G.... 85, 172, 184
Hooke, S. H.... 122, 123, 125
Huxley, A.... 157
Huxley, J.... 145, 146

IRWIN, W. A.... 184

JACK, J. W.... 3
Jefferies, R.... 144
Jirku, A.... 25
Johnson, A. R.... 123

KENNEDY, A. R. S.... 36, 114
Kennett, R. H.... 85, 166
Kraemer, H.... 145, 146, 150

LESSING... 153
Lindblom, J.... 119
Lofthouse, W. F.... 172

MACMURRAY, J.... 29
McNeile, A. H.... 28, 30, 31, 35, 89, 115, 167, 168
Marti, K.... 56
Micklem, N.... 172
Montefiore, C. G.... 144
Moore, G. F.... 39, 95
Mowinckel, S.... 121, 122, 123, 124, 125, 126, 172
Murray, G.... 162

NEALE, J. M.... 187
North, C. R.... 55, 123, 177
Nowack, W.... 56

OESTERLEY & ROBIN-SON... 1, 3, 105, 127, 164, 165, 189

Ottley, R. R.... 1

PALLIS, M.... 144
Peake, A. S.... 49, 74, 85
Pedersen, J.... 41
Pfeiffer, R. H.... 20, 21, 22, 23, 25, 111, 112
Phillips, G. E.... 182
Philo... 193, 194
Phythian - Adams, W. J.... 3, 167, 188
Piper, O.... 138
Porteous, N. W.... 172

RENAN, E.... 152
Rieger, J.... 50, 56
Robinson, H. W.... xii, xiii, xv, 1, 3, 21, 58, 61, 62, 116, 119, 135, 144, 154, 166, 190, 198
Robinson, T. H.... 1, 53, 123, 164, 165, 172
Rowley, H. H.... 3, 119, 137, 172

SELLIN, E.... 56
Schmidt, H.... 121, 126
Schofield, J. N.... 164
Siebens, A. R.... 85
Skinner, J.... 15, 23, 25, 51, 71, 82, 103, 130, 131, 132, 171, 178
Smith, G. A.... 56, 184
Smith, S.... 131
Smith, W. R.... 192

TENNYSON... 142

VAN HOONACKER, A. ... 17
Volz & Rudolph, 35
von Rad, G.... 107

WARDLE, W. L.... 1, 3
Welch, A. C.... 15, 53, 82, 85, 107, 128, 129
Wellhausen, J.... 166
Winkler, R.... xv
Wood, H. G.... 67, 191, 194

BIBLICAL REFERENCES

GENESIS

1...76, 125
1–11...22 (bis)
1^2...49, 200
1^{14}...116
1$^{29f.}$...110
1^{31}...109
2$^{2f.}$...109
2^{4a}...113
2$^{4-25}$...22
2^{4b-25}...77
2$^{10-14}$...77
3...22
3$^{22f.}$...23
4^1...22 (bis)
4$^{17-22}$...112
4$^{17-24}$...22, 23
4^{18}...111
4$^{23f.}$...23
5^1...113
5^{15}...111
6$^{1-4}$...22, 23
6^9...113
6^{11}...111
9$^{3f.}$...110
9$^{8-17}$...110
9$^{18f.}$...112
9$^{21-7}$...22
10^1...113
10^{21}...25, 112 (bis)
10$^{24-30}$...112
11$^{1-9}$...22
11$^{6f.}$...23
11^{10}...113
11^{27}...113
11$^{28f.}$...112
12...22, 112
12$^{1-3}$...26
12^7...32
12$^{16, 17}$...26
13$^{2, 7-11, 15f.}$...26
13$^{15ff.}$...32
14^8...42
15...36
15$^{3f, 13-16}$...27
15^{18}...30, 32
16^2...27
16$^{4-7}$...37
17...110
17^1...110
18$^{11f.}$...27
19$^{1-26}$...22
19$^{30-8}$...22
20...37

20^{13}...36
21$^{8-21}$...37
22...36, 159
23...110
24^3...27
24$^{5-8}$...27
24^7...32, 134
25$^{12, 19}$...113
26^3...32
26$^{34f.}$...112
27$^{33, 37, 39}$...**41**
27^{44}...27
27$^{46-28^9}$...112
28^{13}...32
30$^{37-43}$...37
31$^{5-12}$...37
34...22
35^{21-2a}...22
36...22
36$^{1, 9}$...113
36^{11}...32
36$^{15, 42}$...32
37^2...113
38...22
45^8...28
46^{27}...2
50^{20}...28

EXODUS

1^5...2
1$^{6, 8}$...28
1^{11}...3, 28
2^{23}...28
3...149
3^1...4
4$^{15f.}$...40
4^{22}...45n.
4^{24}...28n.
6...110
6$^{4-8}$...31
7^1...40
7$^{15b, 17b, 20b}$...37
9^{23a}...37
10^9...89
10^{13a}...37
12$^{21-7}$...89
12$^{25-7}$...88
13^4...89
14^{11}...31
14^{16a}...37
14^{21}...3 (bis)
14^{21b}...29
14$^{24f., 27}$...29
15$^{1-18}$...3

15^{10}...3, 29, 170
15$^{23f.}$...31
16$^{14-35}$...168
17$^{3-7}$...31
17$^{10-13}$...59
18...4
19–40...30
19$^{1f.}$...90
19^5...30, 81
20–3...30
20$^{1-17}$...4
20^3...4
20$^{22-3, 33}$...4
21–3...88
23^{15} (bis)...89
24$^{1-2, 7f.}$ (bis)...30
24$^{9-11}$...30
25^8...114
25^9...114, 117
25^{22}...113
25^{40}...114, 117
26^{30}...114
27^8...114
29^{45}...114
30$^{1-10}$...193
31^2...200
32–4...35
32$^{1-24}$...31
32$^{9-14}$...35
32$^{15-35}$...174
32$^{25-34}$...31
33^1...32
33^7...113
33$^{17-23}$...159
34^{10}...30
34$^{10-27}$...4
34^{14}...4
34^{18}...89
34$^{27f.}$...30

LEVITICUS

1^4...18n.
4...18
4$^{23f., 28f.}$...192
6$^{24-30}$ (Heb. 17-22)...185
7$^{26ff.}$...115
14...185
16...113, 185
17–26...185
19$^{9-18}$...185
23$^{5f.}$...89
23^{43}...90
26^{45}...31n.

NUMBERS

1^{53}...113
2...113
2^{17} (bis)...113
3–4...113
3^1...113
5^{11-31}...185
8^4...114
10^{21}...113
11...31, 168
11^{6-9}...168
11^{25}...175
$11^{26f., \, 33-6}$...113
12^1...97
12^4...113
13^{33}...23
14...31
$15^{30f.}$...18
16...31, 92
20...4
20^{1-13}...31
21^4...5
21^{21-32}...93
21^{29}...152
$21^{33ff.}$...93
24^{16}...134
$28^{26f.}$...90
31...130

DEUTERONOMY

1–11...86
1^1...85n.
1^6–3^{39}...86
1^8...86
1^{30}...94
2^{14}...94
2^{26-37}...93
2^{34}...93
$3^{1ff.}$...93
3^6...93
3^{22}...94
$4^{3f.}$...86
4^{10-14}...86
4^{19}...105
4^{32-5}...86
4^{37}...81
4^{44}...85n.
5^{15} (bis)...90
5^{22-31}...86
6^{10}...86
6^{14}...95
6^{20-3}...86
7^6...81
$7^{6ff.}$...90
7^7...81
9^1–10^{11}...86
$9^{5, \, 27}$...86
10^{15}...81
10^{19}...90
11^6...92

12–26...81, 85
12^5...81
$12^{15f.}$...111
$12^{20ff.}$...111
13^{6-11}...91
13^{10}...86
13^{12-18}...91
14^2...81
14^{29}...91
15^{10}...91
15^{15}...86, 90 (bis)
15^{18}...91
16^1...89
16^{1-8}...89
16^3...86, 89
16^{12}...86, 90 (bis)
16^{15}...91
$17^{2f., \, 2-7}$...91
17^3...105
17^{14-20}...98
17^{15}...81
18^5...81
18^{15}...170, 199
18^{18}...170
$19^{11ff.}$...91
19^{21}...91
$20^{4, \, 5-9}$...94
20^{10-14}...93
20^{15}...95
20^{15-18}...94
21^5...81
21^{18-21}...91
22^7...91
22^{22-7}...91
$23^{3f., \, 7}$...86
23^{17}...123
23^{20} (Heb. 21)...91
24^5...94
24^7...91
24^9...86
24^{16}...91
24^{18} (bis)...90
24^{19}...91
24^{22} (bis)...90
$25^{17ff.}$...86
$26^{5, \, 5-8}$...86
28...86, 92
$28^{7, \, 25}$...92
29^{13}...86
29^{23}...42
30^{20}...86
32^8...134, 135
33^2...4, 5
34^{10}...170, 199

JOSHUA

1–12...37 (bis), 87
3^{11-17}...38
3^{16}...167
6...38

6^{17-21}...93
$6^{20f.}$...38
8^{18}...59
8^{26}...38, 59, 93
$9^{3-15a, \, 16, \, 22f.}$...38
10^{1-27}...38
$10^{12ff.}$...38
10^{28-43}...38n., 93
10^{36-9}...94
10^{42}...95
11^{1-9}...38
11^{10-23}...38n.
13^{13}...32
15^{13-19}...94
15^{14-19}...32
15^{17}...32, 97
15^{63}...32
16^{10}...32
17^{11-18}...32
19^{47}...32
$23^{3, \, 10}$...95
24...97
24^{1-28}...37
24^{18}...37
24^{28}...38

JUDGES

1...5, 32
1^{10-15}...94
1^{13}...32, 97
1^{16}...32
2^{6-36}...95
2^{6}–16^{31}...97
2^{11-19}...97
2^{12}...95
$2^{13, \, 14a}$...96
$2^{14b, \, 20f., \, 23}$...95
$3^{2, \, 3, \, 4, \, 5f.}$...95
3^{12}...97
5...6
$5^{4f.}$...4, 5
$6^{ff.}$...97
6^{34}...198
$8^{22f.}$...38, 39
8^{22-8}...38
8^{31}...123
9^{8-20}...38
$10^{6ff.}$...97
11^{24}...63n.
11^{29}...198
$13^{ff.}$...97
13^5...33
13^{25}...33, 198
14^6...198
14^{19}...198
$15^{9ff.}$...33
15^{14}...198
16...97
17–21...97
17^6...33

$18^{1, 2, 8, 11}$...33
19–21...56
19^1...33
21^{25}...33

RUTH
...177
1^2...123

1 SAMUEL
1–12...88, 97
4^{1-3}...33
$4^{1b}-7^1$...33
4^{18}...97
7f....39
7^2-8^{22}...36, 98
7^{5-14}...99
7^{15}...97
8^{9-18}...98
9^1-10^{16}...33
9^{16}...34
$10^{2f.}$...97
10^{17-24}...36, 39, 98
10^{27b}...33
11...33
11^6...198
$11^{14f.}$...56
12...36, 39 (bis), 98
$12^{7, 9, 11, 14}$...97
13f....33
14^{49}...124
15...56
21^2...124
24...117
26^{19}...72

2 SAMUEL
$6^{6f.}$...64
7...99
7^6...9
9–20...34
12^{1-15}...58
$24^{1ff., 10f.}$...63

1 KINGS
1–2...34
3^8...81
8^{14-61}...100
8^{27}...194
9^{26}...3
11^4...100
$11^{11f.}$...100
11^{14-25}...100
$11^{29ff.}$...58
11^{31}...59
11^{41}...87
$12^{26ff.}$...101
14^{24}...123
15^{9-15}...104
15^{12}...123

16^{19}...101
16^{23-8}...102
16^{25}...102
17^{14-16}...166
17^{17-23}...166
18...11
18^{18}...103
18^{21}...167
19^3...39n.
20...103
21^{1-16}...102
21^{16} (bis)...103
21^{17-20a}...102
21^{19}...71
21^{20b-26}...102
21^{27}...103
$21^{27ff.}$...102
22^{11}...60
$22^{41ff.}$...104
22^{46}...123

2 KINGS
2^{19-22}...166
$4^{1-7, 18-37}$...166
4^{38-41}...166
6^{1-7}...166
9...58
10^{11}...68
10^{15}...5
$12^{1ff.}$...104
13^{14-19}...59
14^{1-4}...104
14^{23-9}...102
15^{1-4}...104
$15^{12f.}$...6
15^{13}...101
15^{32-5}...104
16^{10-18}...105
17^2...101
17^{16}...105
$18^{4f.}$...104
18^7...105
20^{21}...71
21^{1-18}...105
21^5...105
22^2...104
22^{11}...86
23^5...105
23^7...6, 123
23^{15}...106
23^{25}...104
24^6...71
25^7...71

1 CHRONICLES
1–9...107, 116
$8^{33ff.}$...5n., 117
10–29...107
10^2...117
10^6...117

11^{1-3}...117
12^5...5n.
21...117
21^1...64, 137
$22^{2, 3ff., 8, 15f.}$...117
23–6...117
$28^{11f., 19}$...117
29^{2-9}...117

2 CHRONICLES
1–9...107
2^6...194
6^{18}...194
10–36...107
20...130
$33^{11ff.}$...105
$36^{22ff.}$...107

EZRA
1^{1-3a}...107
1^2...134
4^{7-23}...118
4^{12-23}...16
4^{24}...118
$5^{1ff., 3}$...118
$5^{11, 12}$...134
6^9...134
10^{25} (bis), 31...124

NEHEMIAH
1^3...118
$1^{3f.}$...16
$1^{4, 5}$...134
$2^{4, 20}$...134
$3^{14, 31}$...124
8^4...124
10^3 (Heb. 4)...124
12^{42}...124

JOB
1–2...137
9^{13}...49, 125
$19^{25f.}$...196
26^{12}...49

PSALMS
1^2...116
$16^{9ff.}$...196
19^{13}...18
29...150
$39^{12f.}$ (Heb. 13f.)...196
$40^{6ff.}$ (Heb. 7ff.)...193
44^{1-3} (Heb. 2-4)...49
44^3 (Heb. 4)...50
47...122
49^{15} (Heb. 16)...196
50^{9-15}...193
51^{11} (Heb. 13)...198
$51^{16f.}$ (Heb. 18f.)...193
68^7 (Heb. 8)...113

73...197
73^{23-6}...196, 197
74^{12-17} (*bis*)...49
74^{13}...49
77^{5-20} (*Heb.* 6-21)...49
80^{8-11} (*Heb.* 9-12)...49
81^{1-10} (*Heb.* 2-11)...49
82...135
84^{2} (*Heb.* 3)...115
87^{4}...49
89...99
89^{11}...49
93...122
$95-100$...122
104^{6}...49
119...116
135^{6-12}...49
136...49
141^{2}...193

PROVERBS
8^{22-30}...200
8^{27}...49
10^{27}...111

ISAIAH
1^{2}...146
1^{b}...45
1^{4}...79
1^{9f}...42
1^{10-17}...183
1^{11-14}...173
2^{1-4}...177
2^{4}...131, 132
$2^{10, 12-17}$...126
3^{9}...42
5^{19}...79
5^{24}...79
6^{5}...79
6^{9ff}...80
7^{1-9}...104
7^{1-17}...58
7^{3}...62, 80
7^{9}...80
8^{1ff}...62
8^{18}...63
$9^{5f, 7}$...132
$10^{5f, 7, 9ff}$...73
10^{12}...74, 126
10^{15}...74
10^{17}...80
10^{20f}...80
11^{1-9}...132
11^{7}...111
$13-14$...130
14^{1f}...130
17^{4-7}...80
19^{18-25}...177
20^{2}...60

$24-7$ (*bis*)...119, 120
26^{19}...197
27^{1}...49
28^{14ff}...51
28^{16}...79
29^{22}...42
30^{7}...49
30^{11f}...79
30^{15}...80
31^{1}...80
37...58
37^{18ff}...73
37^{19}...73
37^{21ff}...79
38^{12}...73
40^{12-15}...76
40^{26}...76
41^{8}...177
41^{8f}...43, 81
$41^{14, 16}$...81
41^{18-20}...16
41^{18ff}...47
$41^{22f, 23}$...75
41^{26}...75
42^{6}...177n.
42^{13-17}...142
$43^{3, 10, 14, 15}$...81
43^{16-20}...47
43^{16-21}...16
43^{20}...81
$44^{1, 2}$...81, 177
44^{7}...75
44^{28}...74
45^{1}...74
45^{1-7}...75
$45^{4, 11}$...81
45^{14}...177
45^{18}...77
45^{21}...75
45^{22}...177
45^{22f}...75
45^{23}...41
46^{10}...75
47^{4}...81
48^{17}...81
49^{6}...177
49^{7} (*bis*)...81
49^{22-6}...177
51^{2}...43
51^{9f}...48, 49
$52^{13}-53^{12}$...198
53...177n.
54^{1-8}...189
54^{5}...75, 81
54^{9}...44
55^{5}...81
55^{10f}...41
$56-66$...16
59^{16f}...130
60^{2}...177

60^{9}...80
60^{10}...177
60^{10-14}...130
60^{14}...80
61^{5f}...130
63^{1-6}...130
63^{5}...130
63^{7-14}...48
63^{10}...43
63^{10f} (*bis*)...198
65^{17}...131
65^{20}...111, 132
66^{22}...131

JEREMIAH
1^{12}...41
2...189
2^{2f}...31, 45
2^{4-28}...54
2^{5ff}...45
2^{23}...54
$4-6$...128
7^{21}...54
7^{21f}...183
7^{22}...54
7^{22f}...52
7^{23}...54
8^{2}...105
9^{4} (*Heb.* 3)...42
11^{3ff}...51
$14^{9b, 21b}$...51
$19^{1f, 10f}$...60
19^{13}...105
20^{8}...175
21^{1}...124
21^{3-10}...74
22^{13-19}...71
23^{5f}...132
23^{29}...41
25^{9} (*bis*)...74
27^{1}...61n.
27^{6}...74
$28^{1-4, 10}$...61
28^{11ff}...175
28^{12-17}...69
28^{13}...61
29^{12f}...181
29^{12ff}...82
31...82
31^{20}...174
31^{31-3}...52
31^{31-4}...82, 171
31^{33}...52n.
32^{6-15}...82
32^{17-23}...49
35...5
37^{11-38}...70
38^{1-4}...58
38^{2f}...74

38⁶...124
42¹⁻⁷...175
43¹⁰...74

EZEKIEL

2⁹⁻³³...62
4⁴⁻¹⁷...62
8...123
8⁹⁻¹⁸...6
11¹³...70
16...189
16³...164
16⁵⁻⁸...52
16¹⁵⁻³⁴...54
16⁵⁹ᶠ...52
17¹¹⁻²¹...71
18...71
20⁵...81
20⁵ᶠ...46, 52
20⁷ᶠ...54
21³⁰...77
23¹⁻²¹...54
23³, ⁸, ¹⁹, ²⁷...31, 54
28¹³, ¹⁵...77
28²⁵...43
33²⁴...43, 52
36¹⁷...82
36¹⁹, ²⁰, ²¹⁻⁴...83
36²⁶ᶠᶠ...83
37²⁵...43
37²⁷ᶠ...114
38–9...128
40–8...16, 84, 85, 108, 118
43⁷...115
47¹⁻¹²...131
48³⁵...114

DANIEL

2³⁴, ³⁵...139
2³⁸, ³⁹ (bis)...137
2⁴⁰ᶠᶠ., ⁴²...137
4¹³, ²³ (Aram. 10, 20)
...134
4¹⁷ (Aram. 14) (bis)...134
4²⁶ (Aram. 23)...134
7⁷...137
8¹³, ¹⁵⁻¹⁹...134
9², ⁴⁻²⁰...133
9²¹⁻³...134
9²⁷...136
10⁵ᶠᶠ, ¹³, ²⁰...134
10²¹...135
11...137
11³⁴...139
11³⁶, ³⁹...137
12¹...135
12²...139, 197

HOSEA

1⁴...56, 62, 68
1⁶, ⁹...62
2²⁻¹³ (Heb. 4-15)...54
2²⁻²³ (Heb. 4-25)...45
2⁸ (Heb. 10)...5, 54
2¹⁵ (Heb. 17)...31
2¹⁶ᶠ. (Heb. 18f.)...54
2¹⁹⁻²³ (Heb. 21-5)...78
3⁴...55
6⁴⁻⁶...183
6⁶...45
6⁷...42, 51
7³...55
8¹...51
8²...51
8⁴...55
8⁴ᶠᶠ...88
8¹⁰...55
8¹¹...88
9⁹, ¹⁵...56
10³...55
10⁵ᶠ...88
10⁹, ¹⁰...56
11¹...44
11⁸...42, 173
12³ᶠ. (Heb. 4f.)...42
12⁷ (Heb. 8)...42
12⁹ (Heb. 10)...44
13¹...54
13²...88
13⁴...44
13¹⁰ᶠ...55
14¹⁻⁸...79

JOEL

(tris)...120
3⁹⁻²¹ (Heb. 4 9-21) (bis)
...130
3¹⁰ (Heb. 4¹⁰)...131
3¹⁶ (Heb. 4¹⁶)...131
3¹⁸ (Heb. 4¹⁸)...131

AMOS

1¹...68
1²...131
1³–2³...65
1¹¹ᶠ...68
2¹⁻²ᵃ...65
2¹ᶠ...73
2⁶...64
2⁹...44
2⁹ᶠᶠ...50
2¹⁰ (bis)...44
2¹¹ᶠ...5, 53
2¹¹ᵇ...44
3²...44, 50, 64, 181
3⁷ᶠ...40
3¹³...42

4⁴...183
4⁶⁻¹¹...68
4¹¹...42
4¹²...68
4¹³...77
5⁶...42
5⁸...77
5¹⁴...50
5¹⁵...42
5¹⁸ᶠᶠ...121, 126 (bis)
5²¹⁻⁵...183
5²⁴...54, 64
5²⁵...53
6⁶...42
6⁸...42, 173
7², ⁵, ⁹...42
7¹⁰...58
7¹⁶...42
7¹⁷...69
8⁷...42
8⁸...68
8⁸ᶠ...126
9⁵...68
9⁷...73
9⁸ᵇ...78
9⁹ᵇ⁻¹⁵...78, 176
9¹⁰...50

JONAH

...177

MICAH

3¹¹...50, 63
4–7...78, 176
4¹⁻⁴...177
4³ᶠᶠ...132
6²⁻⁵...46
6⁶⁻⁸...183
6¹⁶...102
7²⁰...43

NAHUM

3¹⁻⁵ᵃ...66
3⁷, ¹⁹...66

HABAKKUK

3⁷...97

ZEPHANIAH

1⁵...105
1⁷...128
1¹⁴⁻¹⁶...128
2¹⁻¹²...128
2¹³ᶠᶠ...128
3⁸ᶠ...129
3⁸⁻²⁰...176

HAGGAI

2⁶...132
2¹⁰⁻¹³...185

INDEX

2^{20-3}...58
$2^{21f.}$...132

ZECHARIAH
1^{7}–6^{8}...134
3f....58
3^{2}...137
4^{7}...132
12–14 (*tris*)...120
14^{1-15}...130
14^{5}...68
14^{8}...131
14^{16-19}...130

MALACHI
1^{11}...177
2^{11}...152

WISDOM
2^{24}...24
7^{24-7}...201
14^{12}...92

1 MACCABEES
4^{46}...195, 199
9^{27}...199
14^{41}...199

MARK
12^{18}...140

LUKE
$1^{9f.}$...193

ACTS
19^{1-6}...199

JOHN
3^{16}...154
$16^{12ff.}$...199

ROMANS
8^{21}...189
13^{1-7}...133

1 CORINTHIANS
12^{27}...191
15^{14-18}...197

GALATIANS
4^{4}...178

HEBREWS
8^{8}...52n.
9^{1}–10^{25}...194
$10^{26f.}$...18
11^{31}...160

1 JOHN
$4^{9,\ 16}$...154

JUDE
9...135

REVELATION
5^{8}...193
$8^{3f.}$...193
12^{7}...135

SUBJECTS

'ACTUALITY' OF HISTORY...xiif., 1
Aegean Civilization...163
Agni...150
Allegorical Interpretation...149, 160
Ancestry of Hebrews...2
Angelic Intermediaries...134
  Patrons...134ff.
Anthropomorphism...29, 143ff.
Anthropopathism...143
Apocalyptic, Characteristics of...119f.
  Development from Prophecy...120
  and Eschatology...120
  Unrelated to History...129
Assyria, Divine Instrument...73f.
Aufklärung...156

BAAL, BAAL-WORSHIP...5, 11f., 54, 96,
  125, 145, 153, 181, 188f.
Bhagavadgita...159
Bhakti-cults...145f.
Bible, Unity of...159f.
Brahman...146

CAINITE CIVILIZATION...23, 112
Concubine Tribes...5
Conquest of Canaan...4f., 32, 37f., 50,
  87, 93ff., 148
Council of Yahweh...109, 135
Court History of David...34, 39
Covenant, The...4, 30, 50ff.
  Book of the...4, 30, 88
  New...52, 82, 179
Creation, Associated with Redemption
  ...49, 125
  Myth...77, 122
Cyclic Recurrence...124

DAY OF YAHWEH...121, 126ff.
Deism...141f., 169
Determinism, Historical...119, 135f.
Deuteronomic Historians...92ff.
Diaspora...181f.
Divine 'Pathos'...173f., 190
Divine Personality, Problem of...
  143ff.
Divine Suffering...143
Divinity of King...123, 133
Dualism, Historical...138ff., 197
Dying and Rising God...122ff., 190

ELECTION, DOCTRINE OF...25f., 44ff.,
  81, 109, 111f., 162f.
'Envy' of the Gods...23f.

Eschatology, Apocalyptic...120
  Pre-prophetic...121ff.
  Prophetic...121, 126ff.
'Event', Historical...xii, xiv, 1f., 170
Exodus, The...xi, xiii, 2f., 44ff., 52,
  186f.
  Association with Creation...49f.
  Association with Covenant...30, 52

'FACTS' OF HISTORY...xii ff., 1f., 170
Fall, The...111, 160
Festivals, Related to History...88ff.
Foreign Alliances and Religious Policy
  ...104f.
Fundamentalism...xv, 157ff.
Future Life, The...179, 196f.

GENTILES, ATTITUDE TO...115, 181f.
God as Process...143
God of Battles...153
Golden Age...24, 111, 132

habhdālâh...138, 178
Heathen, Conversion of (see also
  GENTILES, ATTITUDE TO)...130
ḥerem...93f.
ḥesedh...13, 45
Hinduism...xiii, 145
Historical, Nature of the...141, 155ff.
History, Philosophy of...19, 67, 155
Holy Spirit...176, 186, 198ff.

Iliad...25
Individual Responsibility...71f., 179
Islam...xiii, 145f., 199

JEALOUSY OF YAHWEH...4, 148

MAGIC...60, 124
Mahabharata...25
Marcionitism...149, 153
Martyr Nation...180
Mediated Immediacy...158f.
Messianic Hope...16, 131f.
midrash...36, 109, 130
Miracle...29, 38, 166ff., 176
Mishna...109
Missionary Vocation, Israel's...177
Mohenjo-daro...163
Monarchy, The...6ff., 33f., 36, 38f.,
  55f., 98f.
  Disruption of...9f., 13, 117, 165
Monolatry...4, 18, 63ff., 150f.
Monotheism...26, 72, 75, 146f.

Moral Retribution...66ff., 87, 90, 195
Myth and Ritual Pattern...121f., 189f.
Mythology...48f., 77, 109, 121f.

NATIONALISM, RELIGIOUS...18, 78, 163, 171, 178
Nazirites...5, 53
Nomadic Tradition...6, 21, 23, 148, 165

PALESTINE, GEOGRAPHY OF...10, 152, 163ff.
Pantheism...141, 144ff.
Patriarchal Tradition...39, 42ff., 50, 53
Pessimistic Interpretation of History ...136
Primeval History...22ff.
Progressive Revelation...147f., 159f.
Prophet and Priest...184f.
Prophetic Clairvoyance...70
Prophetic Consciousness...170, 176
Prophetic Symbolism...58ff., 172, 175
Providence...28, 170, 176
Pseudo-Ecstasy...119f.

RAMANUJA...146
Rechabites...5, 53
Remnant, The...80
Rig Veda...146, 150

SACRIFICE...18, 53f., 110, 183ff.
Sanctuary Legends...24f.
Satan...64, 137
Second Exodus...16, 46f.
Secondary Causes...69
Separation Policy (see also habhdāláh) ...17, 138
Servant of Yahweh...177f.
Sex Metaphor...45, 54, 189
Suffering of the Righteous...72, 196
Symbolic Names...62f., 68

Symbolism, Apocalyptic...119
Prophetic...58ff.
Syncretism...164

TAOISM...146
'Telescoped' History...118
Theocracy...17, 38, 98, 113, 130
Theodicy, Prophetic...195
Thronbesteigungsfest...121ff.
Transcendence and Immanence... 194f.
Transcendentalism...133ff.

UPANISHADS...146

WILDERNESS WANDERINGS...31, 45, 54
Wisdom...200f.
'Word', Prophetic...41, 58, 175
World-ages...110, 136

YAHWEH:
Meaning of Name...149f.
War God...6, 153
Wilderness God...9
A Jealous God...4, 148
Sphere of Control...26, 72
God of Israel...78ff.
as King...121ff.
Holiness of...14, 180
Lovingkindness of...13
Righteousness of...13, 64f.
Lord of Universal Morality...63ff.
Lord of History...26, 72ff.
Lord of Nature...76ff.
Lord of the End of Things...127
as Redeemer-Creator...125
as Personal...143ff.
Reality of...153
'Word' of...41

ZOROASTRIANISM...145, 171, 181

Printed in Great Britain by
The Camelot Press Ltd., London and Southampton